FIRST EDITION

Published by
Manley Goldfine and Donn Larson

Copyright© 2004

Design and Production by
Westmorelandflint LLC.
Advertising/Marketing/Public Relations

Library of Congress Control Number
2004105414

International Standard Book Number
ISBN 0-9747195-2-8 US $26.95

Printed in the United States of America
by ProPrint, Duluth, MN

THE
WILL
and the
WAY

HOW A GENERATION OF ACTIVISTS
WON PUBLIC AND PRIVATE ACHIEVEMENTS
FOR THEIR COMMUNITY AND REGION

Assembled with care and affection
for their community

by

Manley Goldfine and Donn Larson

Gail Trowbridge, Editor

ACKNOWLEDGMENTS AND DEDICATION

I wasn't much of a reader in elementary school but one of the few books I remember reading was Halliburton's *Complete Book of Marvels*. While Duluth's progress in the last 40 years was not one of the wonders of the world, it was one of the wonders of 100,000 population cities in the Midwest.

The more I thought about it, the more I knew that compiling memories of how progress in the Northland happened, as told by some of the people who made projects happen, would be interesting and inspiring to those who will work on projects to improve our area in the future. The result is this history recording first-hand recollections by the civic leaders of most of the many projects that changed our area since the early '60s.

Erwin Goldfine 1923-2002

The book is in memory of my brother Erwin who was active in improving the area, especially during his twelve years as a Regent of the University of Minnesota.

Special thanks to my co-publisher, Donn Larson, for his tireless work, ideas, and most importantly, his knowledge of how to put together a book. His professionalism, perseverance and input kept the project on course during the two-year period that we worked on it. His 40-plus years of active involvement in Duluth's projects were invaluable in keeping us on track. Without Donn's dedication, this book would never have gone to press.

Thanks to Gail Trowbridge, our editor, who researched and reviewed all the many chapters. She had the patience and the ability that this project needed and was undaunted by deadlines and detail.

Thanks to Harold Frederick for his encouragement, input, and knowledge of many of the projects and for contributing the introduction to this book.

We wish to thank the reference department at the Duluth Public Library, especially Kris Aho who tracked down and verified important information for many of our chapters; Maryanne C. Norton who located several photos for the book; Pat Maus, manager and curator of manuscripts for the Northeast Minnesota Historical Center who found great vintage photos for our chapters; Diane Hadrich, editor's assistant at the *Duluth News Tribune* who went the extra mile in locating photos from the newspaper's archives; Bob King at the *Duluth News Tribune* who prepared several photos for the book; Sam Alvar of Seaquest Photography for the cover photo; and Jan Schroeder, retired director of the Duluth Public Library for reviewing several items for historical accuracy.

Thanks to Julie Martin, Westmorelandflint, for design of the book, and to Holly Olson, who coordinated all the details of production.

Most importantly, thanks to the 45 authors, who are listed in the Table of Subjects. They generously agreed to collect information about decades-old projects, search their memories and tell their stories. We are indebted to them for taking on the task. We also want to thank the several hundred unnamed people who provided valuable input to the authors—

extremely valuable and much-appreciated contributions.

Very special thanks to Valerie Jerome at the Manley Office and to Peggy Ahistus at the ZMC Hotels office, whose support and help were essential.

Thanks to my wife Lillian, to our family and to our many associates who supported and encouraged the project.

My parents, Fannie and Abe Goldfine, who were both born in Russia, knew the importance of giving back, of contributing to the area in which all of us are so lucky to live. They passed this on to our generation and we will do our best to pass it on to the next generation.

I'm sure there are many other worthy projects that could have been included here. I apologize to those we missed. All efforts that succeed in improving our community are noteworthy and deserve recognition but I believe that success is its own reward.

Thanks again to everyone who worked on the projects highlighted in the book. Your interest and your contributions made the Twin Ports and the surrounding area a better place to live.

—Manley "Monnie" Goldfine
Co-Publisher

Manley "Monnie" Goldfine, still active in the Goldfine family's diverse business interests, is former CEO of Zenith Management (ZMC Hotels), was president of the Arena/Auditorium Administrative Board and Spirit Mountain during their construction period, and has long been active in promoting the region's tourist industry. He was inducted into the Duluth Hall of Fame at age 35.

TABLE OF SUBJECTS

Duluth harbor and downtown looking southwest toward Superior, circa 1950. Throughout the second half of the century, our city and region would be challenged many times to change our role and appearance. The ship canal, which was dug through Minnesota Point in 1870, and the Aerial Bridge, built in 1905, had already made it possible for Duluth to become one of the busiest harbors in the country. By 1959, the port authority would transform our Great Lakes city into a regular port of call for ocean-going ships. Over the next half-century, many individuals would continue to work to change and improve our corner of the world.

INTRODUCTION

by Harold Frederick

While reading through the many chapters for this book as I prepared to write my introduction, I found myself recalling in vivid detail a few defining moments in the extraordinary transformation of Duluth and the region that has taken place within the last 40 years. Let me share a few anecdotes:

"There is hereby created an arena-auditorium administrative board for the City of Duluth ... [which shall] consist of seven directors who shall serve without compensation [and upon whom] there is hereby conferred the power and duty to contract for and superintend the erection, construction, equipping and furnishing of such arena-auditorium and to administer, promote, control, direct, manage and operate such arena-auditorium as a municipal facility."

The arena-auditorium (now the Duluth Entertainment Convention Center) legislation prepared by City attorney Harry Weinberg was approved by Governor Karl Rolvaag on April 22, 1963. As a young assistant to Mr. Weinberg, helping him with some of the legal work associated with the new arena served as my first exposure to the generation of citizen activists who were responsible for the necessary reshaping of our community that occurred over the next forty years.

While talking business with Monnie Goldfine via telephone one day long ago, Monnie interrupted to ask me the time. I said it was 4:20. Monnie said he needed to cut short the discussion because George Hovland was picking him up behind the store (Goldfines by the Bridge) at 4:30. He explained that George was taking him to a place out on West Skyline Drive in my old neighborhood. George thought that it would be a good place for a ski hill.

━

I recall sitting next to Kay Slack at a committee meeting called to develop a solution to the controversy surrounding the location of the new library. There was concern in the community that the proposed location across Michigan Street from the Depot would block the public view of that wonderful building. The solution developed at the meeting was to vacate a part of Sixth Avenue West, move the library to the West in order to improve the view of the Depot from the Fifth Avenue West Mall. Not all were satisfied with the solution but many today would not understand why such a controversy existed.

━

I remember the day that Mayor Robert Beaudin appointed a citizens' task force to relocate the route of the freeway from Mesabi Avenue to Tenth Avenue East as planned by the Highway Department. The long-established design had routed the freeway over Lake Avenue, out across the corner of Lake Superior and would have mowed down Fitgers and all of the buildings on the lower side of Superior Street, including the Hartley Building. In an unprecedented act, the Highway Department gave the Mayor's Committee, led by Lauren S. Larsen, the staff and authority needed to make the final decision as to the location of the roadway. The relocated route, including Lake Place, the plantings that exist along the road, and the concept for Lakewalk grew out of the committee process.

━

Years later Jack LaVoy invited me to lunch and told me that Minnesota Power and Pentair Corporation had formed a partnership to build a new paper mill in West Duluth. That paper mill and the adjoining recycling facility is now owned by a company headquartered in Finland and which, not many years ago, merged with a Swedish company. Given the ethnic background of many in the community there was a pleasant irony to this turn of events.

━

1960 marked the beginning of a new era for Duluth and the region. The sawmills along the harbor had long ago closed. Two world wars emptied the Mesabi Range of the rich, red ore that had been the backbone of the regional economy. The large wholesale houses, manufacturing plants of nearly every variety, and the other commercial and industrial standbys of the past era had closed, moved south or would do so within the next years.

Only those of my generation still remember the several woolen mills, Klearflax linen looms ("the Carpet of the Hollywood Stars"); a robust steel mill that turned the red iron ore of the Iron Range into rails, nails, woven wire and fencepost; a large cement plant; Clyde Whirley Cranes made in Duluth and used in ports around the world; factories that made Coolerator refrigerators, paint, horseshoes, mattresses and the finest wrenches in North America, as well as a plant that printed the boxes in which Red Dot potato chips arrived at our homes.

Technology had provided a blow to the tourist industry in Duluth and along the North Shore. Long known as the air-conditioned city and a "hay fever haven," the invention of mechanical air conditioning curtailed the need to come north in the summer and dramatically reduced the number of summer visitors.

It seems, therefore, that it was necessity which fostered the individual and collective efforts that are described and remembered in the following pages. The first chapter by Jeno Paulucci certainly makes that point. With the notable exception of the Miller Hill Mall, most of the major developments that occurred in Duluth in the last 40 years were incubated and brought to life from within. Not all of the projects are recorded in this collection, and a further effort must be made to record some of the omissions, including the remarkable growth of higher education and development of the medical facilities in the community. Moreover, during the last 40 years the long-established arts and cultural organizations in the community have been well-maintained and advanced and those organizations, together with some additions like the Blues Festival, Sacred Heart Music Center and the Minnesota Ballet provide a vibrancy to life in Duluth not present in the suburbs of America. Some ventures, including Bayfront Park, are still in process and reporting on them now would be incomplete.

In 2002 Gene Bunnell, a college professor and former director of Planning and Development for the City of Northhampton, Massachusetts, published *Making Places Special, Stories of Real Places Made Better by Planning*. The book chronicles successful planning and development efforts in Chattanooga, Tennessee; Providence, Rhode Island; Charleston, South Carolina; San Diego, California; *and Duluth*. The segment on Duluth covers some of the history of our city and touches on many of the projects and efforts included in this book. It is worth reading, both to provide background for and as a compass to this effort. Duluth's recognition by Mr. Bunnell certainly validates the decision to publish the accounts you will be reading here.

History has, at the same time, been both tough on and kind to our community and region. The prosperity of the period between 1890 and 1920 produced architecturally significant buildings and homes, many of which remain for our use and enjoyment. However, the loss of the red ore and white pine, in part responsible for the prosperity of that earlier era, as well as the exit of manufacturing jobs to the south, have provided the challenges that faced our community in 1960.

The purpose of collecting some of the accomplishments of the last forty years is not to provide a forum for those involved to brag about what occurred, but rather to serve as a navigational aid to the generation that is following.

No less an effort will be required going forward.

Harold Frederick, a partner in the law firm Fryberger, Buchanan, Smith and Frederick, is a former Duluth city attorney who participated in many of the undertakings described in this book.

CHAPTER

1

As I Remember It...

by Jeno F. Paulucci

In the late 1950s and early 1960s, Duluth and Minnesota's Iron Range were suffering the dregs of a private depression. Red ore iron mining was petering out, and so were the fortunes of the communities that relied on that industry so heavily. Double-digit unemployment wracked nearly every town...Superior Street was a silent string of boarded-up stores and shops...our young people took flight to earn a living elsewhere. I still have large photos of five blocks of Superior Street, both sides, showing the desolation of that time.

On New Year's Eve 1960, I met with mining industry executives, steelworker bosses and community leaders behind locked doors in my Chun King offices in Duluth to hammer out an agreement to work together—instead of at cross purposes—to help the industry invest in plants and create jobs through the new taconite technology. That meeting has since been heralded as the birthplace of the Taconite Amendment to the Minnesota Constitution, which triggered more than $2 billion in private capital investment in northeastern

Minnesota and continues as a primary industry today.

That's just one example of what a few dedicated citizens can do for the benefit of a neighborhood, a city, region, or in this case, state and nation, for Minnesota's mining resources remain as critical to the national defense today as they did supplying the backbone of steel to win two world wars.

As a team, we kicked ass. Not one of our projects failed.

Duluth and northeastern Minnesota were blessed in the second half of the 20th century with dedicated, independent community leaders, taking turns in project leadership, but working hand-in-hand for the public good.

The Goldfines—Monnie and Erv; television executives Bob Rich, John LaForge and Fran Befera; newspaper publishers Bernie Ridder and Gene McGuckin; Jim Lee, Jim Tills and my energetic associate Lee Vann who ran NEMO, Inc. (N.E. Minnesota Organization for Economic Education) for me, just to name a few. All shared a common trait—an astounding ability to recognize a good idea and an overpowering desire to make it work—in spite of the fact that all the work they knew was forthcoming wasn't going to add a nickel to their pocket. We were going to do it anyway, for the common good and because it was right.

We didn't rely on the government to do our job. We took it upon ourselves to bring projects to the government, rather than waiting for government to assess our needs. We were thorough in our homework, made certain of our facts, then got the attention of public officials when needed through the power of public opinion expressed through the media.

As a team, we kicked ass. Not one of our projects failed.

So how do you turn business acumen into worthwhile economic development that meets real needs in the community? As a civic activist, you must play the role of an entrepreneur, for it is only the entrepreneur who creates wealth, and the laws of entrepreneurship, as I see them, are the guides to successful activism as well.

AN ENTREPRENEUR'S TEN COMMANDMENTS

Use the Entrepreneur's Ten Commandments as a guide to being an activist and getting things done in your community:

1. **Find that niche.** You determine what the community really needs, what it lacks, what it will benefit from...then put that objective in writing.

2. **Devise a plan...about how to do it.** What does it involve? City? County? State or federal participation? If so, how are you going to get the money and the support that you have determined your community needs? Now you have a business plan.

3. **Be careful.** Don't try to get everybody involved, or try to please everybody. Get two or three activists such as yourself and work out who does what. One person is the leader, the CEO, and he doesn't listen to any of the naysayers, because every person in the community has his or her own idea. You do what is best for the community based on your purpose.

4. **Trade jobs as a commodity for a business,** and the same holds true for your plan to help the community with the new service or building of whatever your goal. Create an economic plan—rough; don't spend a lot of money doing it—showing the jobs your project will create. Remember; when you bring your plan to the city, state or federal government, the bureaucrats are interested in only one aspect: Does it create jobs? Jobs are a commodity you trade for the dollars of support you need.

5. **Find a lawyer who believes in your project;** someone who can look at the different departments and levels of government to learn where

your program fits. What monies do they have? How do you get that money and that support? Find someone who studies these laws, appropriations by Congress and so forth.

6. **Watch your costs.** Since this is a civic project, make sure bidders or contractors don't assume that since this is a public, civic project, there is more profit to be made. You need to look at it like a business; you'll want the lowest costs possible.

7. **Establish and enforce policies** to ensure good communication and control. Get the media—newspapers, radio, television—sold on the project and they become the background drumbeat that helps you with the politicians, who are scared of not being re-elected and wonder whether they should stick their necks out. Don't be worried about any of the people you work with getting jealous or having their own ideas. You are the CEO. You want a team, but if you have to kick someone off the team, do so. The end result is most important, not the people involved. And don't go into it with the belief that everyone is going to love you. In the end, you might end up with a love-hate relationship such as I did after all these years, and that comes with the territory.

8. **Regardless of your title or your success, you'll never be more than a peddler.** The CEO, he or she, has to present the project's message, whether to the county commission, city council, governor, a bureau in Washington or to a member of Congress. This job cannot be delegated. You have to do it yourself. You have to become the peddler of your project.

9. **There always is a battle.** One of the biggest battles often occurs within the organization, but if you are a good CEO and leader of the group, you won't have to worry about that. The other battle is the constant battle for available funds; other communities, other projects want that money. You can't take any prisoners if you want to win this battle for your

project. You really have to be rough, tough—honest, of course—but you have to go after all the funds and the support you need for your project with the understanding that there will be intense competition.

10. **Don't fall in love with your project.** Once it's completed, don't look for laurels. Look for the next project you should be doing, with the same team or a new team of activists. That's exactly what happened during the times we worked together in Duluth from the 1960s on. And the proof of success stands today: the Arena/Auditorium and Pioneer Hall...Spirit Mountain Recreation Area... University of Minnesota School of Medicine Duluth...Duluth Public Library...the Duluth air terminal...the Lake Superior Water Purification Plant...Lyric Block redevelopment...and so much more.

> Curt Carlson called me to say, "Jeno, don't push for a convention center in Duluth; you'll have a white elephant." "Fine," I answered. "I really would love to ride that white elephant."

The Duluth Entertainment and Convention Center was achieved later. I remember Curt Carlson and Carl Pohlad didn't want Duluth to have it; they wanted Minneapolis to have the convention center.

Curt Carlson called me to say, "Jeno, don't push for a convention center in Duluth; you'll have a white elephant."

"Fine," I answered. "I really would love to ride that white elephant. Curt, mind your own business."

That's what it takes to accomplish the seemingly impossible. You don't give a damn about opposition or roadblocks; you just keep your eye on the ball and press on. That's what we did.

I remember sitting down on a Sunday...Monnie and Erv Goldfine, Lee Vann and myself, and Mac Fredin, who was on the Seaway Port Authority of Duluth Board of Directors. We decided that we had four projects; which has priority?

One was the grain meal plant for the port. That's last, I said. We all agreed that we would work together to help one another. Each project would have a different lead person. Bob Rich and I were on the Blatnik Bridge and Airport Terminal projects; Monnie and Erv Goldfine were on Spirit Mountain, and so forth. We all worked together as activists. We didn't worry if the mayor or others supported us because we made them all support our success for the community in the end.

And Mac Fredin, who worked with us to establish that grain meal plant eventually, later wrote to me, "You know, Jeno, I never did like you. But I have to respect you."

That's how we ended up. And that's how I remember it. ∎

Son of immigrants to Minnesota's Iron Range, Duluth industrialist and philanthropist Jeno Paulucci has developed a series of successful national food enterprises, beginning with the Chun King Corporation and most recently Luigino's. Throughout his career he has devoted time, energy and resources to community improvement.

CHAPTER

2

Maurices

BUSINESS FOUNDED DURING GREAT DEPRESSION GROWS INTO THRIVING RETAIL CHAIN STARTING IN THE '60S

by Joel Labovitz

The first Maurices store was located on the northeast corner of 3rd Avenue West and Superior Street where Wells Fargo Bank is today.

Prior to the first Maurices, my dad, E. Maurice Labovitz, and his father had a dry goods store—the Fair Store—in the same location. They were always a bit ahead of their time, and in 1928, a year before the Great Depression, they went bankrupt. After coming out of bankruptcy my dad realized that the Fair Store could not make it. He did not have enough money to inventory a dry goods store so he decided to open a store in the same location with a merchandise focus that would have a more rapid turnover. This required less capital investment, and he had very little money. So on March 28, 1931, in the depth of the Great Depression, Maurices was born.

Sales for 1931 were about $49,000 and the store's first

When ladies wore hats. March 1938 window display shows more hats than coats. Maurices was at 120 West Superior Street from 1933 to 1958, then moved to a larger store at 105 West Superior, formerly Albenberg's. This storefront is a 1937 redesign. Fluorescent lights and air conditioning came in 1940.

profitable month was December 1931. The profit was $4.12. With hard work, a lot of imagination and good luck, the store slowly prospered. In 1933, Maurices moved to 120 W. Superior Street where it stayed until 1958. In 1937 my Dad had installed a new storefront there. In 1940, he installed fluorescent lights and air conditioning. These were certainly among the first, if not the first, such commercial installations in Duluth.

I worked at Maurices in various capacities—janitor, stock boy and cashier—beginning when I was about 14 years old.

In 1948, Maurices opened in Virginia, Minnesota and in 1950 a third store was added in Superior.

I joined my dad in 1950, one year after graduating from UMD and working briefly for a wholesaler of staple goods, I started as the store manager at Maurices in Virginia. At that time, Dan Blehart, who later became a partner, was my dad's merchant and I believe that he was the best of the best. I moved to Duluth in 1951 after training Gloria Aho to be our Virginia store manager. Gloria had begun as the cashier/bookkeeper; I was unsure of what my duties would and should be. This was fortunate, because since Dan Blehart was so effective as a merchant, I turned to store operations, marketing, and sales. We became an effective team.

In 1958, we purchased the Albenberg store just across the street at 105 W. Superior Street and gained more selling space, as well as office, shipping and storage areas. Our stores grew slowly in their sales and profits, but since we had not only our employees to feed, but also the Blehart and Labovitz families, we decided to look for growth. In 1960 we opened a store in Wausau, Wisconsin and then added one in Appleton and another in Green Bay, both in 1963.

I became CEO in 1967. That year we opened a store in downtown Hibbing, and then we got lucky.

A shopping center developer in Manitowoc, Wisconsin dragged us kicking and screaming and resisting paying his high rent (which turned out not to be very high at all) into a center in that city. This was immediately successful and profitable. We had never before been able to turn a profit in a store before perhaps the second or third year. Local downtown merchants were known. Maurices was unknown when we moved into a new city's downtown, and shopping habits were hard to change.

The advent of shopping centers, however, changed consumers' habits. The consumer immediately realized that these big, shiny, clean, well-lit, and open-long-hours shopping centers would provide them a much better, richer and easier shopping experience. So as soon as we discovered that, we made plans to find other locations in which we could open stores.

At that time, very few local women's apparel (and men's apparel store owners for that matter) were willing to take the risk of opening stores in new shopping centers. They were unwilling to make the capital expenditures that were necessary and also in many cases, were unwilling to pay the rents asked.

Because of our success in Manitowoc, we were much more confident that similar results would occur in other shopping center stores. In 1969, we opened three stores; one in Cedar Falls, Iowa; one in Mankato, Minnesota; and the third in Sioux Falls, South Dakota. These stores were also profitable and they led us to look for centers in similar communities and open stores as fast as we could. So we opened about five stores each in 1970 and 1971, and by 1980 we had about 175 stores with more coming. We had put a men's shop in our Duluth downtown Maurices store in 1958, and as that was quite successful, we added some men's shops within the women's stores, and some smaller freestanding men's stores.

We benefited from terrific staff, mostly homegrown. We concentrated very hard in promoting within our ranks. Most of our management was promoted from within and I guess that probably 96% of our people, management included, were female. We were blessed and lucky to have truly outstanding people to take us through that first 50 years.

We sold Maurices to American Retail Group in early 1979 and I stayed until January 1981, meanwhile breaking in Hans Brenninkmeyer as the new CEO. Hans was terrific as was his brother, Mark, who followed him. Another Brenninkmeyer—Roland—has been in charge or Maurices for about eight years. There are now four or five hundred Maurices stores throughout the country!

The business has changed over the years, but I am sure now, as it was in the 50 years with which I am most familiar, it is a great place to work and to shop and is good to and for its communities.

My entire 30-plus years at Maurices were stimulating and fun. ∎

Joel Labovitz was CEO of Maurices 1967-1979 and continues to have business interests in Duluth.

CHAPTER

3

Duluth Seaway Port Authority

OPENING OUR HARBOR TO THE WORLD

by Bill Beck

When the British Motor Vessel Ramon De Larrinaga slipped under the Aerial Lift Bridge on the rainy Sunday of May 3, 1959, it was the beginning of a new era for the Twin Ports of Duluth and Superior. The completion of the Great Lakes-St. Lawrence Seaway that spring truly opened up the mid-continent of North America to world shipping. With the construction of U.S. and Canadian locks on the St. Lawrence River between Montreal and Lake Ontario, ocean-going ships could finally penetrate into the heart of North America, 2,000 miles from saltwater.

Since early in the 19th century, there had been Canadian canals linking the Great Lakes to the Atlantic Ocean. But the canals were small and limited passage to vessels called "canallers," roughly 250 feet in length and 50-feet wide.

Aerial view of the harbor in July 1959 when the Seaway Port Authority of Duluth dedicated the new Arthur M. Clure Public Marine Terminal. The Great Lakes' heaviest lift capacity cranes are unloading general cargo from a German freighter. Across the slip, a Finnish vessel is loading grain from elevators that were acquired by the Port Authority and removed in 2002, while tugs maneuver a Norwegian tanker in the front channel. Yard in foreground can accommodate 3,500 rail cars.

Duluth and Superior shipyards had built coastal vessels during both World War I and World War II, but none was comparable in size to the behemoths that carried iron ore and grain down the Great Lakes. Minnesota politicians and visionaries had been promoting a seaway since at least the 1890s; for many years, the Great Lakes-Tidewater Association—the trade group pushing for construction of a modern seaway—had been headquartered in Duluth.

When President Dwight D. Eisenhower signed the Wiley-Dondero Act in 1954, he committed the United States to participation in a binational effort that resulted in one of the great construction projects of the 20th century. For the next five years, U.S. and Canadian construction crews blasted and moved mountains of rock to create a seaway that allowed passage of the biggest ocean-going ships in the world at the time. President Eisenhower and Queen Elizabeth II formally dedicated the Seaway on June 26, 1959. By that time, Duluth and Superior had been a world port for nearly two months.

THE VALUE OF PREPARATION

Unlike many Great Lakes communities, Duluth and Superior had been preparing for the arrival of ocean-going ships for years. Duluth, in particular, had created a fully functioning port authority in the mid-1950s to oversee shipping activity in the port. And the newly formed port authority had moved quickly to build the infrastructure that the expected influx of ocean-going ships would need to make the Lake Superior port city a regular port of call. The Seaway Port Authority of Duluth[1] had already received funding from a wide range of government agencies and bodies, had bought land at the tip of Rice's Point in the inner harbor and had constructed a ship- and cargo-handling complex to receive the expected foreign commerce. Named the Arthur M. Clure Public Marine Terminal (after the Duluth admiralty lawyer whose leadership in essence created the modern Duluth Port Authority), the 120-acre facility included warehouses, cranes and berths for the saltwater vessels. The concept of an

---

[1] The name was changed to the Duluth Seaway Port Authority in 2000.

independent port authority went back to the 1920s, when an engineering firm recommended that the U.S. Army Corps of Engineers dredge a new, wider entry to the inner harbor across Minnesota Point about 2.4 miles southeast of the present Duluth entry and bore tunnels underneath the proposed new entry. At the time, Minnesota and Wisconsin were attempting to come to an agreement on the appointment of a joint harbor commission for Duluth and Superior. In 1929, the Minnesota legislature finally passed a bill creating a port authority in Duluth. The City of Duluth appointed a three-member commission to oversee the affairs of the harbor. Charter members were J. W. Lyder, Donald S. Holmes and Leroy M. Pharis.

That first port authority never took hold, and it wasn't until the 1950s that the City of Duluth and the Minnesota Legislature made another stab at creating a governing body for the port. The City took the first step, reorganizing the old, three-member port authority in 1954. President Eisenhower's signing of the Wiley-Dondero Act that summer spurred port development and planning around the Great Lakes, including the creation of port authorities in several other lakes ports. Named to head the revived Duluth body was Arthur M. Clure, a long-time admiralty attorney and expert on St. Louis County real estate titles. A native North Dakotan, Clure was a 1925 graduate of the University of Minnesota Law School and had practiced in Duluth for 30 years. Many in the community gave him credit for leading the fight for the establishment of UMD in the late 1940s.

Clure and his colleagues on the reconstituted board—Samuel Atkins and Charles S. Hagan—moved quickly to hire a staff and build the modern facilities that would attract ocean-going general cargo and ships to the Twin Ports. The City's initiative in reforming the port authority did not go unnoticed. The first port authority in the 1920s and 1930s was wrecked on the shoals of a decades-long squabble over the location of what would later become the Blatnik High Bridge, and nobody in city hall wanted partisan bickering to break up the current port authority. Mayor George D. Johnson and the five-member Duluth City Commission[2] also

---

[2] In 1956, the voters elected to change the City Commission form of government to a Mayor-Council form of government.

knew that Duluth could not go it alone when it came to building the port terminal facilities needed to serve the 1959 opening of the Seaway.

In 1955, the City, St. Louis County and the State of Minnesota agreed to share responsibility for establishment of a truly bi-partisan port authority. Under the terms of the agreement, the governmental partners created a seven-member port authority board to govern affairs at the port. The Duluth City Commission was given three appointments to the board, while the St. Louis County Board of Commissioners and the Governor of Minnesota were given two appointments apiece. The 1955 agreement has withstood the test of time. Appointments to the Duluth Seaway Port Authority Board are still made in the same proportion as agreed to in 1955.[3]

In February 1956, the port authority hired Robert T. Smith, a Cunard Lines veteran and president of a New Orleans stevedoring firm, as its first executive director. Smith worked out of port authority offices on the 9th floor of the Alworth Building and began to assemble a staff, including Telford Young, a former Duluthian working in New Orleans, and Richard Sielaff, a professor at UMD. Smith and the staff quickly began organizing the functions of the port authority and promoting the concept of Duluth-Superior as a world port.

Smith and his staff were hardly in place when the maritime community was shocked when Clure collapsed and died suddenly in his Duluth law offices in the first week of April 1956. Clure's death coincided with the opening of another era in Great Lakes shipping. Two days after Clure died, the *C.L. Austin* departed her winter lay-up berth in Superior and made the short trip up the North Shore to the new port of Silver Bay where she took on the first cargo of taconite pellets bound down the Lakes from the Reserve Mining Co.

BUILDING THE CLURE PUBLIC MARINE TERMINAL

The death of Arthur M. Clure cast a pall over the Duluth-Superior

---

[3] In the mid-1980s, Governor Rudy Perpich suggested increasing the size of the port authority board to 9 or 11 members, although nothing ever came of the suggestion.

Dick Magnuson

The first sea-going general cargo vessel at the new port terminal was the *TransMichigan*, which tied up on May 16, 1959. Gathered for the event are, L-R, Capt. Thomas Wilson (pilot), Robert Morris, manager of the Duluth Chamber of Commerce, Duluth Mayor E. Clifford Mork, E. L. "Buster" Slaughter of the International Brotherhood of Longshoremen, *TransMichigan* Captain Oskar Overbeck, Duluth's first Port Director Robert T. Smith, Port Commissioner Matt Antilla, representative of the Seaman's International Union, Dick Stahl, terminal superintendent, and Leonard Theobald, St. Louis county commissioner and port commissioner.

maritime community, but it did not impede progress on the ports' plans to ready themselves for the advent of ocean shipping three years hence. Kenneth Duncan, the longtime general manager for Pickands-Mather's Lake Superior iron ore properties, succeeded Clure as board chairman in the spring of 1956. He and Port Director Smith set about getting commitments from the city, county and state for land purchases and funding of construction of a port terminal. There was never any question of the state's participation. DFL Governor Orville Freeman visited Duluth late in 1956 and pledged the state's support.

In the 1957 session of the Minnesota legislature, Governor Orville

Freeman signed a bill that authorized $10 million ($5 million from the State, $4 million from St. Louis County and $1 million from the City of Duluth) to construct the port terminal. St. Louis County also contributed 80 acres of tax-forfeit property on Rice's Point as a site. The financial package came together quickly during the spring of 1957.

There were several lawsuits questioning the constitutionality of the state appropriation, but by early 1958, all had been settled in favor of the port authority. The authority quickly purchased an additional 21 acres from the Soo Line Railroad and awarded a $2.7 million dredging contract to Duluth's Zenith Dredge. L. Keith Yetter was the project engineer for Zenith Dredge. He recalled in a 2000 interview that the project site for the port terminal was nothing more than a spit of sand that housed a gun club and firing range. In the past, the property had been a dock during the port's heyday of timber shipments early in the 20th century. But the dock had been abandoned since the 1920s.

A Zenith Dredge crew of more than 100 people descended on the Rice's Point site in the summer of 1958. They moved more than a million cubic yards of material, sinking 500 sheet steel pilings 58 feet into the harbor to support the docks and transit sheds which would mark the site as one of the most modern port terminals in North America when it opened in 1959. Crews first dredged the perimeter of the site to a 15-foot depth and used the spoils to reclaim some of the submerged property, eventually expanding the project site to 120 acres. Then they finished dredging the 6,700-foot perimeter to a 30-foot depth along the dock walls so that the largest ocean-going vessels in the world at the time could fully utilize the facilities.

Meanwhile, other contractors swarmed over the site, building a warehouse and transit sheds, installing two "Whirley" gantry cranes (manufactured in Duluth by Clyde Iron Works), blacktopping two miles of roads, installing a 2,200-foot-long concrete ship apron and laying more than 9,000 feet of railroad tracks. By the time the first frost arrived in the fall of 1958, the project was essentially complete. The Seaway Port Authority of Duluth had brought the complex project in on time and under budget. To honor the visionary who had died before the project came to fruition, the Seaway Port Authority of Duluth named the complex the Arthur M. Clure Public Marine Terminal.[4]

The creation of the port authority and the completion of the port terminal project in time for the April 1959 opening of the seaway was an example of a public-private partnership at its best. Duluth and Superior have benefited immeasurably from the vision of those who understood that the Twin Ports must always orient themselves to the water.

Since the *Ramon De Larrinaga* entered the Duluth Ship Canal that blustery May Sunday nearly half a century in the past, the Duluth port authority and the port terminal project have been economic drivers for a substantial portion of the regional economy. By 2003, the port authority also owned an industrial park ("Airpark") near Duluth International Airport as well as other waterfront facilities, and nearly 900 people were employed full-time by some 60 companies on port authority-developed lands. The Clure Public Marine Terminal itself housed 18 tenants and had no remaining space for development. Arthur M. Clure would not have been surprised. ∎

---

[4] Arthur M. Clure's son Thomas Clure, also an admiralty lawyer, was appointed to the port authority board by the Duluth City Council in 2001.

Duluth Seaway Port Authority Executive Directors

Robert T. Smith	1957-1967	Paul D. Pella	1977-1978
David W. Oberlin	1967-1969	Davis Helberg	1979-2003
C. Thomas Burke	1969-1976	Adolph Ojard	2003-present

Bill Beck is an Indianapolis-based writer and historian. He raised his family in Duluth, and from 1982-1988, he served as a city council appointee to the then Seaway Port Authority of Duluth board of commissioners. He and local maritime historian C. Patrick Labadie have written a port authority-sponsored book on the history of the Duluth-Superior port, "Pride of the Inland Seas," published by Afton Historical Society Press in 2004.

CHAPTER

4

Duluth Arena/Auditorium

THE VISITOR INDUSTRY'S BIGGEST LIFT
SINCE THE AERIAL BRIDGE

by Manley "Monnie" Goldfine

In the 1950s there was much conversation about building an arena/auditorium for Duluth. Reidar Lund, sports editor for the *Duluth News Tribune*, pushed the project in his columns on many occasions.

In about 1960, Jeno Paulucci took charge of the project and with the help of a small committee he got the effort launched.

The committee hired the Stanford Research Institute to do a feasibility study. There had been much controversy over whether the Arena/Auditorium should be built in the Miller Hill area or downtown, but the study recommended that it be located in downtown Duluth on the waterfront. Probably the most important decision made early on was that it be located on the site of the Zalk-Josephs scrap yard.

The Stanford Study recommended a 2,500-seat auditorium, a 6,000-seat arena and a convention center. The committee and the Duluth city administration applied for and received a $3 million federal grant to finance half of the construction. It was one of the first Economic Development Administration (EDA) grants for this type of civic project. In order for the city to bond for the balance, it was necessary to hold a referendum ballot. A speakers' committee of 40 members was created to go to all the civic clubs to encourage people to support the general obligation bond issue. We spoke to every group we could find, some as small as five people in a garden club. The project was so controversial that the question was raised as to whether the City should pay the $6,000 that the vote would cost, so Jeno offered to pay for it.

> The project was so controversial that the question was raised as to whether the City should pay the $6,000 that the vote would cost, so Jeno offered to pay for it.

In February 1962, a special referendum was held to authorize the City to issue $3 million of construction bonds and $200,000 of operation bonds. The bond issue passed with 62% in support.

After the election, the Minnesota Legislature authorized the formation of an independent administrative board. Those appointed to the first board were Bob Dettman, Annabelle Gallagher, Paul Miller, Robert Prescott, Lee Vann, Casper "Bud" Visina and myself. Bob Prescott was elected chairman and I was elected vice chairman.

A company composed of five major architectural firms in Duluth was formed to design and build the facility. Each firm was responsible for a different part of the project. They included: Lucas-Peck Associates, Melander & Fugelso Associates, Morgenstern & Stanius, Shefchik & Associates, and Starin & Thorsen, Inc. The Shefchik firm was in charge of construction supervision; Morgenstern & Stanius did the original design.

It took quite an effort to put the land package together. The Minnesota Slip and other parcels had different owners, including the Great Northern Railroad. Groundbreaking took place in January of 1965, with the temperature 15 degrees below zero. As Mayor George D. Johnson picked up the first shovel full of dirt he quipped, "They said it would be a cold day in hell before we could build an Arena/Auditorium."

Many decisions had to be made during the construction. The board was divided into seven different committees, with Bob Dettman serving as chairman of construction. The Arena/Auditorium Board, based on the special law of the State of Minnesota, was extremely independent of city government. They could do everything except levy taxes. The board hired its own attorney and made its own arrangements separate from the City administration. During the construction, Bob Prescott invested the money raised from the bond issue. The money earned over $200,000, which helped the building budget.

The construction had many glitches. In the spring of 1966, construction unions were negotiating new contracts and a citywide strike looked possible. However, the unions agreed that the Arena/Auditorium had to be built on time and voted not to strike its construction. During construction, the board decided to upgrade the facilities and many improvements were made. One of the very important ones was to upgrade the Arena/Auditorium facility by putting in a ceiling and installing upholstered seats instead of wooden benches. This made the room much more popular and versatile than originally anticipated.

To pay for the upgrades, the board scheduled meetings every Thursday evening at the Flame Restaurant where they asked different groups for donations. Those meetings were very successful.

One of the "dog-and-pony" shows at the Flame was presented to the Duluth Clearing House, a group of five local bank presidents. The story has been told that during the meeting, the presidents all excused themselves to adjourn to the restroom, where they held a private meeting and decided to commit the money necessary for the hydraulic orchestra lift in the auditorium.

A plaque is located in the stairway across from the ticketing windows

"They said it would be a cold day..." – Mayor George D. Johnson's words as he turned the first shovel of earth for the Arena/Auditorium on December 19, 1963, using a snow shovel. Others at the groundbreaking ceremony, from left: Donald C. McDonald, president of Zenith Dredge, contractor on the initial construction phase; Paul W. Miller, board member; Robert K. Prescott, board president; Donn Larson, city council president; Robert A. Dettman, board member; Kaarlo Otava, Area Redevelopment Administration field coordinator; Manley "Monnie" Goldfine and Annabelle Gallagher, board members.

acknowledging the many organizations and individuals who donated money to enhance the original facility. A stone mural at the main entrance was designed by Sister Mary Charles of the College of St. Scholastica.

When it became apparent that for the Arena/Auditorium to be successful, more hotel rooms were needed downtown, Bob Prescott resigned from the board to develop the Radisson Hotel and I was named

When the Arena/Auditorium was young. August 1969 photo depicts the facility on Portorama Sailboat Day, with Drill's Arena Marina in the foreground where the *SS William A. Irvin* is now berthed. Describing the community effort to build the Arena/Auditorium, Congressman John Blatnik wrote, "Then something wondrous happened in Duluth." Note Flame restaurant in right background.

chairman. By the time the Arena/Auditorium was ready to open, board members included myself as chairman; Robert Dettman, vice chairman; Annabelle Gallagher, secretary; Lester Dahl, Sylvester Laskin, Lennie Underdahl and Lee Vann. Past board members were Paul Miller and Casper "Bud" Visina.

The Arena/Auditorium officially opened on August 5, 1966 with a ten-day "Hello World" celebration. It was the first facility of this type built after World War II. Most auditoriums built in previous periods consisted of one huge room in which the floor seating could be changed to accommodate both concerts and athletic events. The Duluth Arena/Auditorium had a 2,400-seat music theater, a 5,400 seat athletic arena, plus a 15,000 square foot convention facility, Paulucci Hall. On August 4 a news conference dinner hosted more than 500 members of the media from all over the United States. The main speaker was Paul Harvey, and a board member's wife was Mr. Harvey's hostess. There was a long reception line before the dinner. Everyone was complimenting Mr. Harvey about his radio broadcasts. Finally he turned to his hostess and asked if she enjoyed his program. Her quick answer, "I'm sorry, I don't watch TV." The Grand Opening celebration began on Friday night with a banquet for 2,000 people followed by a show headed by Lorne Green, Buddy Hackett and the Jimmy Dorsey Orchestra. Among the 40 people at the head table were Vice President Hubert H. Humphrey, Gov. Karl F. Rolvaag, Congressman John A. Blatnik, Mayor George D. Johnson, and many other

> ...we were advised that we needed to submit a balanced construction budget. We were short about $250,000 at that point. Now it was time for creative accounting. We prepared a new balanced budget with this item: unpledged donations— $250,000. EDA reviewed the budget and sent the $1 million check!

dignitaries. On Saturday, the Duluth Symphony performed a concert starring opera baritone Robert Merrill—a major event. The celebration continued the following week with events including a yacht club race, a parade and the Blue Angels flying team. A performance took place every night, featuring such performers and notable individuals as the Beach Boys, Walter Reuther, Bennett Cerf, the New Christy Minstrels, Johnny Paycheck and the Ice Capades. Duluth's Arena/Auditorium was launched big time!

The EDA required that our project spend all its own money before it could draw the government's money. The board called Congressman Blatnik for the first $1 million; a check came immediately. A second call and another $1 million check arrived. When we asked for the third million dollars, we were advised that we needed to submit a balanced construction budget. We were short about $250,000 at that point. Now it was time for creative accounting. We prepared a new balanced budget with this item: unpledged donations—$250,000. EDA reviewed the budget and sent the $1 million check! When all the construction bills were in, the actual construction costs were $167,000 over the funds available, despite the fact that $400,000 had been donated for upgrading. Jeno Paulucci donated the final $167,000 so that there was no outstanding debt against the Arena/Auditorium.

The events held during the first two or three years brought every major personality in the United States—Bob Hope, Jack Benny, Maurice Chevalier and Elvis Presley (who performed twice). The Arena/Auditorium, since re-named the Duluth Entertainment and Convention Center (DECC) is undoubtedly the most successful complex of its kind in the U.S. Its location was the first major breakthrough, which created a dynamic new industry and gave a whole fresh look for Duluth. Ignited by Jeno, with great support from its citizens and government and served by outstanding boards and extremely capable managers, the Arena/Auditorium made Duluth a better place to live. Joe Sturckler was its first manager during the construction period and for 21 years thereafter. William Schweiger succeeded Sturckler, followed by Dan Russell who has served as executive director since 1990.

In 1976, Pioneer Hall and the Northwest Passage connected the Arena to the downtown skywalk at a $6 million cost. The City Side Convention Center was added in 1990 for $17.2 million and the Harbor Side Convention Center and parking ramp were added in 2001 for $20 million. The two major tenants were UMD Hockey (an annual sellout) and the Duluth Symphony. The Ice Capades trained at the Arena for a month each summer. On several nights each season, the Symphony would be performing a concert while at the same time UMD played hockey or the Ringling Bros. Circus performed.

In 1963, it was determined that a room tax should be created to contribute support for the Arena/Auditorium. The tourist industry backed the 3% proposal, and it was passed by the city council. The first year the room tax raised approximately $100,000. The money was split 60% to the Arena/Auditorium, 35% to the Visitors and Convention Bureau for advertising and 5% for administration. Duluth was one of the first tourist destinations in the U.S. to back a room tax.

Today the DECC is one of Duluth's major assets and a source of civic pride. The DECC is a huge success as a major venue offering cultural, entertainment and sports activities to the people of Duluth and the entire region. It has been a major factor in attracting conventions and tourists from all over the nation and was the key in making Duluth an outstanding tourist destination. It is estimated over a half a billion dollars has been invested in tourist industry facilities since the Arena/Auditorium was built. ∎

Manley "Monnie" Goldfine was appointed to the first Duluth Arena/Auditorium Board of Directors in 1960. He served as vice chairman of the board during fundraising and construction, and was chairman of the board when the Arena/Auditorium celebrated its grand opening in 1965.

CHAPTER

5

John A. Blatnik Bridge

CONNECTING THE TWIN PORTS
WAS A HIGH-WIRE ACT

*This article first appeared in the Duluth News Tribune April 10, 1985,
entitled "Unlike the High Bridge, the Arena brought the region together."
Reprinted with permission.*

by John A. Blatnik

What has the High Bridge (now the John A.
Blatnik Bridge) got to do with the Arena/Auditorium? They
are seen and used by thousands of appreciative people
regularly, they enhance the spectacular Duluth-Superior
harbor and in turn they are enhanced by the beauty of the
Head of the Lakes. But at their beginnings a quarter of a
century ago, the Arena/Auditorium almost never came to be
because of the bridge.

For years Duluth dreamed and hoped a public bridge would
span the bay. Duluth and Superior talked about building their
own toll bridge, and Congress enacted legislation permitting

them to do so. But the bridge never came.

Shortly after the St. Lawrence Seaway was approved by the Congress, the interstate highway system was also approved. In Minnesota I-35 would run from Minneapolis-St. Paul to Duluth. But I eventually got the high bridge included in the interstate system to link up to the Twin Ports.

The bridge was going to become a reality, and with the incredible good fortune that 90% of its cost would be paid by the Federal Interstate Highway Fund with the remaining 10% split by the two states at no cost whatever to the two port cities!

All the cities had to do was make up their minds on what kind of a bridge they'd prefer, how high it should be and where the two ends should touch ground. That's when the real brouhaha began!

Duluth was a loose conglomerate of contiguous but unlike communities and neighborhoods. Its diverse nature manifested itself in the great difficulty it had in arriving at any community consensus. Now with the proposed bridge there was something big and real to argue about. A crowning blow came when a petition with a substantial number of signatures was sent to Washington recommending the bridge be abandoned and a tunnel be drilled under the bay so it could also be used as a bomb shelter.

However, the real blow came after all the wrangling was over and the Minnesota Highway Department formally submitted its approval to Washington, but incredibly asked that it be limited to a two-lane structure. I was stunned. And Minnesota's share of the bridge cost was only 5%. Things had come to an impasse.

To bring it to a close, I had the Army Corps of Engineers hold a public hearing in Duluth so all interested parties could state their positions. All factors were then reviewed in Washington, and the Federal Bureau of Roads approved the bridge essentially as it now is. One person who did a great deal to bring this to a head was then-Mayor George D. Johnson.

All this wrangling lasted more than two years. The bridge was being given to the cities free; all they had to do was make up their collective minds. And they couldn't!

Shortly after the bridge episode, the late Bob Morris of the Duluth Chamber of Commerce invited me to a meeting to discuss prospects for federal help for a city arena-auditorium facility. My immediate reaction was not to have anything to do with it on the grounds that if such a relatively simple matter as a free bridge became such an obstacle course, what wonderful possibilities lay ahead on the variety of aspects concerning the arena; dealing with size, shape, location, color, cost, type of use and what not. I wanted to have nothing to do with it, and advised promoters to go ahead on their own—they could build their own and pay for their own. I heard nothing about the arena for several months.

Then out of the blue I got a call from Jeno Paulucci, who, in an uncharacteristically calm, easy-going manner began, "John, regarding that Duluth Arena proposal..."

I interrupted, "Jeno, we're good friends, but let me tell you I don't want to have anything to do with it. After all the grief and headaches I got over the bridge that didn't cost them one cent."

"I know, I know, John," continued Jeno, still soothing, "but hear me out. If we get the city of Duluth to vote a bond issue for its half of the project cost ($3 million), will you get the other half from the community facilities provisions of your Area Redevelopment program?"

I chuckled at this, for I couldn't imagine Duluth passing any bond issue, even if it was to help handicapped school children. But the proposition was a sound and fair one. So in good humor I agreed to go along, certain no such bond issue would be approved, and if it by chance were they would never agree on what kind of facility they should have.

Then Paulucci and his team, spearheaded by Lee Vann, launched an all-out promotional campaign the likes of which had never been experienced in the Head of the Lakes. Full page ads in the Duluth papers, ballots clipped out and mailed by readers by the thousands, radio and TV spots and guest appearances. When the referendum was held, the vote was more than two to one in favor of the bond issue. I then got federal approval of the other half of the $6 million project cost.

Then something wondrous happened in Duluth. Quietly, a few people got to work in earnest, finding ways they could combine their efforts, talents and resources to start a coordinated effort, calling upon ingenuity, constructive thought and foresight to conceive more precisely the kind of

NEMHC, Duluth, MN. Photo by Barbara Glick

September 24, 1971. Minnesota 8th District Congressman John A. Blatnik is congratulated by U.S. Secretary of Transportation William Scranton (Nixon administration) and Wisconsin Congressman Alvin O'Konski at ceremonies dedicating the Blatnik Bridge spanning the St. Louis Bay between Rice's Point and Connor's Point.

facility which would best serve the needs of the community and area. A group of architects visited other cities with such centers, adapted the best of what they saw, devised their own concepts and finally came out with the design and plans for the attractive, functional, multi-purpose facility which today still stands in the forefront as one of the largest, most attractive, functionally efficient of its kind in the country.

In addition to the varied activities and events at the Arena/Auditorium which brought pleasure and excitement to so many, there were economic benefits of measurable proportions. The facility brought visitors from an area which stretched through northern Wisconsin to Michigan's Upper Peninsula and westerly to the Dakotas.

Above all, it did something to and for the spirit of the people in this diverse community. One clearly feels a sense of warm pride expressed by so many. The Arena/Auditorium seems to be a focal point drawing their interests and attention and presences together in an atmosphere of warm togetherness. It seems as though the combined hopes, aspirations and dreams of the people that expressed themselves so overwhelmingly and decisively in that smashing referendum were embodied in the structure.

The spirit of the people seems to emanate like a warm glow out of that beautiful edifice. ∎

John A. Blatnik was born in Chisholm, Minnesota in 1911, and enjoyed a long and productive career in Minnesota and national politics, beginning in 1940 when he was elected to the Minnesota Senate. From 1947 to 1974, he represented Minnesota's Eighth Congressional District in the U.S. House. For several years, U.S. Representative Blatnik was chairman of the powerful House Public Works Committee. The High Bridge was completed in 1961, with nearly 26,000 vehicles crossing the bridge during its first 24 hours of operation. In 1971, the High Bridge was renamed the John A. Blatnik Bridge. John A. Blatnik died in 1991.

CHAPTER

6

Pioneer Hall, Duluth Curling Club & Northwest Passage

ARENA/AUDITORIUM EXPANSION BROUGHT MORE
CONVENTIONS, WORLD-CLASS CURLING...AND A
WARM CONNECTION TO DOWNTOWN

by Bob Magie III

Eight years after the Arena/Auditorium was constructed, it became apparent that in order to increase Duluth's ability to attract major sports events and conventions, an expansion was needed. At the time, the Arena/Auditorium pumped $6 million into Duluth's economy, and in a survey, 91% responded that the Duluth Arena/Auditorium was an asset to the community. The annual payroll averaged $300,000 and more than 750 people were employed on a full-time or part-time basis.

A 1972 economic feasibility study, financed by the Paulucci Family Foundation, determined that an expansion would bring $8 or $9 million within the first five years of operation. The

Duluth Curling Club

The Duluth Curling Club hosts a bonspiel in Pioneer Hall. The facility can accommodate eight sheets of ice, the largest facility for curling in the U.S. The Duluth Curling Club's annual House of Hearts Charity Bonspiel allows curlers to share the ice with top curlers from North America.

study took into account the Minnesota Department of Transportation's (Mn/DOT) intention to run Interstate 35 through downtown Duluth and past the old Curling Club at 1330 London Road. The building had been home to Duluth curlers since 1912, and was slated to be demolished.

Rep. John A. Blatnik, his successor Rep. James Oberstar, Duluth Mayor Ben Boo and Jeno Paulucci worked behind the scenes to garner funding for the $4.5 million project. In May 1974, the project received a grant of $400,000 from the Upper Great Lakes Regional Commission. The remaining costs were to be financed through a $2 million general obligation bond issue by the City of Duluth and $2 million from the federal Economic Development Administration (EDA). Construction was expected to require 18 months. It was hoped that the facility would be up and running when the city hosted the Air Canada Silver Broom world curling tournament in March 1976.

Joseph Sturckler (Arena/Auditorium Manager 1964-1985) worked closely with Manley Goldfine and the Arena/Auditorium Administrative Board, headed by President Leonard E. Griffith. Frank Befera, president of the Duluth Curling Club, played a key role in envisioning and planning the addition.

The Duluth Arena/Auditorium Administrative Board selected architect Thomas A. Vecchi to design the addition and covered walkway. He recommended an 87,000 sq. ft. annex, a low-profile building to be constructed at the east end of the Arena, large enough to accommodate both ice hockey and curling, an increased exhibit and trade show area, and a heated skywalk to tie the Arena/Auditorium to the business district. Curling in Duluth was now moving into a public facility. In addition to hosting hockey and curling, the remodeled facility would double the current Arena/Auditorium space available for trade shows and conventions—from 49,000 sq. ft. of floor space to 106,000 sq. ft.

Constructing a skywalk between downtown and the arena presented some obstacles, including air rights and a railroad right-of-way. Air rights were achieved with Chicago North Western, and Mayor Ben Boo worked for months with Burlington Northern railroad officials, representatives of Mn/DOT and the Federal Highway Administration to settle the right-of-way question. It was resolved that the skywalk would pass over a parking area, Commerce Street and railroad areas to Third Avenue West and Michigan Street. The skywalk would open more than 2,000 parking spaces below Michigan Street that were formerly inaccessible to the arena.

On April 7, 1975, the stroke of a sledgehammer marked the beginning of construction. Leonard Griffith, President of the Arena/Auditorium Board, and Duluth Mayor Bob Beaudin presided over the groundbreaking ceremonies.

Excitement mounted in 1976 when Duluth hosted the Silver Broom World Curling Tournament in March, drawing 41,000 fans from ten countries. (Even though it took place before the new Curling Club facility officially opened, it was the largest sports event to date for the Arena/Auditorium.) 1976 also saw the visit of Norway's Christian Radich training ship, which drew 45,000 visitors.

By May 1976, while construction was still underway, costs were expected to be at least $1 million higher than projected. The increased costs were partially due to the expense of the "T" connection between the annex pedestrian bridge and the existing downtown Duluth skywalks. The EDA grant was increased to $2.5 million, and the Upper Great Lakes Regional Commission increased their original grant from $400,000 to $650,000. The Duluth Curling Club contributed $500,000 to complete the curling facility.

Construction of the skyway was expected to begin in early fall of 1976 and was to be completed by 1977. It was also at this time that the Duluth Arena/Auditorium Administrative Board named the annex Pioneer Hall and the skywalk was named the Northwest Passage.

Pioneer Hall, however, was nearing completion, and grand opening ceremonies were scheduled for August 30 through September 12, 1976. The ceremonies were also a celebration of the Arena/Auditorium's ten-year anniversary. Performers included the Ice Capades, singer Bobby Vinton and a Glenn Miller stage show by Ray McKinley and his orchestra. The addition put Duluth in competition with cities five to ten times larger for regional and national conventions.

In 1977, attendance at the Duluth Arena/Auditorium hit the six million mark. Its economic impact was estimated to average more than $9 million a year. ∎

Bob Magie III has been a Duluth attorney since 1970. He has been counsel for the Duluth Curling Club for over 30 years. Mr. Magie was extensively involved in the legal work that accomplished this project.

CHAPTER

7

Duluth Entertainment
Convention Center (DECC)

HOW 6 WEEKS OF LOBBYING WON OUR CITY
ONE OF THE BUSIEST VENUES IN THE U.S.

by Dan Russell

Late in the afternoon at the Radisson Hotel lounge on December 19, 1984, Duluth Mayor John Fedo asked the question, "Why not Duluth?"

A commission appointed by Minnesota's Governor, Rudy Perpich had chosen Minneapolis as the site for Minnesota's world-class convention center. Along with the designation came the state funds to construct the project. The City of Duluth had been totally off the radar screen in regards to the state convention center project, and not a factor in the commission's decision.

With the opening of the 1985 Minnesota legislative session less than six weeks away, Duluth jump-started an incredible, and what turned out to be controversial, effort to build the

Duluth State Convention Center.

Mayor Fedo rallied support from the Duluth Convention and Visitors Bureau, Duluth Chamber of Commerce, the business community and perhaps most importantly, Jeno Paulucci. Jeno, with his larger-than-life reputation, brought instant credibility to the lobbying effort.

When State Senator Sam Solon joined in, Duluth virtually became an overnight competitor to become designated as Minnesota's State Convention Center. As with any major state project, the city needed a feasibility study—the best and fastest study $30,000 could buy. To no one's surprise, the study—funded by the Chamber of Commerce, Duluth Convention and Visitors Bureau and Jeno and conducted by Gladstone & Associates—said Duluth would be a perfect location for the center. Then the lobbying effort began in earnest.

Early on, a memorable evening meeting took place in Carl Pohlad's office in Minneapolis. Present were Mr. Pohlad; Governor Perpich and his wife Lola; Jeno Paulucci; Paul Ridgeway (representing Curt Carlson); Mayor Fedo with supporters Ray Rizzi and Randy Asuma; and Dan Russell, Director of the Duluth Convention and Visitors Bureau.

The Minneapolis representatives asked why Duluth was interfering with what had been a clear path for Minneapolis to receive major state funding for a convention center they had been planning for years. Governor Perpich stated his theory that Duluth was just using the convention center destination as a bluff to get state support for Duluth's effort to turn the vacant Sears building in downtown Duluth into an Indian gaming facility. Mayor Fedo pointedly explained that the Duluth effort was for real and the battle for funding was just the beginning.

After Duluth's successful lobbying effort during the 1985 legislative session, Governor Perpich signed a bonding bill including $16 million dollars for Duluth to build a world-class convention center. (Minneapolis was unsuccessful in its efforts to get funding from the

Continued on page 39

Duluth OMNIMAX Theater

BIG SCREEN ENTERTAINMENT COMES
TO THE WATERFRONT

by Dennis Medjo

The thought of bringing an IMAX/OMNIMAX theater to the Bayfront was first considered in the late '80s. Minnesota Power was looking for a way to honor CEO Jack Rowe who would retire in 1989. The company's generating plants and principal facilities already bore the names of previous chief executives. Ray Erickson, Minnesota Power vice president, sought advice from public relations advisor Donn Larson, who suggested that the company sponsor construction of a wide-screen IMAX/OMNIMAX theater in Rowe's name. The company contracted for a study, which concluded that a big-screen theater was viable in the Bayfront area, but then chose not to pursue the idea and elected to name its energy control center for Rowe.

Jeff Frey & Associates Photography

The Duluth OMNIMAX, with 270 seats and a state-of-the-art sound system, was unveiled on April 18, 1996.

Only a few years later, when the retired ore boat *SS William A. Irvin* became a DECC satellite, the DECC directors and administration were looking for ways to make use of the carrier's cavernous cargo hold. An intriguing proposal—building a big screen theater inside the vessel—won serious consideration. They invited IMAX representatives to Duluth to size up the proposal. The IMAX experts judged that the idea was unrealistic. But this helps explain why the design of the Duluth OMNIMAX shows hints of ore boat in its form and color. (IMAX and OMNIMAX use similar film, but a different lens and screen. The IMAX projects a flat picture, while OMNIMAX is parabolic.)

Groundbreaking for the new theater took place on a corner of the DECC parking lot in March 1995. The theater was financed through a recreational revenue bond for $8 million, to be paid off in 15 years. Because the DECC took responsibility for the financing, with no general obligation by taxpayers, the project did not become a political issue.

Continued on page 39

Duluth's crowning achievement. From symphony concerts to monster truck rallies, the DECC has become the showplace for the city's growing entertainment and tourism industry. It has been cited as one of the busiest convention centers in the country. Photo circa 1997, before addition of parking ramp and harbor side expansion.

DULUTH OMNIMAX
Continued from page 37

state, but did get authority to impose additional hospitality taxes to finance the Minneapolis Convention Center.)

During the session, there were accusations of impropriety that will remain part of Duluth's political lore. Mayor Fedo collected $13,500 from Duluth businessmen Jeno Paulucci, Wing Huey and Bill Meierhoff for lobbying purposes. However, the use of the cash delivered in a paper bag was questioned and was later included in a number of criminal charges against Mayor Fedo. A Duluth jury found the mayor innocent of the charges November 16, 1988.

On December 9, 1985, an architectural design team headed by Thomas & Vecchi was selected by the Duluth Arena/Auditorium Board to design the facility. In May 1986, Senator Sam Solon was successful in his efforts to obtain an additional $1.2 million for the project from the Minnesota legislature. During this time, the retired U.S. Steel ore carrier *SS William A. Irvin* was purchased and renovated with Convention Center funds and opened to the public on July 10, 1986.

On October 5, 1987, A. H. Hedenberg Construction was selected as the general contractor for the project.

The board voted to change the facility's name to the Duluth Entertainment Convention Center (DECC) on August 31, 1987.

Grand opening of the new DECC took place on June 18, 1990 when over 1,000 people were

Continued on page 41

Key DECC directors fostering the project included Charles Andresen, Monte Wittmann, Jim Shearer, Kurt Soderberg and Phil Rolle. They chose Duluth architects/engineers LHB, and Minneapolis architects Hammel, Green and Abrahamson to design the new attraction. Mortenson Construction won the contract to build it.

Only 13 months later a new, unique, never-before-seen theater in Duluth was ready. The pressure was on to be open in time for the important springtime influx of student tour groups. Beginning April 18, 1996, the Duluth OMNIMAX, with 270 seats and a state-of-the-art sound system, first revealed all its excitement.

The grand opening of the theater would kick off with a reception and the film *The Dream is Alive*. To help celebrate, astronaut George "Pinky" Nelson made a special appearance. Nelson, a veteran of NASA's Space Shuttle program, was a mission specialist aboard the Challenger's flight 41-C. He shot much of the film featured

Continued on page 41

SS *William A. Irvin*

A STALWART FLAGSHIP SERVES AS A LASTING TRIBUTE TO GREAT LAKES SHIPPING

by Bob Hom

The steel bulk freighter SS *William A. Irvin* was built by the American Shipbuilding Company in 1938. Named after the president of U.S. Steel, the Irvin was the first major vessel to be constructed on the Great Lakes after the Depression, and it incorporated a number of technical advances in the shipbuilding industry. Hauling 14,000 tons of cargo per trip with a crew of 36 and a top speed of 12 miles per hour, the *Irvin* served as the flagship of the fleet until bigger and faster ships came along in the early 1970s.

The *SS William A. Irvin* makes its final trip to its permanent berth in the Minnesota Slip. More than a million people have toured the ship since it opened to tourists in 1986.

The last trip for the *Irvin* as a Great Lakes Fleet vessel occurred on December 11, 1978.

In the fall of 1985, a group of farsighted Duluthians—led by Don Shank and Julia Marshall— signed an option to purchase the vessel to save the ship from the scrap yard. They held this option until other plans could be made.

In 1985, an appropriation by the Minnesota Legislature made it possible for the Duluth Arena/Auditorium to expand its facility by building the City Side Convention Center addition. On April 15, 1986, the DECC board agreed to buy the SS *William A. Irvin* for $110,000 from the U.S. Steel Great Lakes Fleet, using funds from the appropriation. On May 8, the board approved a contract with Fraser Shipyard for $210,000 to renovate the vessel. The renovations consisted of sandblasting, scraping, painting, and closing off all underwater openings that were necessary for the operation of the vessel.

On June 17, the Irvin was towed from the Fraser Shipyard in Superior to the dock on the harbor side of the DECC by two North American Towing Company tugs, the *Sioux* and the *Dakota*. The boat was opened to the public as a tourist attraction two weeks later. The original thinking by the board was to have it open by the spring of 1987. Due to the determined hard work board by president Bob Heimbach, the boat opened to

Continued on page 42

THE WILL and the WAY

welcomed by Governor Perpich to tour the new facility. It included a 26,000 sq. ft. Lake Superior Ballroom, 16 meeting rooms, the Edmund Fitzgerald Exhibit Hall, a lobby/registration area, and a new kitchen and support space.

DECC HARBOR SIDE CONVENTION CENTER AND PARKING RAMP

The DECC proved to be very successful—It soon was operating near capacity. In 1996, the national publication *Meeting News*, rated the DECC as the 11th busiest convention center in North America.

The additional traffic also added to the ongoing problem of a shortage of parking at DECC events. The DECC Board of Directors once again started planning for expansion, this time for additional meeting space and a parking ramp.

In May 1997, the board approved a funding package requesting financial help from both the State of Minnesota and the City of Duluth.

Politically, Duluth's request to the State of Minnesota for help was timed to coincide with similar requests from the City of Minneapolis for their convention center expansion and St. Paul's request for funds for the Xcel Center.

After visits to Duluth by the State House of Representatives Capital Investment Committee and Minnesota Finance Department officials, Governor Carlson included $12 million for the DECC expansion in the bonding bill he presented to the 1998 legislature.

DULUTH OMNIMAX
Continued from page 39

in *The Dream is Alive*. Two months and 35,000 customers later the OMNIMAX was flourishing.

July 4, 1996, just one month later, the theater shared a world premier with five other cities, featuring the film *Special Effects*. The audience grew steadily, and a new attendance record was set in 1998, enhanced by booking the film *Everest* in June.

As the theater's popularity grew, so did the number of school groups that were attracted. In February 2001, vice-presidential candidate Winona LaDuke taught a lesson in cultural diversity to a group of students from our stage.

In 2002 the OMNIMAX showed its first feature-length film, *The Rolling Stones*. Most films in the 70-millimeter big screen format are about 40 minutes. By this season the popularity of our gift shop prompted us to offer videos, DVDs and other merchandise online. 2002 brought another special attraction for school groups: Amy Mosset, who portrayed Sacagawea, telling her story to the youngsters who came to view *Lewis and*

Continued on page 43

SS WILLIAM A. IRVIN

Continued from page 40

tourists on July 1, 1986.

In October of 1986, the *Irvin* was towed to its present location in the Minnesota Slip where it continues to operate as one of the premier tourist attractions in the state. In the first 17 years, the *Irvin* has been open as an attraction, more than 1,360,000 people have toured the boat.

In October of 1991 the *Irvin* began what has become a yearly tradition by opening up for the Halloween season with the haunted *Irvin*. The haunted version of the *Irvin* has scared more than a quarter of a million people since the production began. In 2000 it was decided to kick it up a notch in the scary department. The DECC bought out the entire contents (eight semi trailer loads) from one of the nation's largest haunted house operations in Chicago. By doing this, new attendance records continue to be set. ∎

A DECC employee since 1977, Bob Horn is director of operations for the entertainment and convention complex.

The state contribution called for a local match and early in 1998, Mayor Gary Doty led the effort to convince the city council to add a .5% food and beverage and .5% hotel/motel tax to fund the $8 million city's share.

With his legendary skill, Senator Sam Solon secured legislative support for the $12 million state grant which the governor signed into law in May 1998.

Special acknowledgement should be given to Representatives Mike Jaros and Tom Huntley and State Senator Jerry Janezich for their efforts. The DECC Board began work on both projects.

PARKING RAMP

On June 29, 1998, the DECC Building Committee recommended to the board that the team of LHB Engineers & Architects and Carl Walker Consultants be retained to design a 600-space ramp at the DECC. The ramp was placed along the Northwest Passage, not only to provide guest parking for DECC events but also for downtown workers and visitors to the Duluth OMNIMAX® Theatre. In December 1998, Reuben Johnson Contractors, Superior, was awarded a $4,480,000 contract to construct the ramp. The parking facility opened with great fanfare 14 months later in February 2000. A "Monster Truck" drove over a fake City of Duluth car driven by Mayor Doty to claim the distinction of being the first vehicle to park in the new ramp.

HARBOR SIDE CONVENTION CENTER

After starting the parking ramp project, the DECC board began work on planning new convention space. The goal was to take advantage of the views from the DECC toward the harbor. The initial plan called for construction over Harbor Drive directly behind the Arena/Auditorium lobby, but that location was soon to change. The DECC Building Committee interviewed several design teams consisting of nationally recognized convention center architects partnered with local firms.

On September 28, 1998 they recommended that the board select Stanius Johnson Architects with Seattle based LMN Architects to design the new facility. The team identified an unused corner of the DECC complex across from the Vista Fleet dock and Minnesota Slip Bridge. The location provided outstanding views of the Harbor and Aerial Lift Bridge from its glass façade. An additional bonus was a panoramic vista of Lake Superior from the upper level ballroom.

A contract of $12,546,000 was awarded to Johnson-Wilson Constructors of Duluth to construct the new facility. The Harbor Side Convention Center included a 12,000 sq. ft. ballroom and with the use of movable partitions, ten new meeting rooms. The new facility also featured a new kitchen, support space and a covered loading area. The building also became the new home to Duluth Superior Excursions.

DULUTH OMNIMAX
Continued from page 41

Clark.

In 2003, Richard Pyle, the scientist who was in the film *Coral Reef Adventure*, made a live presentation to school groups. In this year the theater's projection system was upgraded with a digital improvement that allowed playing longer films without an intermission. Our second feature length presentation, *The Lion King*, drew over 23,000 people.

The appeal of big screen entertainment continues to grow and our Duluth theater is part of the pattern, attracting 160,000 to 200,000 annually, another successful and complementary magnet for our downtown waterfront. We're pleased that our OMNIMAX building resembles an ore boat, where the concept for today's busy theater was born. ∎

Dennis Medjo is director of attractions at the DECC. He is responsible for the OMNIMAX and SS William A. Irvin. He joined the DECC in 1993 and has been with the theater since its opening in 1996.

Grandmaison Studios

The DECC Harbor Side Convention Center under construction in the summer of 2000 by Johnson-Wilson Constructors. It includes a 12,000 sq. ft. ballroom and an imposing view of the harbor, aerial bridge and Lake Superior. (See front cover.)

A grand opening celebration was held on January 31, 2001. The first convention booked in the new center, International Ship Masters Association, began their meeting the following day.

The board presidents during both expansions were Monte Wittmann and Vern Amundson. Other board members were: M. George Downs, Gary Kelleher, Steve Bianchi, John Bray, Bob Eaton, Greg Fox, Yvonne Prettner Solon, Karen Evens, Richard Pearson, Riki McManus, John Scott, Jim Shearer, Amy Weidman, Peter Sneve, Bob Heimbach, Philip Rolle and Peter Bye. ∎

Dan Russell served as the director of the Duluth Convention and Visitors Bureau from 1979-1989. He was appointed executive director of the DECC in 1990.

CHAPTER

8

Davidson-Ojibway Press/HBJ/Advanstar

A RIDE TO REMEMBER

by Orlando "Lars" Fladmark

When I arrived for my first day of employment with Ojibway Press on December 4, 1962, the company occupied roughly three floors of the building at 1 East First Street. In addition, the company owned Davidson Printing Company, which operated out of rented quarters two blocks away. The total number of business publications owned by Ojibway at that time was 12. Total local employment was about 100.

The principal owner of Ojibway Press at that time was Marshall Reinig. He, along with a group of local investors, had formed Ojibway Press after first acquiring Davidson Printing Company from South Haven, Michigan and a magazine that came with the company called *American Fur Breeder*. Marshall was already a very successful mink rancher and had formerly been an advertising salesman in the Chicago area. Once he moved the printing plant to Duluth and began publishing *American Fur Breeder*, his interest in growing the company increased by leaps and bounds. He then set out on a program of acquiring other business publications to add to his vision of a large, multi-faceted business publishing house. It was that early vision we all followed faithfully in later years.

His second in command and junior partner was Robert Edgell. Bob brought a magazine he owned in the hearing health care field to the new company and became the sales executive for the company. Both he and Marshall were great business colleagues, good leaders and good, reliable friends.

My first assignment was to straighten out the circulation system currently in use. After that was accomplished, my assignment became to prepare the company for computerization. In 1962, there were very few companies that knew what a computer was, most certainly not in the publishing field. I, however, had gained some systems and programming skills while working for the National Security Agency in Washington, D.C. and it was this background Ojibway hoped to utilize.

By 1964, I was in charge of the entire circulation department, the company had grown to about 16 publications doing about $12 million annually and I was given the green light to go ahead and pursue computerization for the company.

This was a truly embryonic project at the time since no software existed for handling circulation records and the requirements of circulation auditing. The task of which computer to rent (one didn't purchase them in those days) and writing all the software fell totally on myself and John Kessler, our electronic data processing manager.

At that point in time, only two computer manufacturers served the Duluth market, IBM and NCR. Having come from an IBM background, I certainly expected that we would go with IBM. To my surprise, I received the best system support and proposal from NCR and, in due course, we wound up throwing our lot in with that company. Once we had selected the hardware, we then sat down to begin the arduous task of computer programming all the functions, which at that point were primarily manual in nature. Our initial system consisted of a 4K, 60-millisecond computer, 2 magnetic tape drives, a card reader and a paper tape reader. For us, at the time, it was a magnificent piece of hardware. Today, there is more computing power in a cheap calculator than existed in our entire system!

Needless to say, with the limited computer memory available in those days, programming was extremely difficult and conserving programming space was of paramount concern. We bravely set out evenings and weekends to write the necessary software, meanwhile maintaining our regular duties during the day. The upshot of all this was that for an almost two-year period, from 1964 to 1966, there were only 13 days in which I did not work nights, days and all weekends. The 13 days were days that I was either ill or out of town. We would write our programs in Duluth and then travel to Dayton, Ohio to test and debug them on hardware at NCR headquarters. Today, it seems like an impossible task. In those days, it was a challenge I couldn't let go. It wasn't work, it was fun! Lo and behold, in the spring of 1966, we put our first publication on line and, by the end of the summer we had computerized our entire circulation and John Kessler's reader service functions. At that time, we were one of the very few computerized companies in the publishing field. McGraw Hill was the only other exception. Our system was extremely good for its time and enabled us to also begin selling circulation services to other publishers, which resulted in our circulation department becoming one of the significant profit centers in the company.

Our advanced computerization brought us to the attention of Harcourt, Brace and World (H.B.W.), a major New York publishing house. This led to the purchase of Ojibway Press by Harcourt Brace and World in 1968 and to the retirement of Marshall Reinig and Bob Edgell in that year. By mid-1969, however, the projections made for the sale had not materialized and H.B.W. was unhappy with the purchase. Plans were made at the corporate level to close down the Duluth operation and move everything to New York. I was not enamored of moving to New York because I had left the East Coast and come to Duluth by choice, not by chance. I therefore began what was perhaps the most important event of my career, convincing H.B.W. to remain in Duluth.

Most of my publishing peers could never understand our Duluth location and its success. In my talks throughout the country, I used to list a number

Harcourt Brace Jovanovich employees, Duluth 1985. At its height, the publishing company occupied 11 buildings in Duluth and employed 1,100.

of reasons, but there were three primary reasons I always emphasized. One, square footage costs were very favorable in Duluth compared to large metropolitan areas. That's why we purchased and remodeled eleven buildings. Two, the educational level attained in Minnesota was (and still is) much better for a publisher than many other areas of the country. Deplore as we might public education, the average high school or college graduate here can read and write well. That's the essence of publishing, in all areas. The third reason, however, was the most important of all, the absolute quality, integrity, dedication and loyalty of our Duluth employees. I could never say enough good things about them because they always surpassed themselves! And we all enjoyed working together.

In June of 1969, I was placed in charge of the entire operation in Duluth. At that point, Davidson Printing Company was our primary printing supplier and their equipment was, to say the least, obsolete. In early 1970, I went to New York to negotiate with William Jovanovich, the chairman of the company, for a new printing press for Davidson and a chance to keep the company going rather than throwing in the towel. The net result of the meeting was that Bill Jovanovich agreed to purchase a new two-color sheet-fed offset press for Davidson and gave us a one-year chance to prove that the company could be profitable.

In 1969, the company had lost $750,000, a rather significant sum based on revenues of about $16 million. I spent most of 1970 trying to figure out how to reduce costs and streamline the company in order to at least reduce the loss. During that year, we implemented a large number of cost-saving measures, the net result of which was that in 1971 we made a $15,000 profit. To his credit, Bill Jovanovich honored his word and Duluth was spared the ax.

In late 1971 we also successfully lured Robert Edgell out of retirement to assume the presidency of the company in New York. Bob was a highly entrepreneurial sort and, with the help of a publicly traded Fortune 500 stock, we embarked on a large acquisition program in the business publication field. The logic of the company became that sales and editorial were primarily in New York and Chicago and all the service components of the company were in Duluth. On that operational platform we eventually grew the company to something over 110 different titles and annual revenues of about $230 million. From one building on Lake Avenue we grew to occupy 11 buildings in Duluth. From 100 employees at the outset, we grew to over 1,100 employees locally and about 1,600 nationally.

In 1985, Bill Jovanovich also determined that we should take over a company called Beckley Cardy, a national school supply distributor. We wound up computerizing the entire company, moving it to Duluth and turning it into a profitable business. I also operated as the CEO of that company from 1985 to 1993. The wheels, however, fell off when Robert Maxwell, the British financier, made a takeover offer for what was now Harcourt Brace Jovanovich, our parent company. To combat the offer, Bill Jovanovich leveraged the company $3.5 billion into debt. The net result was that everything wound up in bankruptcy and many parts were sold off. Out of the wreckage of what I term late '80s Wall Street greed came what is today Advanstar Communications in downtown Duluth.

On New Year's Day 1991, Bob Edgell leaped to his death, unable to cope with the ruin of his life's work. The death of a friend, who always called me "little brother," was the greatest tragedy of all.

By 1993, nearly all members of senior management, including myself, were replaced, along with many of our wonderful employees. This led me back to publishing on my own, a course which has been rewarding but nowhere near as exciting as the growth years with Harcourt Brace Jovanovich. During a period of economic uncertainty in Duluth, our company experienced its greatest growth. Now those days are just memories…a pleasant beginning and a sad ending. But, like me, I think all our past employees would agree that it was a fun-filled, exciting and glorious ride. ∎

Orlando "Lars" Fladmark joined Ojibway Press in 1962, served as executive vice-president of HBJ Publications from 1978-1992, and was CEO of Beckley Cardy 1985-1993. Throughout his Duluth career he has been active in community development.

CHAPTER

9

The Taconite Amendment

STATEWIDE EFFORTS HELPED TO FIRE UP
THE IRON RANGE MINING INDUSTRY

by Al France

The taconite industry has experienced its highs and lows since 1964, but it has remained a significant source of strength for the economy of northeastern Minnesota. The people in the early 1960s perceived a problem, worked to do something about it, and succeeded.

Following the United Steel Workers strike across Minnesota's Iron Range in 1959, economic conditions in 1960 gave rise to concerns that iron mining would not continue to be the singular strength in the regional economy. Natural ore mining was in decline as mines became depleted, and expected investments in new taconite facilities were not being made. Techniques for mining and concentrating lower grade taconite ore were known—the Reserve and Erie taconite operations had come on stream in 1955 and 1956—but new and additional taconite facilities had not been built, partly because of state tax policies.

A group of mayors from Iron Range communities, led by Mayor Ben Constantine of Babbitt, sought to improve the investment climate for taconite. They recommended that the mining companies, banks and insurance companies that would be asked to provide investment capital first needed the assurance that mining operations would not be singled out for tax increases, as had occurred in 1957 and 1959. This effort by Iron Range mayors prompted the notion of an amendment to the state constitution that would limit the increases in state occupation and royalty taxes on taconite operations. The idea of a constitutional amendment was seen as necessary because the mining occupation tax was already a constitutional provision, having been adopted as a part of the constitution by a vote of the people in 1922.

Elmer L. Anderson, the Republican candidate for Governor, endorsed the proposal, and when he won the 1960 election, the proposed taconite amendment became a priority issue. A bill for the amendment was introduced and easily passed in the Senate. When the bill was heard in the House Tax Committee, however, committee Chairman Donald Wozniak opposed it and the bill failed.

The ensuing 1962 election was dominated by the taconite tax issue with Governor Anderson and conservative[1] candidates for the House made it one of their principal causes. The DFL, unions and liberal candidates generally opposed the amendment with Congressman John Blatnik declaring it "dead as a dodo bird."

It was a hard fought, and sometimes bitter election campaign. Elmer L. Anderson was defeated by Karl Rolvaag by some 90 votes after a lengthy recount that stretched into the middle of March of 1963. Conservative candidates, however, won the House by a substantial margin, and they were determined to put the taconite amendment on the ballot in the 1964 election. Liberals, on the other hand, reflecting their DFL and union constituencies remained strongly opposed to it. Just as the proposed amendment had been a divisive issue in the 1962 campaign, it continued

---

[1] In those days the Minnesota legislature was nonpartisan. Members generally aligned with Republican values were known as conservatives, while members accepting Democrat-Famer-Labor (DFL) philosophy were called liberals.

as a major issue in the 1963 legislative session.

Some mining companies were not enthusiastic about pursuing the amendment, fearing that it would fail in a statewide vote. Some of their representatives approached the Speaker of the House, Lloyd Duxbury, and the tax committee chairman, Roy Dunn, to express their concerns and head off a vote on the issue. They were told that the issue was not theirs to control. The conservative caucus, having campaigned so strongly for the amendment, would decide its outcome in the House.

While the House leadership and some of its new members who had campaigned for the amendment began to plan steps necessary to move a bill for the amendment, there were efforts being made to work up a compromise approach that would defuse the issue. Senator Hubert Humphrey began to engineer a *volte-face* for the DFL, and mining and steel company officials met with David McDonald, president of the United Steel Workers. These meetings between Humphrey, McDonald and mining company executives led to an agreement of support for an amendment that would be submitted to the people for ratification in the 1964 election. The key to the compromise was an agreement to sunset the provision after 25 years, in 1989, assuming the people adopted the amendment.

The conservative leadership and majority in the House were determined to pass a bill for an amendment regardless of DFL opposition. People outside of the legislative environment knew that the amendment could never be ratified without the support of both political parties, the union and business communities. Only by forging a coalition of these interests during the legislative process could the foundation be laid for a successful referendum outcome at the polls in 1964.

House tax committee chairman Roy Dunn decided that passing a measure authored by individual legislators would not have the impact he wanted. Rather, he preferred that the bill would be a committee bill, carrying with it the imprimatur of the entire tax committee. Three hearings were held in the auditorium of the State Office Building to accommodate all who wanted to testify for or against the bill. Support for the amendment was overwhelming.

National Steel Pellet Plant, Keewatin, MN, was among the first new taconite operations spawned by the taconite constitutional amendment. It was operated by one of the Range's premier merchant iron ore companies, the Hanna Mining Company. 1997 photo.

Working with their counterparts in the state Senate, it was agreed that a statute setting out the terms of the agreement would be passed. A companion measure containing the language of the amendment, itself, would also be passed. Sen. Donald O. Wright of Minneapolis, chairman of the Senate tax committee, headed the Senate effort.

In the House, the tax committee's bill was introduced on March 12, given special order status on March 14, and was passed by a vote of 121 to 4. In the Senate, the house bill was given a speedy hearing and was passed on March 20 by a vote of 56 to 9. House and Senate conservatives wanted to pass the amendment while Elmer L. Anderson was still governor, and he was able to sign the bill on March 22, even though a governor's signature was not necessary for a constitutional amendment.

So the Taconite Amendment would go to the people for ratification at the general election on November 3. The amendment did not freeze taconite taxes, as some asserted, and it did not affect local production taxes which mining companies would later have reason to regret. The amendment gave voters the option of voting "yes" or "no" as to whether the provisions of Chapter 81 of the Laws of 1963 should prevail for a period of 25 years. Chapter 81 provided that State Occupation and Royalty taxes imposed on taconite companies would not be raised in an amount greater than any increase of the corporate income or franchise tax that might be imposed on the manufacturing industry of the state. Language addressing the potentials of copper-nickel was also included.

Passing the amendment through the legislature was one thing, passing it in a general election was another. No simple majority of those voting on the amendment question would suffice. Rather, a majority of all of those voting in the election would be necessary for ratification. Those who chose not to vote for the amendment, or who overlooked it would be voting "no."

Mining companies, with their future at stake, decided to keep their profiles low. For instance, a popular television program, sponsored by the industry and featuring Earl Henton as commentator, was not to be used to promote the amendment. It did, however, continue to familiarize Minnesotans with the industry's importance.

Duluth newscaster Earl Henton represented the iron mining industry on statewide television and radio during the 1960s and '70s. Although he didn't directly promote the taconite amendment, his interpretation set the stage for public acceptance by acquainting the people of Minnesota with the industry's importance.

Instead, those concerned with passage of the amendment turned to the Duluth Industrial Bureau as a vehicle to fund the campaign effort. The Bureau, run by Emery Hoenshell, was an economic development agency funded by Duluth and regional business interests. Its president was Howard Cooper, a vice president of Minnesota Power and Light Co. The bureau, in turn, retained H. E. Westmoreland Co., a Duluth public relations and advertising agency, to coordinate a campaign for the amendment.

Wes Westmoreland turned his full energies toward the campaign. Working with Dr. Charles Mayo of the Mayo Clinic, backers began framing a citizens committee, which would develop statewide support. Gov. Karl Rolvaag appointed Dr. Mayo as Chairman of the Committee. Earl Bester, district director of the United Steel Workers and Mrs. Scott Schoen, Redwood Falls, the immediate past president of the Minnesota Federation of Women's Clubs, were named vice-chairpersons. Members of the executive committee included former governor Elmer L. Anderson, State Treasurer Val Bjornson, Congressman John Blatnik, DFL state chairman George Farr, Republican party state chairman Robert Forsythe, the state secretary of the AFL-CIO, Robert Hess, Lt. Gov. A. M. Keith, Attorney General Walter Mondale, Congressman Ancher Nelsen of the Second District and Stanley J. Wenberg, V.P. of the University of Minnesota.

A key move in organizing the campaign was the recruitment of Rita Shemesh as director of the effort. Recommended by Elmer L. Anderson, Mrs. Shemesh was indefatigable in her efforts to enlist local and state organizations to support the amendment. Before she was done, she had recruited hundreds of local and state groups to the cause, ranging from local co-ops and chambers of commerce to major statewide groups such

The first new plant to open after approval of the taconite amendment was Eveleth Taconite, but Oglebay Norton had jumped the gun by starting construction before the ballot. This 1966 opening ceremony includes Lt. Gov. A. M. "Sandy" Keith, former governor Elmer L. Anderson, Senator Hubert Humphrey, 2nd District Congressman Ancher Nelsen and Governor Karl Rolvaag. Humphrey activated the mine's "first blast" by pushing a Ford Thunderbird shift lever (Ford was a major owner of the new operation).

as the Minnesota Grange, Farm Bureau Federation, Bar Association, and others.

Meanwhile other efforts were being mounted. Carl D'Aquila of Hibbing, organized a stamp campaign. He had taconite amendment stamps printed by the thousands for people to affix to their letters. A speakers bureau was also active. One such speakers tour included Earl Bester, H. E. Westmoreland, Val Bjornson, George Rossman, publisher of the Grand Rapids Herald Review, and this writer. For a full week, this group barnstormed the state, riding in a stretch limousine to Winona, Rochester, Marshall, Mankato, Detroit Lakes, Moorhead and other communities. Bjornson's grand sense of humor and his Icelandic tales kept the group friendly and happy throughout the mission.

Many, many people worked on behalf of the amendment, and from the likes of Jeno Paulucci, to the barber on mainstreet, they all deserve credit for their efforts.

And their efforts, taken together, did the job. When the votes were counted, more than 80% of those voting on that November 3rd voted for the taconite amendment, an unprecedented measure of support for a constitutional amendment.

And what about the real aim of the amendment effort? Within days after its passage, mining companies announced new taconite projects as well as expansions at the Erie and Reserve operations. Around half a billion dollars of new investment were committed in that wave of taconite investment. Future investments in the industry would bring the total to more than $3 billion. ∎

Al France was a public relations executive at the Westmoreland Agency during the amendment campaign, and served in the Minnesota Legislature, 1962-1969. He was president of the Lake Superior Industrial Bureau (known today as the Iron Mining Association of Minnesota), the iron mining industry trade association, 1972-1992.

Gateway Urban Renewal Project and Fifth Avenue West Mall

A FACE-LIFT FOR DOWNTOWN DULUTH'S WESTERN APPROACH

by Walker Jamar, Jr.

The Duluth Gateway story is really several stories. This chapter is an overview of the entire effort. The details of the major features are each told separately in stories on the Radisson-Duluth Hotel, the Duluth Public Library and the Fifth Avenue West Mall, which is recounted as a second part of this chapter.

In 1960 the federal government initiated a program under the name of "Urban Renewal" designed to provide an incentive for individual municipalities to substantially upgrade depressed sections of their city. Duluth Mayor E. Clifford Mork secured an entry to some of this program for Duluth, and borrowed the

NEMHC, Duluth, MN. Detail, Basgen Studios

The Fifth Ave. W. Mall area before the Gateway project removed the buildings to make way for widening the approach to the civic center, at top of picture. Spalding Hotel, built in 1898, is the large building in the center, foreground, obscuring Lyceum Theater just behind it. Right, corner windows on Spalding's second floor illuminated Parlor X, where many political and business decisions were wrought.

"Gateway" name from Minneapolis' urban renewal effort. Mayor Mork created a broad-based advisory board of 15 citizens who selected Odin Ramsland (KDAL radio and TV) as chairman and established the city's planning department, with the task of examining the "Bowery Area" of downtown Duluth, bounded generally by Fourth Avenue West, Mesabi Avenue, Michigan Street and First Street.

By the fall of 1961, the project had received some publicity, but not much else in the way of action. The similar program that had been started in Minneapolis progressed to the point where developer Donald Knutson had been selected and action started. The Duluth Kiwanis Club had invited him to speak to it and the Rotary Club followed in September 1961. At both meetings, Knutson spoke enthusiastically about the Minneapolis project and offered the thought that if no one in Duluth were going to do anything about our project, he would come up and take it over!

To fill a perceived void, and stimulated by Knutson's talk, I recruited a small group including Roger Bowman (Bowman Realty), Herb Burns (attorney), Joe Veranth (a general contractor), Jerry Jyring (architect) and H. E. Westmoreland (public relations). Each of us contributed $500 towards out-of-pocket expenses. The Duluth Urban Development Company (DUDC) now had $3,000 for starters!

By April 1962, the group had studied the area and visited with potential occupants of the project. Our brochure and news release were simple and low key, envisioning a major department store, a number of specialty shops, upscale office buildings, a small motor hotel and parking. Now was the time to sign up some clients! In retrospect, there were a couple of problems with the proposal. Major retail stores were not moving into city centers—they were beginning to leave for the suburbs. Also, Duluth already had a slight surplus of office space; and although not all of it was new, it was available.

The urban renewal part of the project was moving along, however slowly. The acquisition of property by the city became predictably entangled with the valuations put on the many parcels in the area. 1963 came and went. Eventually in May of 1964 the Housing and Redevelopment Authority approved the third reappraisal of property. At last the relocation of those still in the area and the securing of bids for the demolition could begin.

In the meantime, in addition to the efforts by DUDC to secure occupants of stature, proposals to upgrade the existing downtown were presented to the public. The Chamber of Commerce published a report developed by its manager, Robert Morris, that envisioned, among other things, the razing of almost 20% of the existing downtown buildings and

Facelift for the Zenith City, 1960s. An ambitious project to renew the "Bowery Area" of downtown Duluth—bounded by 4th Avenue West, Mesabi Avenue, Michigan Street and 1st Street—laid the groundwork for many successful projects, including the Duluth Public Library, Radisson Hotel, and the 5th Avenue West Mall.

suggesting seven major sites for the development of parking. The Metropolitan Improvement Association headed by R. J. Higgins questioned the uses to which Gateway land should be put to use. Mark Flaherty, one of the deputy city planners, cautioned against spreading the retail district into the Gateway. Understandably, much of this reflected the concerns of the owners of the existing major retail stores and office buildings. Some were less than enthusiastic about what they visualized as government-sponsored competition.

It became apparent to all that, one way or another, something was going to be put into the Gateway. What, when, and under what leadership was

an open question. It was also obvious that DUDC could succeed only by joining those interests in Duluth that had the most to gain by a well-conceived Gateway, and the most to lose by a poorly executed development. In 1964 the DUDC went out of business, but a successor was about to surface.

Our concept and organization were replaced in the fall of 1965 by the Duluth Development Association (DDA) whose officers were Robert Prescott (Oneida Realty) as its president, Roger Bowman (Bowman Properties) as vice-president and Hubert Nelson (mining and real estate) as secretary-treasurer. Financial support from the sponsoring organizations, Northwest Publications (The Duluth Herald and News Tribune), Minnesota Power and Light, and Oneida Realty (a major owner of downtown real estate) among others, was assured. A renewed effort at meaningful redevelopment was underway. The DDA's announced focus was on the securing of a motor hotel, specialty shops and high-rise apartments.

In March of 1966, the DDA asked the city for exclusive rights to develop the entire Gateway area for the sum of $770,000, the entire area to be completed in six years with one-sixth of it being completed each year. Included in their offer was the commitment of Northwest Publications to expand its facilities on First Street to occupy the area to Fifth Avenue West and a plan by radio and TV station KDAL to build an entirely new studio and office complex on the upper side of Superior Street, between Fourth Avenue West and Fifth Avenue West. The offer was accepted. The search for a hotel, which resulted in the construction of the Radisson Hotel, began.

Also, on a slightly different level of civic activity, a substantial effort had materialized to join the three buildings of the Civic Center to the rest of the town with a conversion of Fifth Avenue West into the Fifth Avenue West Mall, as described later in this chapter.

Of the major parcels of land still open for development, the largest and most visible was the block between Fifth and Sixth Avenues West on the lower side of Superior Street. The DDA was asked and agreed to hold that open for two years for a new Duluth Public Library.

The land west of the Radisson Hotel side, both above and below Superior Street, was still uncommitted. Its relatively remote location, between Sixth Avenue West and Mesabi Avenue, made it an unlikely site for commercial use, but attractive for apartment construction. (Gateway Tower and Lenox Place, high-rise apartments for senior and disabled citizens, built in the mid 1970s and early 1980s, now occupy these sites.)

FIFTH AVENUE WEST MALL

In the spring of 1965, in the community's search for suitable uses for the land available for development in the Gateway, Duluth philanthropist

Julia Marshall had a wonderful idea.

Duluth's Civic Center consisted of the Federal Building, the County Courthouse and City Hall, all handsome buildings, located around a small park between Fourth and Sixth Avenues West at the "head" of Fifth Avenue West on the First Street. The buildings faced three sides of the small central park, the fourth side of the park being the First Street entrance to a circular drive.

Plans for construction of a freeway into the center of downtown Duluth included an interchange at Fifth Avenue West. It would be between Michigan Street and the harbor and require the demolition of the old

In the spring of 1965, in the community's search for suitable uses for the land available for development in the Gateway, Duluth philanthropist Julia Marshall had a wonderful idea.

warehouse buildings on the west side of the avenue between the freeway and the harbor. The eastern side of the avenue was already committed to the newly constructed Arena/Auditorium complex at the harbor's edge.

Would it be possible to increase the width of all of Fifth Avenue West so that the instead of just a typical commercial street, Fifth Avenue West would be a divided roadway, the two 26-ft. traffic lanes separated by a 36-ft. landscaped park, connecting the Civic Center with the harbor?

Miss Julia Marshall enlisted her sister, Miss Caroline Marshall and family friend Dorothy Congdon, and the three formed a coordinating committee with this in mind. There were some problems, however. Not scheduled for demolition as part of the Gateway were the Holland Hotel and the Fifth Avenue Hotel as well as the Lyceum Theater. Each was a substantial building and each abutted the existing Fifth Avenue West. Further, the design of the new freeway to be built between Michigan Street and the harbor had progressed to the point where making changes to the bridge scheduled to carry Fifth Avenue West over it was next to impossible.

The women of vision were determined. They contributed $100,000 for starters. They had already purchased one of the hotels and were proceeding to purchase the other. The committee had concept drawings made of the mall (as it was now being called) cut short at Michigan Street, accepting defeat on the issue of the bridges over the freeway. Their ideas and accomplishments were presented to the public in July 1965.

Such effort and commitment could not be ignored. The mall was incorporated into the Gateway and highway project. It was further enhanced by a proposal to build two pedestrian plazas, one on either side of the mall between Superior and Michigan Streets, with public accommodations off the Michigan Street level. In time, the western plaza gave way to the construction of the Duluth Public Library. The eastern plaza was built and today serves as the front door to the handsome Ordean Building, which the Ordean Foundation built on the remaining Gateway land to the east.

A formal city dedication of the Mall was held at Fifth Avenue West and Michigan Street on the evening of September 12, 1971. ∎

Walker Jamar, Jr. was a Duluth businessman and member of the Duluth City Council when the Gateway Urban Renewal program was undertaken. He was instrumental in organizing local business interests to redevelop the blighted Gateway area.

CHAPTER

11

The Radisson Hotel

HOW A FIRST-CLASS HOTEL
(WITH REVOLVING RESTAURANT)
ROSE OUT OF A DUSTY VACANT LOT

by Bob Prescott

Starting in the early 1960s, the Gateway Urban Renewal Project was underway. At that time, the Housing and Redevelopment Authority acquired most of the properties and demolished the buildings in an area encompassing the upper side of Michigan Street to the lower side of First Street and from Seventh Avenue West to between Fourth and Fifth Avenues West. The buildings demolished included the Soo Line RR Depot, the Spalding, Holland and Fifth Avenue Hotels, Lyceum Theatre, Greyhound Bus Depot and various other properties. In the main, the properties were unsightly and uneconomic in their operations, and the area was a blight on downtown Duluth.

The land remained vacant for several years. A small group of Duluth businessmen became concerned the area would not be

View east from freeway ramp at foot of Mesaba Avenue, fall 1971, is dominated by new Radisson. Soo Line Depot is in center of photo, where Duluth's library now stands. Northern City National Bank sign on Alworth Building dominates skyline. Greyhound terminal is still downtown. Cigarette billboard would now be illegal.

developed at all, or alternatively used for unsuitable purposes. We formed the Duluth Development Association to undertake a redevelopment of the area, contracting with the Housing Authority for the rights to do so. The principals of the Duluth Development Association included myself as President; Roger Bowman, Principal of Bowman Properties as Vice President; and Hubert Nelson, a mining and real estate executive, as Secretary-Treasurer.

Thereafter the association, or its individual members, through their efforts and negotiations with other business interests, were successful in the locating and construction in the area of the KDAL building, the Ordean building, expansion of the Duluth News Tribune building, the Duluth Public Library and the Gateway Tower. Concurrently, a prime objective was to have a large, first-class hotel developed in downtown Duluth. Promotional work was done, nationwide and throughout the Midwest, in efforts to persuade various hotel companies to come to Duluth and build, own and operate a modern hotel facility. Extensive negotiations took place with the Hilton, Sheraton, Marriott and other hotel organizations in efforts to attract them to the city. Interest was shown by some, but not on terms either acceptable to the group nor with facilities that would be in the best interests of Duluth.

It became evident that to achieve our objective of developing a first-class facility—of the right size, with the best amenities, and with a potential for successful operation—that the association would have to undertake the hotel project themselves. Accordingly, we became the catalyst for organizing a new company: the Greysolon Mall Corporation, which later became the developer and owner of the Radisson Hotel.

Aggressive efforts by the Association continued to enlist the interest of an established hotel organization to become an investor in and manager of the hotel operations. Finally, after long and intensive negotiations with

> It became evident that to achieve our objective of developing a first-class facility—of the right size, with the best amenities, and with a potential for successful operation—that the association would have to undertake the hotel project themselves.

Curtis Carlson, owner of Radisson Hotels, he committed to become a participant. I later became president of the Greysolon Mall Corporation, and headed efforts to raise funds from investors and also to secure mortgage financing to proceed with the project. In addition to Carlson, principal investors were the Chicago Tribune Co. (KDAL), Minnesota Power, Northwest Publications (Duluth News Tribune), Oneida Realty Company, Jeno Paulucci, and Zenith Dredge Company. Financing was arranged with a consortium of local savings and loan associations and banks.

William Tabler, a prominent hotel architect from New York City, was retained to develop architectural plans. A. Hedenberg Company of Duluth was selected as the general contractor. Groundbreaking took place in the fall of 1968.

When the building and site development of the new 208-room Radisson Duluth Hotel was completed, furnishings were installed and a gala grand opening took place in May 1970. Additional rooms were added in 1975. The 268-room hotel stands today, prominent on the skyline of Duluth with its revolving Top of the Harbor Restaurant where patrons may enjoy a spectacular 360-degree view of the city. ∎

Robert Prescott, president of Oneida Realty, served on the Duluth City Council in the early '60s, was the first president of the Arena/Auditorium Administrative Board, and has been active in civic ventures throughout his business career. He once advised Manley "Monnie" Goldfine, "The most important thing you can do for your community is to manage your own business well."

CHAPTER

12

Lyric Block Renovation

HOW PUBLIC AND PRIVATE INVESTMENT
TRANSFORMED DOWNTOWN DULUTH

by Walker Jamar, Jr.

with assistance from Jim Gustafson,

Joel Labovitz and Bruce Stender

In the early '70s, it was apparent that Duluth was beginning to come out of its post World War II malaise. The Gateway improvements were working. Interstate 35 had arrived. The downtown was relatively healthy and city leaders were dreaming of developing a skywalk system similar to the Twin Cities.

The most prominent vacant building in the downtown was the Lyric Theatre on the upper side of Superior Street between Second and Third Avenues West. This once-grand theatre occupied about 75 feet in the center of the block and had been closed and abandoned for several years. The neighbors of this blighted building starting from Third Avenue West and proceeding eastward were: a parking lot which resulted from

Lyric Development Corporation 1976. Left to right: Joseph B. Johnson,
Thomas Thibodeau, Mitchell Sill, James Gustafson, Dennis Dunne, Burt
Dahlberg, Tom Noble, John Owens, Robert Prescott, James Claypool, and
Robert Heller.

the razing in the mid '60s of the old First and American National Bank
building. Next to the parking lot was a tired Woolworth store;
McGregor-Soderstrom men's clothing; Gustafson's Bakery and Coffee
Shop; Lyric Theatre; Norm's Reliable, a jewelry, sporting goods and
discount store; a small loan storefront office and an elderly Montgomery
Wards store which occupied about 50 feet of frontage on Superior Street.
Across the street on the southeast corner of Third Avenue West stood the
relatively modern First American National Bank building (now Wells-
Fargo). Adjoining the east wall of the bank was Livingston's Big Duluth,
a men's clothing store. Heading east from Livingston's were Nick's Burger
King; a stairway leading to the Silver Hammer Bar; Minnesota Surplus
Store; Paul Bunyan Bar and Grill; A&E Gift, Card and Luggage store;
Ace Hardware; Edward's Shoes; a stairway up to Gallery Five; Bud's
Clothing; and the Sellwood Building on the corner of Second Avenue

West. Community leadership generally agreed that something should be done about the Lyric Theater building, an eyesore which was depreciating property values on the whole area.

ORIGINAL CONCEPT AND LEADERSHIP
1972 - 1974

In the 1972 City budget, Duluth Mayor Ben Boo included $25,000 to tear the Lyric Theater down. The city council voted its approval in May 1972. However, demolition was postponed when Montgomery Wards revealed plans to move to the Miller Hill Mall area. Northwestern Bank of Commerce announced its intention to build a drive-in banking facility in the area, and other proposals and suggestions for alternative uses for the building and the surrounding area surfaced. Growing out of several ideas of the 1960s for improving the central business district and using the experience that came out of development of the Gateway, the Downtown Development Corporation (DDC) was formed in 1972. Its vision was to improve the core of the downtown through construction of shops, a new hotel and other commercial activities all connected by skywalks and supported by adequate parking

While the City's focus at this time involved only the Lyric Theater, the DDC vision encompassed a large portion of downtown Duluth. In early 1973, its main effort was narrowed to the entire block bounded by Second and Third Avenues West and Superior and First Streets—the Lyric Block. A Lyric Block Committee of the DDC was formed with Roger Bowman (Bowman Company) and Bob Prescott (Oneida Realty) at the front of the new organization, which now included Sylvester Laskin (Minnesota Power), Jack Owens (Northwestern Bank of Commerce) and Chester Lind (First American National Bank). Plans focused on a major hotel with specialty shops and adequate parking for the development. Significant work was undertaken in 1973 to compile land valuations and acquisition costs, as well as develop architectural schematics and construction costs. There were also extended discussions during the year with potential builders and operators of a hotel. However, except for the possibility of City funds to demolish the Lyric Theater itself, there were no government funds or support for the project and it stalled in late 1973.

1974 - 1975

During 1974, the federal government established the Economic Development Authority (EDA), a program similar to the Urban Development program of the 1960s which gave birth to the Gateway Project. The City designated the area between First and Third Avenues West and Michigan and First Streets, which included the Lyric Block, as a Development District eligible for EDA support, financial guarantees and tax increment financing. Conversation was reopened with several hotel operators and builders. One new feature of great interest to the new hotel operators was the proposal to construct an elevated skywalk extending from the downtown to the Arena/Auditorium complex on the harbor. Financing for both the hotel and the skywalk appeared to be possible, but not without major creative effort and commitments from multiple governmental agencies and private interests.

This creative effort came from the DDC itself. The composition of the DDC executive committee was expanded from 7 to 20 members to include a broad representation of downtown businesses, real estate owners and financial institutions. A full-time executive manager, Vincent Coughlin was engaged. Mayor Bob Beaudin and Eugene Lambert, publisher of the *Duluth News Tribune*, kept up contact with EDA representatives in Washington, including many personal visits, and together with the active support of Congressman James Oberstar, EDA approval was secured.

By March 1975 it seemed that all of the homework had been done and the projects were ready to go. Hometels of America, Inc. announced it would build a 10-story, 220-room hotel supported by a parking ramp and specialty shops. It was to be a $12.8 million dollar project involving $10 million of private financing supported by an EDA grant of $3 million on the commercial portion of the project. In addition, there would be $2.8 million of public improvements in the area financed by various government programs and tax increment bonds. Construction was slated to be under way by June 1975.

The EDA participation required that Hometel submit a formal application detailing its financing and capabilities for completion of the project. The June deadline for the application was extended twice into the fall of 1975. Hometel appeared unable to furnish the private financing assurances that EDA required.

1975 – 1976

By this time two additional developers had expressed serious interest in the project.

Bob Flackne, a Twin Cities mortgage broker, called the opportunity to the attention of Tom Noble, who owned the Normandy Hotel in downtown Minneapolis, suggesting the concept of a high-rise hotel in downtown Duluth. Sometime in late 1975, Noble, Coughlin and Flackne paid a visit to Burt Dahlberg, executive vice president for development of Krause-Anderson Company, with the idea of redeveloping the 200 block in Duluth with a Normandy Hotel as the centerpiece. Following that initial meeting, Dahlberg who had close ties to Duluth and was a former employee of Oneida Realty Company, visited Mayor Bob Beaudin as well as senior executives of Minnesota Power, the banks and other business leaders to gauge their interest in investing in the project. Once he received the support of Mayor Beaudin and several city councilors and the tentative financial commitments from the business community, Dahlberg proceeded with preliminary work on the project. The Lyric Block Development Company was formed. It hired the local architecture firm of Damberg and Peck as architects. The Larsen and Harvala firm was named the principal engineers.

At the same time the Lyric block project was conceived and moving forward, the skywalk project was moving ahead through several downtown buildings. The Lyric project was designed to tie into the skywalk. In addition, concurrent with the building of the hotel, the Northwest Passage connecting the downtown through the First American National Bank building was to be built. The Normandy Hotel along with the restaurant and shops in the project would be connected directly to the Arena/Auditorium.

During this period the DDC was engaged in assembling the real estate package necessary for the project. The property involved all of the upper side of Superior Street between 2nd and 3rd Avenues West as well as parcels on First Street. It was a section of town where some of the owners of the land were different from the owners of the buildings that occupied the land. Most of the ownership involved Duluth individuals or firms.

However, some parcels were owned by trusts and individuals who had no current connection with Duluth other than the property and its potential value and annual income. The most interesting—and challenging—of these involved the lease that ran until 2027 with the F. W. Woolworth Company (a major national retail chain at this time). Roger Bowman tells the story:

"The F. W. Woolworth store was located on the upper side of Superior Street just east of the former First National Bank, which was on the Northeast corner of Third Avenue West and Superior Street. In the 1920s the building was owned by a Mr. Espenschied, a non-Duluthian, and managed by the Lawrence F. Bowman Company. It was leased to F. W. Woolworth Company on a 99-year lease commencing in 1927.

"Mr. Espenschied's daughter, Ruth Davis from St. Louis, Missouri, was the sole beneficiary of her father's estate. Her husband, Fred Davis, informed us they had no interest in selling the Woolworth building. The lease was triple net; the Davis's received $1,000 free and clear each month and although the store was doing poorly, it was apparent F. W. Woolworth was not going broke anytime soon.

"There were numerous letters and phone calls between Fred Davis and me…but all to no avail. Finally, I went to St. Louis to meet with Mr. and Mrs. Davis in a last-ditch effort to persuade them to sell at a price we could afford. Armed with plans, specifications, architect's rendering and financial data, I made my presentation (I can't remember the exact dollar offer). Fred Davis, however, was adamant and thought the price should reflect an amount that would pay them $12,000 annually in interest.

"It was difficult to appeal to Fred Davis's civic duty as he had never lived in Duluth. However, Ruth Davis had fond memories of Duluth when she visited there frequently as a young girl with her father. Fortunately, most of the Davis assets were in Ruth Davis's name. With her happy memories of Duluth, she finally agreed to our proposal and signed the necessary documents."

FUNDING

The Lyric project was truly a public/private partnership.

Mayor Beaudin was a strong advocate of the project and exerted a great deal of leadership in seeing the project to completion. The principle financial assistance from the city was the sale of $3.5 million of Tax Increment Finance bonds. The City also provided $75,000 of general funds for demolition costs. The Federal Economic Development Agency (EDA) provided a grant of $3.0 million. This money was used to acquire all the properties for the project. Community Development Funds provided a $1.9 million grant. The Upper Great Lakes Regional Commission provided $400,000, and the Minnesota Highway Department $150,000. The city was to acquire the property, relocate the businesses and demolish the buildings. The land was then to be sold to the developers for $4 million.

Approximately $500,000 was invested privately with Minnesota Power and the three downtown banks—First American, Northern City, and Northwestern Bank of Commerce—participating both as lenders and equity investors.

Altogether there were 18 members of the initial investment group including three Twin Cities businessmen who were friends of Tom Noble. Great West Insurance Company agreed to carry the mortgage and Bob Flackne was retained by both Lyric Block Development Company and the insurance company.

BOARD OF DIRECTORS

The Board of Directors of the Lyric Block Development Company included: George Barnum, Burton Dahlberg, Dennis Dunn, Paul Flament, James Gustafson, Robert Heller (representing Jeno Paulucci), Sylvester Laskin, Sidney Mason (representing Dorothy Congdon), John McMillion, Thomas Noble, Kenneth Nordling, John Owens, Robert Prescott, Dr. David E. Raab, Glenn Rye, Paul Schanno, Gordon Seitz and Mitchell Sill.

REALIZATION

In February 1976 the Lyric Block Development Company signed an

Groundbreaking for Lyric Block renovation, July 4, 1976. Left to right: Mayor Robert Beaudin; Al France, Duluth Bicentennial Committee; (at podium) Vince Coughlin, executive director, Downtown Development Corporation; Rep. James Oberstar; and Burt Dahlberg, president, Lyric Block Development Corp.

agreement with the City to purchase the land after it had been cleared. In March 1976, the city council authorized purchase and demolition of the Lyric Block property. In June 1976, the City sold the $3.5 million of tax increment revenue bonds necessary for the project. Shortly thereafter demolition was started.

Ground was broken for construction of the new hotel, parking ramp, shopping complex on July 4, 1976, the 200th anniversary of our country. Instead of the owners wielding shovels, a Liberty Bell replica was rung to mark the occasion and participants in the ceremony received small replicas of the bell. The official grand opening of the building was on New Year's Eve, December 31, 1977. The final product was 16 stories, 240 luxurious rooms, banquet and convention facilities and several restaurants. There was also a 66,000 square foot shopping complex and a 240-car parking facility.

CONSOLIDATION AND GROWTH

Even though the hotel and the mall connected to it were the centerpiece of downtown Duluth, the property struggled financially. About a year after opening, there was a second round of financing and most of the investors made additional equity investments. Later, with the financial picture fairly well stabilized, Tom Noble, through his company Inn Management, Inc., purchased the majority of the stock from the original investors at a price slightly more than their investment.

Joel Labovitz's Maurices was one of the early commercial occupants of the center with a 6,600 square foot store on the corner of Superior Street and Second Avenue West. In the early 1980s, after the sale of the Maurices organization, Labovitz, with his partners Manley and Erwin Goldfine and Mitch Sill, joined by Bruce Stender, purchased 100% of the stock in the project from Noble and the remaining stockholders. The corporation was reconstituted as a partnership, the Normandy Hotel was changed into a Holiday Inn, and the ownership of this prime facility in the center of Duluth was in the hands of Duluthians.

By 1988, Labovitz Enterprises had invested an additional $6 million into an expansion of the parking ramp, a realignment and expansion of the shopping facilities and redecoration and major maintenance. Again, in the late 1990s, the $9.5 million Atrium addition added 113 large rooms and suites, a second swimming pool and sauna. They are again in the midst of an additional $6 million remodeling and upgrade scheduled to be completed in 2005. The Holiday Inn and Suites Downtown Waterfront was a Holiday Inn Torchbearer Award winner in 1989 and 1991, and was named Hotel of the Year in 1996.

SUMMARY

The Lyric Block project was the centerpiece of a good deal of economic activity in the mid 1970s. The Northwest Passage to connect the Arena Auditorium/Pioneer Hall complex was funded by several federal government agencies. With this funding in place, the mayor and city leaders began concentrating on connecting the entire downtown through a skywalk system. With the new Lyric Block development beginning to

...the Lyric block, the Normandy Hotel, the skywalk system, Northwest Passage, and the freeway all became a reality at about the same time, because of a great coming together of the business community, city government and the community at large.

look like a reality and the vision of a skywalk system with the Normandy Hotel as its centerpiece, the dream began to take shape. Further, a commitment by the City that this skywalk would become the center of a skywalk system was the main inducement for Krause-Anderson and the investors to proceed with the project. In the meantime, the decade-long community dispute over the location and design of the freeway was starting to be resolved. It was becoming clear that the railroad tracks running through the downtown had to be removed so parking and other elements could be put in place to link the arena and the waterfront to the downtown. The result was that the Lyric block, the Normandy Hotel, the skywalk system, Northwest Passage, and the freeway all became a reality at about the same time, because of a great coming together of the business community, city government and the community at large. This example of community cooperation drew national recognition. In 1978, Duluth was selected as the winner of a national competition process to receive the All-American City Award. ■

Duluth native Walker Jamar, Jr. is a retired Duluth businessman who served on the City Council during the years following the 1956 charter change to the strong mayor-council form of government, and continued to be active in community development.

CHAPTER

13

Duluth's Skywalk System

WEATHERPROOFING OUR DOWNTOWN

by Robert Asleson

Duluth's downtown skywalk system has truly been a "public/private partnership" and credit for its success is shared by many individuals and organizations. Included are several mayors, city councilors, city staff persons, citizen participants on various boards and commissions, the leadership of the Downtown Development Corporation/Greater Downtown Council, business leaders and property owners in downtown Duluth, as well as various design firms and contractors.

A special thank you needs to made to John Ivey Thomas, who originally was involved through the architectural firm of Thomas and Vecchi, AIA, and served as the design architect for most of the system. He deserves credit not only for his design work, but also for his ability and willingness to address concerns of property owners while still keeping the integrity and quality of the skywalk system as a first priority.

Our downtown skywalk system began with a number of factors coming together. One was the realization that U.S. Steel, Duluth's last remaining major "smokestack" industrial employer, was "pulling the pin" on its Duluth operations and taking what had once been the city's largest payroll with it. Duluth's governmental and community leaders realized that the city must take a new approach to the economic vitality of the community or face the fate of older "rust belt" communities, predominantly in the eastern part of the country.

The only problem was that the Arena/Auditorium and the downtown were separated by major rail yard facilities...exacerbated by the construction of Interstate 35. The answer was to construct a skywalk to unite the two locations. Thus the "Northwest Passage," Duluth's first skywalk was born.

One area of need was Duluth's downtown. The so-called "100% Block" was no longer 100%—the Lyric Theater building was vacant and decaying and the largest merchant on the block, Montgomery Ward, moved operations to the new Miller Hill Mall. A number of vacant lots in the block were being used for parking instead of retail.

Fortunately, some in leadership positions saw this condition as an opportunity to redevelop and reorient the direction of the downtown, especially in conjunction with the Arena/Auditorium on the Duluth harbor front. These leaders saw that, if the Arena/Auditorium could be linked to a new and complementary development in the downtown, Duluth could enhance its economy as a convention and entertainment center and strengthen the entire downtown. The only problem was that the Arena/Auditorium and the downtown were separated by major rail yard facilities and this problem would be exacerbated by the construction of Interstate 35. The answer was to construct a skywalk to unite the two locations. Thus the "Northwest Passage," Duluth's first skywalk was born.

Another fortunate element arrived at this time: *tax increment financing* (TIF). This new tool captured the increased valuation created by a development and channeled the dollars back to pay some of the development costs. In 1973, the City of Duluth secured special legislation to authorize it to create development districts. In 1974, the statewide Municipal Development District Law authorized all cities to create development districts and to capture the tax increase created by projects to help fund developments. This created a new funding source, which would make it possible for the city and downtown to support a variety of projects, including the proposed redevelopment of the Lyric Block and skywalk connections to the Northwest Passage (which was paid for primarily by transportation funding).

As planning proceed for the Lyric Block development and the Northwest Passage, civic leaders looked south of Duluth to the Twin Cities, and other places where the idea of elevated, weather-protected connections between buildings was taking hold as an enhancement to downtown shopping, office and entertainment districts.

It soon became apparent that if ever a downtown needed a weather-protected environment to encourage workers and shoppers, Duluth was it. In April, 1975, the city contracted with Architectural Resources, Inc. to: 1) design a skywalk into the Lyric Block facility; 2) recommend a route and connection for the Northwest Passage; 3) do schematic designs for skywalk connections from the Lyric Block to adjacent buildings; and 4) determine elevations of streets and buildings around the Lyric Block development. Later that year, the city further contracted with the Downtown Development Corporation, predecessor to the current Greater Downtown Council, to develop schematic plans for a skywalk system that would serve the entire downtown area.

By 1976 a design for the skeletal structure of the future downtown skywalk system had been developed. At its center stood the new Lyric Block. From there, connections would radiate out from Lake Avenue to

4th Avenue West. It included connections through the First American National Bank (now Wells Fargo) to the Arena/Auditorium with a connection along Michigan Street to the Medical Arts Building, a connection along the north side of Superior Street to the MacDonald Building with a bridge to Minnesota Power, and back along the south side of Superior Street to the bank, to City Hall through the Missabe Building and the Board of Trade Building and to Shoppers Auto Park and Town Park (now the First Bank Place Parking Ramp). Almost all of these elements were included in the plan and have been the backbone of the system.

The year 1976 also saw the commencement of the Northwest Passage and the Lyric Block Development, which included a Normandy Hotel (now the Holiday Inn), two floors of retail space, a two-level skywalk development which boasted elevators, an escalator, and a major three story courtyard and five levels of parking. Also under construction at about this time were the skywalk bridge across Superior Street to the First American National Bank building, the connection to the existing pedestrian bridge over Michigan Street into the bank's parking ramp, and connections to the Northwest Passage and the Northern City National Bank (soon to become a First Bank Systems bank, then US Bank) parking ramp across 3rd Avenue West from the First American ramp.

In early 1977, another piece of the puzzle fell into place. Minnesota Power, which then occupied an office building on the southeast corner of First Avenue West and Superior Street, needed to expand their administrative offices and wanted to do so downtown. The City, Minnesota Power and a group of local developers entered into an agreement, which resulted in the existing Minnesota Power building being integrated into an office, parking and skywalk development. This included a retail component and public plaza, taking up the entire block between Lake and First Avenue West between Superior and Michigan Streets. Once this project was underway, it and the impending completion of the Lyric Block development generated substantial impetus to make a skywalk connection between them.

At this time, I became actively involved in the extension of the skywalk system. Until then, most negotiations for downtown projects had been conducted directly by Duluth's director of planning and development, Richard Loraas. However in 1980, Mr. Loraas suffered a serious heart attack; Ken Johnson, then a city business developer, and I were assigned to continue work on the downtown skywalk plan. Subsequently, when Johnson left for other employment, I was detailed to proceed with skywalk negotiations.

Unlike the skywalk systems in the Twin Cities, where many blocks had only one or two buildings, Duluth's downtown consisted primarily of smaller 25 and 50-foot buildings; this meant, first, that the City would have to get concurrence from many property owners to extend the skywalk system a relatively short distance. Also, the buildings had not been constructed in a manner that coordinated the heights of the second floor levels; so some kind of vertical adjustments would have to be constructed. This was further complicated by the requirement that the system be "handicapped accessible" which meant that ramping and elevators had to be used for access between buildings. These elevation accommodations took up space in buildings that were small and further stressed the ability of the building to accommodate the skywalk.

But perhaps the greatest concern was that of some building owners that benefits would be insufficient to outweigh the potential negative impacts. In addition to loss of rentable area, owners were concerned about operating expenses, potential fire danger to staff and customers and after-hours security. They were also, of course, concerned about the cost for construction of the skywalk through their building. The City took the position that the system was to be a public-private partnership and, as such, the benefiting building owners were expected to share some of the costs of constructing it.

In response to these concerns, the City developed policies to guide development of the system and allocation of costs. The first and most fundamental decision was that the city skywalk system would be constructed only on public easements. This allowed the City to use public resources to help defray a portion of the costs. It also meant that system would be open to the public just like sidewalks.

Then, the City established minimum parameters for design of skywalks within buildings which included choosing a standard skywalk tile for the flooring material (to help people know when they were "on the skywalk"), standard minimum widths, and adherence to handicapped accessability standards.

The City agreed that the cost of constructing skywalk bridges over streets was appropriately a public cost, to be borne by the Development District. Additionally, the Planning Commission had voted to require that there be at least one "vertical transit node" consisting of an elevator and stairs or an escalator, in each block having skywalks and this too was treated as a public cost. Also, when some vertical accommodation was required from one property to the next, such as ramping, or when major building utilities needed to be relocated to accommodate the skywalk corridor, the City paid those costs. Finally, openings between buildings and fire doors would be paid for by the public.

The main cost which the property owner was expected to pay was the cost of skywalk tile floor. In addition, property owners were expected to donate the necessary easements for the skywalk. The rest of the costs were negotiated, based on the principal that the system was a partnership between the public and the owner and each should pay a fair share. Fairness took into account the impact the skywalk had on the building, the relative benefits to the building, the costs of operation and the ability of the buildings to support any costs. While this allocation system was not scientific, it served to allow the system as it exists now to be completed.

Minimum skywalk operating hours were established for the system, depending on the anticipated primary use of the space adjacent to the skywalks in the various legs. These were minimum hours for the operation of the system and owners were free to agree with other owners or to themselves establish longer hours. Then the City provided the fire doors between buildings with a lock and keying system which allowed each owner to lock his own space from his neighbors with his own discrete key, thereby giving security control if the owner chose to exercise it; in many case owners chose never to exercise this right, depending on owners at "public access points" to lock those access doors and thereby provide security to the system.

As the final condition, maintenance and operation of the space, including insuring, would be the building owner's responsibility. In addition, the owners of the buildings at either end would share routine maintenance of the bridges. The City has historically taken care of major, non-reoccurring maintenance and structural repair. This system has worked well. The City passed an ordinance in 1985 providing for Duluth's skywalk administrator to give notice to an offending property owner of any failures to maintain their skywalk property and, if no adequate response was forthcoming, perform the necessary maintenance and assess the cost back against the affected property. This power has not been often used.

The first major objective of the system, after the Northwest Passage was opened, was to complete a skywalk connection from the Lyric Block to the MacDonald Building and to the Lake Superior Plaza Development and Minnesota Power. The westerly portion of that leg, from the Lyric Block to the building occupied by Snyder's, was opened in 1981 and enthusiasm in the downtown began to build rapidly. The next year, the rest of the section was completed and the city had its first "retail" skywalk leg.

Up until the early 1980s, one of the major anchors to retail downtown was the Glass Block Department Store, at the southeast corner of Second Avenue West and Superior Street. Early on, the City tried to induce its owner, Mercantile Stores, to connect the department store into the system, with the objective of adding a major retail facility to the skywalk and encouraging them to maintain their store in the downtown since they had also chosen to open a competing store at the Miller Hill Mall. Unfortunately, that effort was in vain and the Glass Block store was closed in the early 1980s.

The silver lining in this disappointment was that the site met the requirements of First Bank Systems, which was looking for a new location downtown. They purchased the old Glass Block site and constructed a new, ten story office and banking building which included a skywalk connection from the Northwestern Bank of Commerce (now the

Northshore Bank of Commerce) on the north side of Superior Street, a connection to the Sellwood Building on the southwest corner of Second Avenue West and Superior Street and a new connection across Michigan Street to the Town Park Ramp which they also purchased and refurbished, providing skywalk access to this parking facility. These connections were opened in 1984.

At the same time, work was in progress to connect the downtown system to City Hall and thereby to the government complex at Fifth Avenue West and First Street. As part of the development of the new Government Services Center located between Third and Fourth Avenues West and between Second Alley and Second Street, a skywalk was extended through the entire office building and parking ramp facility and a skywalk bridge was constructed connecting it with City Hall. Subsequently the system was completed through the Board of Trade Building, the Missabe Building, and two other buildings on the north side of First Street before crossing to the Lyric Block parking Ramp and then, by glass elevators, connected down into the Skywalk Court in the Lyric Block. This leg was passable before Christmas of 1983 and formally opened in early 1984.

In 1983 work was completed on the skywalk leg from the Northwest Passage along the back of the Alworth-Lonsdale Buildings through the Torrey Building and into the Medical Arts Building. In addition, the owners of Medical Arts Building agreed to allow the owners of the Providence Building to build a private connection to the Medical Arts Building Lobby.

The growing success of the skywalk system was leading to requests for expansion beyond the bounds of what was originally planned. Early among those seeking such expansion were most of the owners of the properties on the upper side of Superior Street between Third and Fourth Avenues West. Negotiations were opened with these property owners which resulted in a connection from the Lyric Block through to the building occupied by the Frame Corner business immediately to the east of the Phoenix Building and a bridge from the neighboring Duluth Camera Exchange Building across Superior Street to the Medical Arts

Building. This portion of the system opened in 1987.

Once the work was done on the First Bank Place and Sellwood Building skywalks, work began to connect them along the south side of Superior Street to Norwest Bank. The last agreement in that skywalk segment was approved in October of 1989 and the leg was opened to the public the next year.

Early in discussions about expanding the reach of the skywalk system, a connection to the Radisson Hotel was broached. This would provide obvious benefits including connecting another major "traffic generator" to the downtown, a hotel facility with a direct, weather-protected connection to the DECC. The major stumbling block to such a connection was the Fifth Avenue West Mall, which was developed at substantial expense in the mid-1960s as a joint public-private venture to remove blighted properties, to enhance the Civic Center and to create a view corridor from the Civic Center to the Harbor. Any type of skywalk bridge across Fifth would have a negative effect on the Mall and the view. Many solutions to the problem were considered before the city settled on a route which would extend the skywalk from the Frame Corner Building through the Phoenix Building, across Fourth Avenue West into the Palladio Building, through the Palladio Building into the rear of the KDAL Building, and then under Fifth Avenue West and into the Radisson. Development of this leg led to the only use of eminent domain required by the extension of the system when an easement was condemned through the Phoenix Building. It also saw the only major casualty in the history of the system. In 1995, after skywalk construction had been completed and a bridge built across Fourth Avenue West, the Phoenix Building was destroyed by fire, literally taking the skywalk down with it. Completion of this skywalk connection required the Duluth Economic Development Authority, now the city's tax increment district administrator, to purchase the property and build a new building on the site. This leg—which included a tunnel with display cases, water wall and reflecting pool under Fifth Avenue West—opened in 1997.

Since then, connections have been made to the Fourth Avenue West Parking Ramp through the Phase II Building and the Duluth Plumbing

Supply Building, a connection from the Radisson to the Library and connections through the Palladio Building to the Duluth Athletic Club and the City's Water and Gas Building.

Not all proposed connections have been made. Some, which are not yet being actively pursued, include connection to Shoppers Auto Park, a connection from Duluth Plumbing Supply to the Northwest Passage, and from the Duluth Public Library through the Depot across I-35 to Bayfront.

Other connections still being worked on include a connection from the MacDonald Building through the Tech Village development to the proposed expansion of SMDC.

The skywalk system by most criteria must be judged to be highly successful. It has fulfilled its primary goal of making downtown Duluth a more friendly and comfortable place to work and to shop and, as such, has contributed greatly to retaining the viability of the downtown area. ■

Robert Asleson is Assistant City Attorney for the City of Duluth. Bob has worked on planning and negotiations for the Duluth downtown skywalk system since 1980.

14

Town View Improvement Company

LOCAL WOMEN ROLL UP THEIR SLEEVES TO HELP THE HILLSIDE

by Beverly Goldfine

Town View was the dream of Judge Gerald Heaney who felt that someone, with time and determination, could help Duluth's Hillside community out of its slump. He cared enough to make his dream into something more than a passing fantasy.

Gerald's philosophy was that Duluth, as a city, had a tremendous land area that was experiencing a change. As people built new homes in suburban areas, the old houses and the old neighborhoods were being "thrown away" as if they were old beer cans. The population was declining in the East Hillside, the Central Hillside and West End.

Along with the decline came school closings. Meanwhile, the City had to continue to maintain its streets, sewers, fire

NEMHC, Duluth, MN

Town View members and supporters at Munger Terrace, 1978. (Several participants are missing.) Back row, left to right: John Ivey Thomas, Eleanor Heaney, Karen Fillenworth, Geraldine Heller, Betty Halvorson, Katherine Watters; middle and first row, left to right: Gerald Heaney, Cliff Olson, Lois Swanson, Bill Burns, Ingrid Wells, MHFA representative, Candace Moberg, Beverly Goldfine, Margie Laughman, MHFA representative.

protection, and police protection—and that was a major problem.

It was our hope that by providing improvements in old neighborhoods, people would want to return—and that is what we wanted to see happen on the Hillside. Gerald gathered a few of us together and through his optimism, sold us on his idea of reversing the downward trend in the Hillside by buying the most rundown homes and then renewing them and reselling them. We ladies took to it like "ducks to water." The original group included his wife Eleanor, myself, and Katherine Watters. We pooled our experiences together and in 1967, created Town View Improvement Company, a nonprofit organization.

We enlisted more women to the project, which created the Town View Board. It consisted of myself as president, Katherine Watters as vice president; Luella Dettman, secretary; Ingrid Wells, treasurer; Grace Bridges; Geraldine Heller—"a graduate architect who never practiced" who was the architect for our very first house; Lois Swanson; Eleanor Heaney; Betty Halvorson; Virginia King; Ruth Frederick; Alice Shershon; Florence Finkelstein; Roberlene Carter; Karen Fillenworth, who took over management and continued to serve the company that purchased us; Eleanor Nichol; Harriet Fredin; Dee Anthony; Audrey Berkelman; Ann Arndt; and Candace Moberg, who was the manager for all the years that I was a part of Town View and did a phenomenal job. (There are some other women whose names I unfortunately can't remember anymore who were also a

> Gerald gathered a few of us together and through his optimism, sold us on his idea of reversing the downward trend in the Hillside by buying the most rundown homes and then renewing them and reselling them.

part of Town View for a short time.)

We started the project by canvassing the entire Central Hillside area to determine which homes were worth saving and which should be torn down. At the same time, we had to find seed money to begin our first remodeling project. Skepticism was high, financial backers thought this dream was just that, but we did finally raise enough money, about $5,000, to start the project. In 1968, only six months after the group was formally chartered, the not-for-profit Town View Improvement Company bought our first house. Thanks to a bank officer who had lived and grown up in the Central Hillside and believed in the possibilities for the area, we acquired a conventional bank mortgage. The real work then began and the women were terrific. We hired a contractor to install a new kitchen and bathroom. The walls and the ceilings were replastered and much of it was repainted...and the work went on and on. The women felt very strongly about providing the essential appliances as part of the home, so a washer and dryer were included. As a group, we were divided up into our responsibilities—we ran a little short of money—so at the very end we became the cleaning crew. I can remember not only working on the cleaning crew, but working with Grace Bridges, who brought her husband, Bob, to help clean up. At that time Bob was vice chancellor at the University of Minnesota Duluth.

When families had problems with financing and relocation, we became involved in that area as well. Eleanor Nichols was especially good at that

> ...we ran a little short of money—so at the very end we became the cleaning crew. I can remember not only working on the cleaning crew, but working with Grace Bridges, who brought her husband, Bob, to help clean up.

and she had the compassion and understanding that went with this. It was remarkable how she worked with the families that needed help. We took the money from the first house and we reinvested it into another project. At the end of 1968, President Lyndon Johnson signed the Federal Housing Act, which was aimed at helping low and moderate income families buy their own homes with low-cost mortgages insured by the government. A section of the Act provided for nonprofit developers to attain low interest loans for rehabilitating old homes in groups of five or more, and the doors swung open for Town View, and we just forged ahead. We then began a five-house rehabilitation program that stopped at a neglected, rat-infested, brick apartment building. After learning that the landlord was selling the building, and finding it structurally sound, we continued the project by having the interior of that building gutted. We ended up with nineteen apartments in that building all with new stoves, refrigerators and carpeting. Town View then became a landlord of rental units. The new housing laws and long-term low interest loans made it possible for Town View to rent to low-income families at relatively low rates. We weren't successful at building new units and selling them, but we were successful at rehabilitating 250 units of housing in the Central Hillside.

Our major projects were:
- **The 8th Street mini-renewal project.** We removed a group of older homes and built 14 new homes there.

- **The Town View Villas** consisted of 44 townhouses on West Second Street.

- **Town View Apartments** consisted of a 19-unit apartment house and another 3-unit apartment located on West Second Street.

- **Town View Villas South** included 27 new townhouses at Mesaba and First Street and a restored 12-unit brownstone on West Second Street, plus three additional townhouses and a converted duplex.

We then went on to do Munger Terrace, which consisted of 32 apartments. It was our biggest project and was completed in 1979. We also renovated the old Fire Hall at Ninth Street and 7th Avenue East, which was converted into apartment units.

Because we had received such good publicity, low-income homeowners contacted us to help them. The volunteer board would send representatives to help them decide what had to be done, get estimates, contractors and arrange financing. It really became an important part of Town View. We renovated about 45 individual homes that were scattered throughout the area.

> We then went on to do Munger Terrace, which consisted of 32 apartments. It was our biggest project and was completed in 1979.

In 1973, Town View received the "National Volunteer Award of the Year" in Washington D.C. It was really quite a remarkable, exciting thing for us. Katherine Watters, Ann Arndt and I went to Washington to receive the award. To this day, Town View is one of the highlights of my life. During the last few years of Town View, I stepped down when President Betty Halvorson took over, and she did a wonderful job.

In 1980, we phased out Town View and sold our company to Thies and Talle Enterprises out of Edina, Minnesota for $100,000. The money was given to the Humphrey Institute for Public Affairs in Gerald Heaney's name. We established a fellowship for graduate students from Duluth and Northeastern Minnesota which exists to this day.

Some of the Federal programs that helped us in our work were:
- Section 221 (d)(3) of the 1961 Housing Act that provided 100%, forty-year mortgages at below-market interest rates for company sponsors to build moderate income housing projects.
- Section 236 of the 1965 Housing Act replaced and expanded this

program and offered tax shelters as an incentive to encourage private enterprise. This also offered low-income people rent supplements to assist them in renting housing in the private sector.

- As the 1968 legislation expanded the rent supplement program under which a person certified as eligible paid 25% of their income as rent, with the federal government making up the difference between that figure and the market rent of the apartment.

- Section 235 allowed low income people to purchase houses.

- In 1974, Section 8 of the Housing and Community Development Act provided more housing subsidies for low-income people renting housing in privately-owned buildings.

Of course, all of this would have never happened without Gerald Heaney being our mentor and our faithful inspiration to make Town View a reality.

You can see how all these programs that were made available led to the success of Town View. We were also in the Model Cities project area which meant additional help to us, and we worked very closely with the City on all of our projects.

If you go by the West Hillside neighborhood today you will see how wonderful those properties look and what an important part they played in the revitalization of the Central Hillside. It was a wonderful, wonderful project for each of us who gave of our time. What came back to us was far more than we ever gave. Of course, all of this would have never happened without Gerald Heaney being our mentor and our faithful inspiration to make Town View a reality.

At the time our organization was chosen the "National Volunteer of the Year," Ben Boo was Mayor of Duluth and there was great publicity in the Duluth papers. When he honored us at a ceremony in Duluth, one of the signs read, "Duluth Salutes Town View Improvements Super Citizens." We were a great group of women who worked wonderfully together. Those thirteen years were magical moments in all of our lives. ▮

Beverly Goldfine is one of the founders of Town View Improvement Company. She was president when Town View Improvement Company was named "National Volunteer of the Year."

CHAPTER

15

Duluth Area Family YMCA

A HEALTH CLUB FOR MEN
TRANSFORMS ITSELF INTO A FITNESS
CENTER FOR EVERYONE

by Bruce Buchanan

In the spring of 1908, the Duluth Young Men's Christian Association (YMCA) opened the doors of its new building at the southwest corner of Third Avenue West and Second Street. This building—containing two full floors of sleeping rooms for young men, a full complement of athletic facilities including a gym, pool, running track, handball courts, meeting rooms and a small restaurant—serviced the needs of its members for almost 60 years.

By the late 1950s, it became obvious that the building was nearing the end of its useful life and if the YMCA was going to continue to have a presence in the city, it was imperative that a location for a new building, preferably in the downtown area, be acquired, and that a campaign be organized to raise the anticipated construction costs. The new YMCA would focus

Harry Neimeyer pumps iron (shovel) for the new YMCA. Groundbreaking for the new facility at the southwest corner of Third Ave. W. and First St. led to the establishment of a modern family health club in 1967. Membership was opened to women and girls in 1975.

on offering recreational and social opportunities, but would not provide overnight accommodations. In 1961, the site that previously housed the Rudolph Furniture Store at the southwest corner of Third Avenue West and First Street, one block down from the original building, was purchased from Morris Rudolph. A campaign committee was formed, chaired by Warren Moore. Construction costs were estimated at $1.44 million, and a capital campaign committee raised over $1 million by May 1964. When the new building was completed in 1967, its final cost of $2 million was underwritten by gifts from individuals and businesses, as well as a mortgage.

Designed by Duluth architects Melander, Fugelso and Associates, the new facility provided 50,000 sq. ft. of space, including a modern health club, a 66x92 ft. gymnasium, a 25x75 ft. swimming pool, an all-purpose assembly room and lounge, several club and craft activity rooms, and a coffee shop with a seating capacity for 200.

In 1975, membership was opened to women and girls.

Many civic leaders were instrumental in making the campaign a success. Notable among them were Seth Marshall, Harry Neimeyer, Donald McDonald and Hugh Wheeler.

In 1975, membership was opened to women and girls, and by 1977 it was evident that the new building was no longer large enough to serve our membership. Initial sketches by Architects IV called for a training pool, a whirlpool, a women's fitness center, a multi-fitness center with a 100-meter running track, an improved laundry and several energy and accessibility modifications—plus three additional racquetball courts and a second gymnasium with a suspended running track.

Fundraising began in 1980, but when costs increased, the racquetball courts and the third-floor gymnasium were eliminated. Arend Sandbulte, Joseph Johnson, Fred Wylie and I led a successful capital funds campaign to raise $1.5 million for the improvements, and construction began when we reached our goal in February 1983. The expansion was completed in 1984, and included the Whiteside Family Pool, a warm-water training pool for pre-schoolers, the elderly and the handicapped. The Whiteside Family Pool was made possible by a gift from Muriel Whiteside.

In 1988, the old free weight/universal exercise room on the lower level was converted into two completely barrier-free, adapted locker rooms. Two new locker rooms plus a new poolside restroom were added in 1991, and in 1995 the YMCA added a new strength training and cardiovascular center.

Today the Duluth YMCA services a total membership of 4,262 men, women and children. ∎

Bruce R. Buchanan has served on the YMCA board of directors since the 1960s. He was in charge of pattern gifts for the $1.4 million fundraising effort to build the new YMCA in 1963, and played a major role in the success of the $1.5 million capital campaign to expand the facility in 1980.

CHAPTER

16

Duluth Public Library

CITIZENS NAVIGATE 18 YEARS OF
ROCKY SHOALS TO BRING
NAUTICAL-STYLE LIBRARY DOWNTOWN

by Mary C. Van Evera

After Duluth's eagerly anticipated first public library building[1] opened its doors on West Second Street in 1902, it wasn't long before the library's annual reports began to refer to crowded conditions. Even after an addition to the Carnegie Library was constructed in 1927, library staffers had to resort to storing some items off-site, including an empty swimming pool in the Barnes-Ames building at Lake Avenue and Second Street.

During the 1960s, voices in the community began to urge the city to give attention to the public library and its branches. When Mrs. John C. Dwan presented $25,000 to the library in 1966, Mrs. Dwan made a point of letting the city officials know that contributions such as hers should not lessen the responsibility of

---

[1] Prior to the Carnegie building, the public library was in shared space.

Before the books, the bowery. The Union Depot overlooked Duluth's Bowery on the upper side of Michigan Ave. until the area was razed in the 1960s to make way for redevelopment. The land was purchased by the City in 1968 and designated for the library, but it took more than a decade to resolve disputes over the site.

the city to equip and maintain an adequate library system.

That year, the City of Duluth hired the director of the Library School of the State University of Iowa, Frederick Wezeman, to conduct a library study. Wezeman deemed the Carnegie library to be inadequate and recommended a new main library building be built and that the book collections of the main and branch libraries be brought up to proper standards. He further recommended that a site on Fifth Avenue West in downtown Duluth's designated Gateway Urban Renewal District would make the library more accessible to Duluthians.

Discussions began about how to pay for a new library. The Duluth Housing and Redevelopment Authority (HRA) owned the Gateway District lot, which was valued at $59,800, and in 1969 the City Council

The new library nears completion. Those opposed to the site feared the building would obscure the view of the Depot, so the plan was changed by moving the building 40 ft. west.

approved an option to purchase the site. Library board members began to explore all private and public sources of money. A gift from Mrs. Dorothy H. Congdon and Miss Elisabeth Congdon to the City funded purchase of the land and the selection of an architect.

In 1968, Mayor Ben Boo authorized the library board and Library Director Lucile Roemer to begin work towards the construction of a new library. In July 1968, the Duluth City Council approved the site for the library between Fifth and Sixth Avenues West and between Michigan and Superior Streets. The City purchased this land from the Housing and Redevelopment Authority in 1969 and the board promptly launched a local fundraising campaign that would eventually raise $860,000 from private contributors.

The board hired the Michigan architectural firm of Gunnar Birkerts & Associates to design the new library, and began to lay the groundwork to obtain state and federal funds. In Minnesota, Birkerts' firm was known for its design of the Federal Reserve Bank Building in downtown Minneapolis.

Birkerts presented his dramatic nautical design for the library and mall to the board in 1970, a design that immediately provoked strong feelings—both pro and con.

Function was one of Birkerts' primary concerns in his design of the building, but the controversy about the design never touched upon what the design would be like for users of the library. Fears were that the library would obscure the view of the Depot.

1971 to 1979 were years of planning, fundraising and frustration. Federal funding for the library project went on hold until 1974, due to priorities for a new airport terminal, Spirit Mountain, a new fire hall, and improvements at the port terminal. By 1976, Jeno Paulucci became convinced that it was the library's turn to be project number one and he spoke for it with force, both locally and in Washington, D.C.

1976 was the stormy year of disputes about the location and funding of the library. The public works employment bill intended to support projects that created jobs, but it failed. Board member Robert F. Eaton, with advice from citizens and government staff (both pessimistic and energized) led the request for funding from the Economic Development Authority (EDA). Bob did a yeoman's job of presenting the arguments for the location and for EDA funding.

During this time, some Duluth citizens voiced concerns about the Superior Street location of the library, fearing the it would ruin the view the Norman French-styled Depot just across Michigan Street. The Depot had just achieved a listing on the Federal Register of Historic Places to become the St. Louis County Heritage and Arts Center. A grassroots group asked that the site be changed, since the original plans for redevelopment of the Gateway area called for a ten-foot setback for each new building, as well as off-street parking.

Julia Marshall and Dorothy Moore Congdon, as well as some Depot board members offered funding for a parking lot, instead, on the library site. The *Duluth News Tribune* conducted a limited poll of about 1,500 people that coincided with a campaign against the site by KDAL radio and TV. The response to the poll found that a majority opposed the site.

Some citizens suggested that the HRA-owned, so-called Lenox Block between Superior and First Street west of Sixth Avenue West would be better, though it would require redesign of the building and the time factor for redesign limited the chance of 100% funding on the Lenox Block. Another suggested location was Superior Street east of Lake Avenue.

The Library Board preferred the Fifth Avenue West and Superior Street location because of its accessibility, bus service, and its downtown location. The board's recommendation says it best: "Above all, remote locations should be avoided...The library must be located in the mainstream of the business and economic area of the city so that it can serve as a dynamic educational and research center whose facilities and resources are accessible to the greatest number of potential users."

A letter from the State Historic Preservation officer affirmed the site and design: "The modern design of the library is not in the same style of the Depot but in its curved surfaces and massing does not detract from the Depot. Therefore, the new building...does not introduce visual elements which are out of character with the Depot."

The HRA offered an exhaustive review of the two sites and its position paper in February 1976 recommended the present location.

In 1977, the EDA provided a grant of $5 million towards construction costs, but added a stipulation that a new site be found. This came as a surprise to Duluth Mayor Robert Beaudin, who quickly sent City Planner Richard Loraas and City Planning Office Special Projects Director Ernest Petersen to Washington to convince EDA officials to allow Duluth to use its existing site. The controversy continued at home. In March 1977, Mayor Beaudin appointed a "blue ribbon" citizens' committee to evaluate the Superior Street site and come up with a final recommendation. Committee members included Sister Joan Braun, Lawrence Caven, Thomas Dougherty, Harold Frederick, Manley

A new chapter for the Duluth Public Library. Dedication day, June 28, 1980. U.S. Representative James Oberstar is at podium; back row, left to right: Mae Wicklund, Gunnar Birkerts, Warren Moore, [last two individuals not identified]. Middle row, left to right: John Moriarity, Robert Eaton, Gil Harries. First row, left to right: Donald Harries, Lillian Goldfine.

Goldfine, Thomas Gruesen, James Gustafson, John Hawley, Sylvester Laskin, Earl Liljegren, Helen Lind, Odin Ramsland, Donald Shank, Kay Slack, Richard Whiteman, Donald Wirtanen and myself.

As the *Duluth News Tribune* reported it, "Just when the committee seemed hopelessly divided, Harold Frederick and Manley Goldfine proposed a compromise that consisted of moving the building 40 feet west to allow a better view of the Depot, and stipulated the building of a city parking ramp west of the Depot to serve both facilities."

The compromise was endorsed. Adolfson and Peterson, Inc. of Minneapolis were given the building contract with a bid of $3,917,000 and groundbreaking ceremonies were held on July 5, 1977.

The original design of the building called for a steel frame with a long cantilever at the east end, but the design had to be amended to meet EDA requirements for more "labor intensive" construction methods, resulting in reinforced concrete and exposed columns.

A 258-space parking lot was financed by a $1.86 million bond issue, which also paid for library construction changes, furnishings, land acquisition costs, engineering costs, and operating costs for the first year.

Upon the completion of the building, Bernard Jacob, architecture critic of the *Minneapolis Tribune*, praised the nautically themed building for its "drama and vigor," calling it "an intriguing ship."

After 15 years of planning and three years of construction, the new Duluth Public Library celebrated its dedication week June 28 through July 3, 1980. The dedication ceremonies included a traditional ship-style launching when Mayor John Fedo smashed a bottle of champagne against the building. A short program featured Library Board President Lillian Goldfine, Library Friend Earl Henton, Emeritus Board Member Donald D. Harries, U.S. Representative James L. Oberstar and Library Director Janet K. Schroeder. Later in the day, a screening of *The Seventh Seal*, a 1957 film by Swedish director Ingmar Bergman, led to a discussion of Swedish films and art. Activities throughout the week included tours, lectures on geneology, storytelling and a book sale. Besides celebrating a new library, perhaps the best news was for those who held long-overdue library materials. During dedication week, they were invited to return their items that week, no questions asked. Ten thousand people visited the library over the course of dedication week.

For its time, the new library was among the most modern libraries in the U.S. Library planners were particularly proud of the North Shore Room, which houses the Americana collection and the Duluth and Minnesota collections; as well as a large children's library with an activity center.

It would take several months before books were moved and shelved in the new building and the old card system was converted to a computer-based system. Lillian Goldfine quipped that for much of 1980, the book-less new building was "open for looks if not books." The library opened to the public in November 1980.

Gunnar Birkerts' daughter designed banners which were intended to circle the performance area under the overhang on the east side of the library. They were never hung after the first year, however, as they were a nuisance to maintain.

The Duluth Public Library has continued to adapt to the times while providing excellent services to the community. A great deal of credit should go to the cadre of volunteers especially the Duluth chapter of the Friends of the Library. Charlotte Moyer reorganized the group in June 1979, just before the building was completed.

The Duluth Library Board members who encouraged the project between 1968 and 1980 included: Thomas W. Chamberlin, Robert F. Eaton, Lillian Goldfine, Donald D. Harries, Gilbert W. Harries, Matilda T. McDonnell, Warren S. Moore, John M. Moriarity, Mary Jean Olson, Mary R. Pooley, Arend V. Sandbulte, Jeanne A. Vecchi, Katherine B. Watters, Mae E. Wicklund, Frank A. Young and Margaret Culkin Banning (Honorary Lifetime Member).

The planning and building of the Duluth Public Library spanned the careers of three library directors: Lucile Roemer, 1963-1975; William Gordon, 1975-1977; and Janet K. Schroeder, 1977-1993.

Duluthians have continued to have a love/hate relationship with the architecture of the library, which has been compared to a space ship...or a parking ramp. Perhaps the idea that a perfect view of the Depot was violated rankles its detractors as much as the design. Yet the treasures it holds inside—and the wonderful key to those treasures that a library card represents—cannot be minimized. A patron who visited the fully-stocked library for the first time was quoted in the *Duluth News Tribune* as saying, "At first I thought it was the homeliest building I ever saw, but now I think it's beautiful." ∎

Mary C. Van Evera served as a member of the Duluth Library Board 1969 to 1980 and was active in fundraising in support of the project and library services. She was president of the Duluth Library Board 1976-1978, co-chaired the Site and Architecture Committee for the new library in 1968 and chaired the committee in 1971.

CHAPTER

17

Duluth's New Airport Terminal and Industrial Park

MEETING A $9 MILLION NEED WITH SPUNK AND INGENUITY

by Ben Boo

In the late 1960s, community leaders were expressing concern over the condition of the Duluth Airport Terminal. Jet planes were replacing props and traffic was increasing at a rapid rate. The existing building was decrepit, old, inefficient and crowded. The need for a new terminal was obvious. A terminal that would present a pleasing gateway to the city, one with adequate space, improved luggage handling and ample parking was overdue.

In 1969 the City of Duluth drafted state legislation to create the Airport Authority. Ultimately, similar legislation was requested to create the Spirit Mountain Authority and Duluth Transit Authority. Senator Sam Solon carried the legislation

Passengers at Duluth's new "port," 1974. The creative financing package for Duluth's new airport terminal involved the creation of AirPark, an industrial park owned and managed by the Seaway Port Authority.

and deputy city attorney Dan Berglund lobbied the bill through the legislature. On enactment, Jack Owens, Bob Rich, Mitch Sill, Keith Yetter, Gil Hartley, Sid Mason and Frank Befera were appointed to the first board. As mayor, I charged this new board with the responsibility for construction of a new terminal and to find the means of financing. Tom Schindler, deputy city attorney, was appointed to provide organizational and legal assistance.

Initial efforts to secure federal Economic Development Administration (EDA) grants were rebuffed. The EDA did not consider terminals to be within the scope of its mission, which was to create jobs.

Bob Rich lead the finance effort, while Jeno Paulucci was persuading the EDA to be a little more flexible. Under Jeno's pressure, the EDA relented to the point that funding would be approved if a job creation element could be included. Bob Rich invented an ingenious solution. An industrial park (later dubbed AirPark) would be built contiguous to the terminal and become part of the revised EDA application. Conrad "Mac" Fredin, Port Authority Board member, entered the picture and became representative of the port. The two, Bob Rich and Mac Fredin, suggested that the city own the terminal and the Port Authority own and manage AirPark. The EDA's job component requirement would be met by the proposed industrial park.

Ernie Petersen, City grants chief, wrote the unusual application. Upon council approval, Jeno and I met with the undersecretary of commerce in Washington, DC to expedite acceptance. Congressman John Blatnik stayed closely involved with the project, as did his successor in 1974, Jim Oberstar.

In 1970, all the pieces of the funding puzzle fell into place. The EDA approved a grant of $2.5 million followed by an Upper Great Lakes Regional Commission grant of $746,000 and a Minnesota Aeronautic Commission grant of $400,000. The city council responded by authorizing $3.8 million in general obligation (GO) bonds for the terminal and $1.6 million in GO bonds for AirPark. In all, more than $9 million was garnered for the project.

> Frank Befera, serving as a member of the Airport Authority and as chairman of the Metropolitan Airport Commission, coerced North Central Airlines into providing modern second-level passenger loading bridges.

Frank Befera, serving as a member of the Airport Authority and as chairman of the Metropolitan Airport Commission, coerced North Central Airlines into providing modern second-level passenger loading bridges. The jet bridges greatly enhanced the facility and came at a significant savings to the Airport Authority.

The new terminal and facilities were built at a cost of $7 million. David Morgenstern of Morgenstern and Stanius was the architect and A. W. Hedenberg was the general contractor.

In the meantime, the Seaway Port Authority, with $1.6 million in GO bonds and the EDA and Upper Great Lakes grants, began construction of AirPark. Of the 300 acres, 150 were deemed non-wetland and became available for sale and development. The 1978 legislature authorized the park to be a tax increment finance (TIF) district. Proceeds from the sale of land and TIF income were used to amortize the GO bonds. Although the TIF expired in 2001, land sales continued. Today, over $30 million in new construction stands in AirPark with over 600 people employed, readily meeting EDA's 1969 requirement!

The successful project demonstrated, again, that energetic, imaginative and resolute civic leaders can provide the solution to a public challenge. The council and I entrusted several special assignments to community leaders. They contributed influence and finesse, while city hall provided the tools of government such as planning, grantsmanship skills, legal support—and in particular on this venture, the adroit supervision of John Grinden, who managed our airport from April 1970 until February 1998. ∎

Ben Boo was mayor of Duluth, 1967-1975. He managed the Western Lake Superior Sanitary District during its construction, 1975-1979, was director of the Upper Great Lakes Regional Commission, 1979-1983, and represented district 8B in the Minnesota legislature, 1983-1993.

CHAPTER

18

Marshall School

FROM CATHEDRAL HIGH SCHOOL
TO AN INDEPENDENT
COLLEGE-PREPARATORY INSTITUTION

by Gracia Swensen

Marshall School holds a unique and prominent place in the history of education in northern Minnesota. It grew out of Duluth Cathedral High School, and has transformed with the times and changing needs of the community to become an integral part of the area, providing a high-quality, college preparatory education for young people in the Northland.

EARLY HISTORY

Parochial education had a shaky start in Duluth in 1881 under the direction of the Benedictine Sisters. Mother Scholastica Kerst opened Sacred Heart School in January, but it closed after only six months. Her second attempt in September 1884 was successful, and Sacred Heart School was

The original Cathedral School, located at the corner of 2nd Ave. W. and 4th Street in Duluth, opened in 1904. It was a boys' high school until the Cathedral Boys' and Girls' schools merged in 1943.

Marshall School's current building on the "top of the hill" on Rice Lake Road was completed in 1963, known then as Duluth Cathedral High School. It was renamed Marshall School in 1987, and today provides education for students in grades 5 through 12.

a fixture on the Duluth hillside for many years. From Sacred Heart, the Benedictine Sisters of St. Scholastica founded the Cathedral School for Girls. The Christian Brothers opened the Cathedral Boys' School in 1904 to serve the boys of this area.

The Duluth Catholic Diocese took over operation of Boys' Cathedral High School from the Christian Brothers in the early '40s, and the Cathedral Boys' and Girls' schools were merged under the direction of the Benedictine Sisters and the Diocesan Priests in 1943.

The original school building on the corner of Second Avenue West and Fourth Street was difficult to maintain, and the structure was failing. The need for a new building was imminent. Monsignor Michael J. Hogan, principal, and Monsignor Patrick McDowell, among others, chose a new location at the top of the hill on Rice Lake Road, the location of Marshall School today.

The current building was completed in 1963 as Duluth Cathedral High School. For the first time, Cathedral boys and girls learned under the same roof, although most classes were still segregated by gender. Rising operational debt and decreasing enrollment made it increasingly difficult for the Diocese of Duluth to continue operating the school. The community at the time was well aware of Cathedral's financial problems, and the Diocese gave serious consideration to closing the school. However, people in the community had a keen interest in preserving the opportunities and freedom of choice in secondary education that Cathedral offered.

TRANSFORMATION TO AN INDEPENDENT, ALL-FAITH SCHOOL

In 1971, a group of independent trustees took over the operation of Cathedral. The school was transformed from a Catholic school to an independent, all-faith school—The Ecumenical Duluth Cathedral High School.

The Board of Trustees guided the school through the changes necessary to ensure its survival. Because of their community involvement, sense of civic duty, and belief in the importance of the existence of educational choice in northern Minnesota, these dedicated individuals worked to preserve the option of independent education in Duluth.

"It was the people. Amazing *people.*
The best board in the world.
I felt it was a great honor to be on that board."

—**Mary Dwan**, a founder, remembers how several key people who believed so much in the need for an educational option were adamant that they succeed.

To ensure a smooth transition, an agreement was drawn up between the Duluth Diocese and the Board of Trustees. Features of this understanding included:

- The Diocese retains title to property and buildings.
- The board of Trustees leases buildings and grounds from the Diocese at the fee of $1 per year.
- The board assumes immediate decision-making authority for the school's guidance, becoming financially responsible at the start of the 1972-73 school year.
- The board is made up of no fewer than 18 members, including the original incorporating members named by the Bishop of Duluth.

In addition, the board agreed to assume responsibility for the following:

- Repair and upkeep of the school building.
- Employment of teaching staff.
- Curriculum oversight.
- Recruitment of students.
- Establishment of realistic tuition amounts.
- Academic excellence.
- Religious study requirement, offering a selection of courses from which students are allowed to choose.
- Establishment of a trust fund.
- Establishment of a scholarship fund.
- Socio-economic diversity among the school population.

- Cooperation with the public school system to promote and make available courses unique to Cathedral to public school students.

- High ethical, moral and religious standards, to include community service, in order to maintain and develop the school's reputation of excellence.

Under the board's direction, Cathedral High School continued to change through the decade of the 1970s. To meet the needs of the school through these years of financial insecurity, all constituents worked together to keep Cathedral's doors open. The faculty accepted lower-than-average salaries and inadequate equipment in exchange for the autonomy they appreciated, and the smaller class sizes. Gifts from the board, alumni, and parents helped to keep Cathedral afloat and the board made the decision to raise tuition. Despite the financial problems of this time, the board never lost sight of its commitment to provide scholarships for deserving students.

"We didn't have a plan for failure.
We just came up with the money.
There was always something *that kept us afloat."*

—**Jim Claypool**, a founding board member, describes the early days of Marshall School in 1971.

"We used next year's tuition to pay this year's expenses." Everyone on the board had something to offer the school, be it financial assistance or gifts of time and talent. And the board recruited heavily to find new members to help with this enormous undertaking. When asked why, Claypool answered, "You do it. You want to see it happen. And you see it through."

NEW IDENTITY

In 1981, grades seven and eight were added, and the school's name was changed to The Duluth Cathedral School. The Cathedral name held a strong identification for the school, so the Board had resisted serious consideration of a name change since 1972, when it became an all-faith school. As the focus and position of the school changed, however, to become one of the finest independent college preparatory schools in the Northland, the Priest's Senate of the Diocese of Duluth requested that the name be changed to reflect more accurately the new identity. Effective July 1, 1987, Cathedral was renamed Marshall School.

> ...the Priest's Senate of the Diocese of Duluth requested that the name be changed to reflect more accurately the new identity. Effective July 1, 1987, Cathedral was renamed Marshall School.

WHY MARSHALL SCHOOL?

Since 1893, when A. M. Marshall came to Duluth and founded the Marshall Wells Company, the Marshall name has held a prominent place in northern Minnesota. The Marshalls had five children, four of whom remained in Duluth and dedicated their energies, civic commitment and financial resources to a long list of accomplishments, focusing on community service, development, and improvement. These included the Marshall Performing Arts Center at the University of Minnesota Duluth, the Marine Museum at Canal Park, the Bayfront Development project, the Duluth Art Institute, the American Indian Fellowship Center, the Duluth Public Library, the Duluth Center for Learning and Recreation, and Discover Duluth. Julia Marshall was a long-time member of the Cathedral Board of Trustees, and along with her sister Caroline, was active all her life in support of education. The choice of the Marshall name for the school celebrates a theme of service to others, which has been a school tradition since its founding by the Catholic Diocese, and a way of life for the Marshall family.

In 1993, Marshall was reorganized into Middle and Upper Schools, and grades 5 and 6 were added. The school embarked on a successful capital campaign in 1995, which enabled Marshall School to purchase the campus from the Catholic Diocese. The purchase of the campus was a pivotal move for Marshall as it allowed the school to commence with building improvements. Deferred maintenance issues were addressed along with improvements to the campus that promote its college-preparatory mission. This includes providing quality teaching spaces as well as adequate opportunities for co-curricular learning.

VISION FOR THE FUTURE

A strategic planning process was completed in 2001 to guide the school for the next five years. Major tenets of the plan include updating the facility to meet today's needs, ensuring educational excellence, enhancing communication, expanding the internal and external sense of community, and increasing the school's financial strength.

A focus of the plan includes keeping a strong commitment to faculty—the heart and soul of any educational institution—to ensure that compensation is adequate. At the time of this publication, Marshall teachers earn less than 80% of the median of their independent school counterparts in the Midwest and less than 60% of the median of their colleagues in the Duluth public schools. The school's ability to retain and attract highly qualified teachers in the future depends on improving compensation.

Keeping with the original board's commitment to socio-economic diversity, the school stretches to ensure that qualified students can afford to attend Marshall, even when their families do not have the means to pay full tuition. Need-based financial aid enables the school to award tuition assistance to 18% of its student body. Marshall can afford, however, only to meet 66% of the determined need of families while many other independent school counterparts can meet a far greater percentage.

Overall, the vision of Marshall School today is to permanently ensure the future of an excellent independent college-preparatory school for Duluth and surrounding communities. The rich Hilltopper history of community commitment is a strong foundation to be built upon by future generations of Marshall students, faculty, and alumni. ∎

Gracia Swenson is Marshall School's Director of Alumni Relations.

[handwritten notes: THE IRON ORES OF LAKE SUPERIOR, CROWELL & MURRAY, THE PENTON PRESS CO., 1923]

CHAPTER

19

Central Administration Building

RESTORATION OF DULUTH'S
"TOWER OF LEARNING" WAS A MONUMENTAL TASK

by Richard Pearson

The discovery of iron on Minnesota's Iron Range in the 1870s led to active mining in the 1880s. Those developments, along with an active lumber industry, produced a rapid growth in the area's population. Duluth, as a shipping center and service center was to grow from 3,131 in 1870 to about 100,000 people by 1920.

The citizens of Duluth, anticipating the huge population influx that was to occur due to rapid expansion of iron mining in northeast Minnesota, committed themselves to development of a first-rate network of public schools. The most significant single school to be built was Central High School. It was constructed during the 1890-1892 period.

What developed under the architectural leadership of

[handwritten annotations: 1884; ore; VERMILLION; THAT SAME YEAR]

NEMHC, Duluth, MN. Photo by H. Rykken

Central High School, 1962. Built to be a symbol of Duluth's lofty education goals at the end of the 19th century, the Romanesque building remains a landmark of towering proportions. As home to the Duluth school district's administrative offices at the beginning of the 21st century, it has also come to serve as lightning rod for a community dealing with the realities of a declining school population and reduced budgets.

Emmet Palmer and Lucien Hall was to be a landmark of towering proportions. They designed a building in the Romanesque style, which had been popularized by Henry Hobson Richardson. The description of this building, written in 1975 for its rededication, follows:

...the architects joined masonry walls, unadorned arches and a massive lofty (clock) tower to create an enduring presence on Duluth's Central Hillside. Built of Minnesota sandstone, the building is decorated with stone carvings by George Thrana. Its steep roof sections were covered with hand-split slate.

The foregoing description could have been written in 1892 when Central High School was first occupied. A masterpiece for its time, the building was "doomed" to be preserved.

TERMINATING CENTRAL HIGH SCHOOL FROM SERVICE

On April 10, 1961, the School Board was nearing the end of a long series of Principal/PTA reports on facility needs at each of the individual schools. On this date, the venerable and highly respected George A. Beck, principal of Central High School, presented his commentary regarding "his" school. What follows is an excerpt from his oral presentation:

"...fine children and high quality teachers guarantee an excellent educational product, even though the quarters are no better than a hovel. But certainly, no thinking person would argue that a better job cannot be done with modern—superior—equipment and a desirable environment. Here and there, about us, we see the demolition of structures built in the 1890 period—being replaced by modern, efficient structures—an outstanding example of which is the new bank building located at Third Avenue West and Superior Street. One does not see the horse and buggy on Superior Street today. They are a casualty of progress, just as 1890 equipment should be in our schools. The public is demanding a 1970 product of our schools; it cannot be produced with 1890 educational facilities."

Mr. Beck sounded the death knell. The final push to replace Central High School was now underway.

In November of 1962, just three months after becoming superintendent, Dr. Bud Rasmussen recommended that the University of Minnesota's Bureau of Field Studies and Surveys be retained to evaluate all school district facilities and recommend a comprehensive plan for facility modernization. The report was submitted in February 1963, and once again it was deemed advisable to correct elementary school deficiencies as a first priority. The report did, however, recommend that a new high school be built "over the hill."

In the fall of 1963, the need to replace Central High School was accented when several tons of heavy plaster fell from the cafeteria ceiling. The Board of Education quickly authorized repairs and replacement and thoroughly studied ceiling conditions throughout the school. Shortly thereafter, Russell Doty, on behalf of the Central PTA, told the board that the Central PTA was opposed to permanent remodeling in favor of a new high school. The issue of pupil safety now became a rallying cry for a new high school.

Subsequently, a 50-member committee, to be known as CAUSE (Citizens Association for Upgrading Secondary Education) was created, with Richard Gurske as chair of the committee, and G. Dell Daedo as the chief administrator on the committee.

Events moved rapidly in the fall of 1964. CAUSE submitted its report on October 6, recommending a new Central High School. Simultaneously, a Vocational Education Committee, co-chaired by Frank Young and Curtis Miller recommended a new post-secondary Vocational Technical School. The Board of Education quickly outlined the parameters of a $6,710,000 bond issue to be submitted to voters in February 1965. The three major elements of the proposal were:

Vocational Technical School	$2,315,000
New high school and site	$3,310,000
Chester Park Elementary addition	$585,000

The bond issue was approved 13,387 to 7,140.

Within a month, the Board of Education retained Duluth architects Morgenstern & Stanius, to work in association with Reid and Tarics of San Francisco, to design a new Central High School.

After 26 years of service to Central High School, Principal George A. Beck retired. He became General Manager of WDSE-Channel 8 TV, but would be heard from again when "Old" Central High School was slated for demolition.

1965-67 became years of programmatic planning for the new high school. It soon became apparent that projected costs of a new high school would rise from $3.3 million to nearly $6 million. In April 1968 voters approved construction of a new high school at the "reservoir" site; the bonding included an allowance for demolition of old Central.

Community members began to sense a scene in which old Central High School would be demolished. Responding to a question at the March 1968 Board meeting, President Don Crassweller was quoted as follows:

> "The Board has already made plans for the demolition of Central High School when the new school is built and this was part of the bond issue. Central will be torn down."

"The Board has already made plans for the demolition of Central High School when the new school is built and this was part of the bond issue. Central will be torn down."

Over the past two years of site acquisition and construction, community voices to "preserve and save" old Central High School began to speak out and the School Board in April 1971 agreed to permit Washington Jr. to use the 1926 wing of Central to alleviate overcrowding at Washington Jr. (Prophetically, that section of old Central has been in some form of student use ever since.)

As the completion of new Central neared, there was increasing speculation that school district administrative services should leave the "ancient" Liberty School and Annex and occupy old Central space. Supporters and detractors were numerous and were becoming more vocal as the months passed. New Central would open on September 1971 and the old Central would become a vacant entity. There were no firm plans to preserve and use, or to demolish.

In May 1971, M. George Downs was elected president of the board and was thanked by member Ruth Bagley for encouraging the board to actively resolve a disposition plan for old Central.

Another catalyst to encourage preservation occurred in late July 1971, when nearly 8,000 Central H.S. graduates convened for an All-Class Reunion.

The All-Class Reunion Committee, led by Robert Livingston, would become a forum for the preservation of old Central, and Arnold Nides, Class of 1929, would provide enthusiastic, prodding leadership to that effort. He, along with Myrtle Marshall and George Beck, would become the three foremost public voices in the "Save Old Central" movement.

In early 1972, the School Board authorized creation of a task force to investigate and recommend:

- Possible uses of old Central
- Plans/sketches for a final plan
- Means to finance alterations and long-term maintenance
- A method by which the public can express approval or disapproval

Task force membership announced on January 4, 1972: Charles Barnes, Chair, George Beck, Donald Bowen, Lawrence Caven, G. Dell Daedo, Mrs. Y. B. Davis, Norton Gross, David Haglin, Mrs. Clifford Hedman, James Lee, Robert Livingston, Julia Marshall, Mrs. Lyman T. (Myrtle) Marshall, Lee Mooers, Arnold Nides, Dr. J. M. Runquist, Thomas Shefchik, John Ivey Thomas, Mrs. William (Mary) Van Evera, Mrs. Ward (Ingrid) Wells, Joseph Weisinger, Mrs. Kenneth Worthing, Frank Young. The presence of Arnold Nides on this committee would ensure that the preservation option would receive powerful consideration.

Meanwhile, the same questions, concerns, statements are repeated month after month:

- If old Central is to be saved, it must be used!
- If used, for what purpose?
- Who is responsible, or should be, for preservation?
- How will preservation be financed? By whom?
- Did the bond issue commit the board to demolition?
- If it was unsafe in 1968, why would it be safe now?

On April 25, 1972, task force chair Charles Barnes presented the final report to the School Board. He emphasized that the group was unanimous in its recommendations:

1. Preserve the building for use as the school district administrative center.
2. The School Board should ultimately decide on the disposition of the former administrative office space and the Barnes-Ames building.
3. Seek financial assistance from the National Trust for Historic Preservation.

Board president Downs and newly appointed acting superintendent Richard Pearson, (both Denfeld grads) became convinced that the building should be saved and used. The only potential appropriate savior was the school district, and therefore, the best use would be to centralize administrative services. To that end, on August 1972 the board approved a contract for architectural services with Fugelso, Porter, Simich & Whiteman to develop a possible restoration plan, timetable for occupancy, and cost estimates. The principal preservation architect would be Richard Frank Whiteman.

On November 9, 1972, the building was declared to be an historic site and was listed in the National Register of Historic Places. No federal dollars would be forthcoming, nor would the State of Minnesota ever include the project in state bonding programs. The school district was on its own.

For several years, overly enthusiastic people had suggested that re-use plans could take place at a minimum cost. Most suggested from nothing up to $250,000. Fortunately, knowledgeable school board members and director of physical plant LeRoy Moore knew such cavalier thinking was not realistic. Early on, architect Whiteman convinced everyone that the building would need more than cursory attention. Concrete reinforced floors, new windows and a new roof would not come on the cheap.

FINANCING RESTORATION AND PRESERVATION

During the 1965-1971 period when a new high school was on its way, the only way for a school district to make major investments in school building improvements was through a voter-approved bond issue. In the 1960s, Duluth voters approved three separate issues. General political belief in about 1970 was that a bond issue proposal to save old Central would not be successful without including improvements to schools elsewhere in the district. It must be remembered that the "pill" and the closing of the steel mill would soon create massive enrollment declines and the district would be closing buildings rather than expanding or building new schools.

A critical Minnesota education funding change occurred in 1971. All during the 1960s the school district was able to make a Capital Outlay Fund tax levy which produced about $425,000 annually. Proceeds from this levy were to be used for equipment acquisition or building improvements. Legislation in 1971 greatly improved school district funding generally. Specifically, the old Capital Outlay Fund would now be called the Capital Expenditure Fund (with no change in purpose) but with a more than quadrupled tax levy limit. The school board, therefore, had better access to building improvement monies.

The board created a "dedicated fund" within the capital expenditure fund for purposes of major improvements to old Central. On average, about $1.2 million was annually placed in a "dedicated" reserve. Over four years, the board would have access to about $5 million for school district capital improvements.

COMMITMENT TO USE AND PRESERVE

In December 1973, the school board committed the district to expend nearly $1.7 million to restore, preserve and use old Central High School. This school board became the brave saviors of old Central High School. From this commitment, there could be no turning back.

During the years from 1971-75, a separate committee under chair Myrtle Marshall faithfully collected memorabilia, relics, and artifacts for placement in an 1890 classroom which was reserved in the northeast corner of the first floor. Old timers remember algebra, geometry and trigonometry classes in that room. (The room is still in use today.)

A Duluthian, Al Lueck, would be construction foreman. The reconstruction would not be complete for nearly two years. Offices began moving to their new quarters in November 1975 and the dedication day took place on January 5, 1976.

Once the building was occupied, it would have been easy for the school board to conclude that they had done enough, but Architect Whiteman and director LeRoy Moore relentlessly badgered superintendent Pearson for a place on the agenda to remind the school board that replacement windows, a new roof and masonry repair were absolutely essential.

By 1986, architect Whiteman, after nurturing and encouraging several school boards over a 14-year period, was finally satisfied that his originally proposed work program had been fulfilled.

In the late 1980s, the Central Hillside Community Club created the Central Clock Tower Restoration Project Fund, chaired by Patty Martin. This group's successful efforts are noticeable, especially in the evenings as the Tower of Learning, with restored clockwork, is now lighted in the belfry and from the exterior.

More recently, in an effort to maintain citizen interest and support for the continued guardianship and ongoing care of the preserved building, the Central Preservation Committee was formed under the leadership of co-chairs Gary and Fayth Glass. This group is inspired to maintain the 1890 classroom and raise funds to assist the school board in recognizing and supporting the ongoing needs associated with prideful and proper maintenance of building preservation.

EPILOGUE

In many recurring instances since 1986, the preservation and use of "Old" Central High School was to become a "political albatross" hanging around the neck of later school boards. As enrollments shrank and school buildings were closed, it was difficult for many citizens to understand how and why this monument of public education should remain worthy of public use and support. Thirty years after a commitment to preserve the building was confirmed, it has now become:

A valued and symbolic landmark of Duluth educational history that merits the continued investment of public monies; or...a fiscal liability to the school district that should be released for private redevelopment; or...a building which has simply outlived its usefulness to the school district and has no redeeming ancillary value; or...an historic building that deserves everlasting love and maintenance by the citizens of Duluth; or... ∎

Richard Pearson served as superintendent of Duluth Public Schools 1972-1986. From being an early skeptic of preservation to becoming an enthusiastic believer that the building should be "saved," he, along with abundant and vocal Central alumni, and lovers of the building itself, were successful in garnering the 1973 School Board decision to preserve the building. Helping the School Board to piece together a long-term financing plan was his major contribution.

CHAPTER

20

Lake Superior Maritime Visitor Center

THE CORPS OF ENGINEERS' INVESTMENT IN A GREAT LAKES COMMERCE MUSEUM ENRICHES VISITOR EXPERIENCE AT CANAL PARK

by C. Patrick Labadie

I came to Duluth in 1973, and I still get the same thrill that I did then when I first approached it from the south shore and saw the city spread across the hillside. The most pleasant surprise in the end was not that visual one, though. It came when I was introduced to Duluth's people.

Upon our arrival, my wife and I were immediately swept into the dizzying vortex of energy and excitement that surrounded Duluth's '70s revival. The I-35 expressway was coming to town, the Miller Hill Mall was under construction, the Depot was coming to life again after its long renovation, the Normandy Hotel was on the drawing board, a new Public Library was only a year or two away, and Canal Park was experiencing a major

Participating in the ground breaking ceremonies for the Canal Park museum are: (left to right) Herbert Klippen, Duluth contractor; William Moser, Duluth architect; Col. Rodney Cox, St. Paul district engineer, U.S. Army Corps of Engineers; Maj. Gen. Earnest Graves, division engineer, Corps' North Central Division, Chicago; U. S. Rep. John A. Blatnik; and Duluth Mayor Ben Boo.

face-lift. It was absolutely breathtaking!

The scale of changes was impressive, but the spirit with which those changes were undertaken was exhilarating and infectious. There were long, often contentious meetings at City Hall and at the Chamber of Commerce, but some of the most productive meetings were at Julia and Caroline Marshall's London Road home, where there was standing room only but free and open discussion and thinking outside the proverbial box. There were also a lot of new faces in the crowd—people like my wife, June, and me, who had been attracted to Duluth by its ambitious plans.

The concept for the Corps of Engineers Visitor Center and Marine

Following the ground breaking ceremonies in 1972, sisters and local philanthropists Julia and Caroline Marshall talk with Ralph Knowlton.

Museum came from the Corps' St. Paul District commander, Colonel Robert Hesse. He proposed improvements to the Corps' Administrative Office building in Canal Park around 1969, beginning with simple restroom accommodations for visitors to Canal Park. Statistics indicated that at least a half-million people visited the popular site annually, and local Corps employees were flooded (no pun intended) with appeals for restrooms.

Colonel Hesse turned to Corps Duluth Administrative Officer Ralph Knowlton. Ralph was recently retired, and the colonel invited him to sound out local officials about ideas for Canal Park and then to generate support for improvements there. If funding could be obtained, the Corps would build and staff the facilities. Ralph organized a committee and they almost immediately reached a consensus that there should be a marine museum in Canal Park. Knowlton's "Museum Advisory Committee" sketched out plans and presented them to Col. Hesse early in 1971. The committee also began petitioning Minnesota's venerable 8th District Congressman John Blatnik for the funds to construct the proposed facility. The funds were authorized in the 1972 Corps budget.

> Visitation continued climbing until it averaged 420,000 for the next 15 years. The Canal Park Visitor Center and Marine Museum had become one of the most popular Corps of Engineers sites in the country.

Knowlton's vision for the Visitor Center and Marine Museum was to illustrate the history of Great Lakes watercraft "from canoes to bulk freighters." He began to collect artifacts from the community in 1971. Caroline Marshall contributed the first ship model, a replica of a small sailing craft. A closet in the Corps' office building quickly filled with charts, ship parts, photographs, and models, all while the design process was still underway for the new building. In a truly inspired move, Knowlton and attorney Bill Van Evera incorporated the "Museum Advisory Committee" as the non-profit "Lake Superior Marine Museum Association" in the spring of 1974, with Arthur King as its first president. The association would play a key role in making the museum a success, and it would eventually become the model for "cooperating associations" at Corps of Engineers public facilities all over the nation. The association is still a partner in the Marine Museum, which was re-christened as the "Lake Superior Maritime

Visitor Center" in 1997.

The new Visitor Center and Museum began construction in 1972 and it was opened to the public on September 29, 1973. It was constructed at a cost of $275,000, and opened year-round, free of charge. It soon proved inadequate for the attendance it received. Visits during the 1970s averaged over 300,000 annually. When the staff greeted its one-millionth visitor in the fall of 1976, the Corps announced plans to enlarge the facility. The building was expanded to three times its original size during 1979-80 at a cost of another $750,000. Visitation continued climbing until it averaged 420,000 for the next 15 years. The Canal Park Visitor Center and Marine Museum had become one of the most popular Corps of Engineers sites in the country.

The City, then under the leadership of Mayor Ben Boo and City Planner Dick Loraas, and with considerable support from the Marshall sisters, began substantial improvements to complement the Visitors Center. The street was straightened and the public parking areas paved. The adjoining Paulucci property was also paved and opened up for public parking. Two years later, the old Sand Bar was bought by the Pauluccis and turned into the enormously popular Grandma's Restaurant. A scrap yard on Buchanan Street was vacated around 1981, adding further parking to the area. The improvements changed the whole character of what had just a few years before been an uninviting industrial neighborhood.

Ralph Knowlton didn't live long enough to see all of the improvements, but the Museum and Visitors Center were prospering when he passed away in 1975.[1] Julia and Caroline Marshall survived Ralph by several years and saw many of their visions become reality. Dozens of Duluth and Superior residents have served on the Museum Association's board since 1973 and have made enormous contributions to this worthwhile civic attraction and to the renaissance that has made Duluth so desirable a community.

---

[1] Ralph's estate included a generous bequest, which is managed by the Duluth Superior Area Community Foundation. The Ralph S. Knowlton Endowment Fund continues to receive contributions to support services and exhibits consistent with the museum's public education mission.

The Army Corps of Engineers, first the St. Paul District and more recently the Detroit District, has quietly supported and enhanced the Visitors Center for thirty years now, and it has, for the most part, been too modest about it. The Corps deserves a great deal of credit for the impact the Visitor Center has had on Duluth's tourist economy. For those of us who have worked for the Corps at Canal Park, the greatest rewards were always the kind words we received from our visitors and the generous support we were given by the community. It has always been a "win-win" relationship. ▮

C. Patrick Labadie served as director of the Canal Park Visitor Center and Marine Museum from August 1973 through March 2000. He is resident historian for the National Oceanic & Atmospheric Administration's Thunder Bay National Marine Sanctuary at Alpena, Michigan.

CHAPTER

21

Spirit Mountain
Recreation Area

THE RUN TO BRING A WORLD-CLASS
SKI AREA TO DULUTH

by Ben Boo

In the early 1970s, commercial alpine ski areas
became popular in the United States. At that time, there was
just a small ski facility at Mont du Lac on Highway 23, across
the St. Louis River from Fond du Lac, southwest of Duluth.

George Hovland, a lifelong cross-country and alpine skier
who competed at the 1952 Olympics, was a friend of the
owners of ski areas around the country, and wanted to develop
a large ski facility that would benefit Duluth. In about 1971, he
chose a slope on 950 acres between Riverside and Highway 61
on Thompson Hill. Hovland studied the grades and
orientation of the hill, and determined that it would be perfect
for a ski facility. He then researched the ownership of the many
different pieces of land that made up the hill and learned that
much of the property was tax forfeited and owned by the

It was all downhill from here. Spirit Mountain Ski School Instructor Karl Petter (on left) and Gov. Wendell Anderson prepare for a run on Spirit Mountain's opening day, Dec. 20, 1974.

county. Hovland called Manley Goldfine, and they went together to look over the hill. Goldfine agreed it was a promising site and a great idea. They took the concept to the city administration, which was supportive. Don Salo, an independent civil engineer, was asked to review Hovland's preliminary analysis of the slopes, and he agreed that the area would make an excellent ski facility. The rest is history.

A committee was formed to raise $8 million. The committee included the mayor, Jeno Paulucci, Manley Goldfine, Lee Vann, Conrad Fredin, Charles Westin, Thomas Smrekar, Michael Pintar, Jack Arnold and

Freeman Johnson. Jeno Paulucci and other members of the committee made appointments to meet with Governor Wendell Anderson and U.S. Interior Secretary James Watt to secure state and federal funds. Governor Anderson committed $850,000 and the Economic Development Administration (EDA) committed $600,000. Other funding sources included $2 million in Spirit Mountain Revenue Bonds to be repaid from future ski hill income; $1 million of General Obligation Bonds from the City of Duluth; $800,000 of City of Duluth utility bonds; $700,000 from private funders; $550,000 from the U.S. Bureau of Outdoor Recreation, Land & Water Conservation Fund; $450,000 from the Legislative Commission on Minnesota Resources; and $250,000 from the U.S. Upper Great Lakes Regional Commission.

A development board was installed with co-chairs Robert E. Mathias and Dr. Donald J. Van Ryzin, and members John Z. Dahl, Elnora Johnson, Orville S. Peterson, Paul Vesterstein and George Hovland. In 1971, the state legislature, led by Sam Solon, passed the necessary legislation and created a board to build and operate the project. The first operating board included: Manley Goldfine, chairman; Harold Hultberg, vice-chairman; Gene Borg, Mary Evans, secretary (and later vice-chair); Gloria DeSmedt, Lewis Erickson and Ray Morrison. The name Spirit Mountain was the idea of Donn Wiski of the city planning department, who suggested it spontaneously during a meeting at city hall.

Ernie Petersen was the city coordinator and Richard Waide was appointed the first general manager. Ski Hills, Inc. was contracted to design the ski hill and Architectural Resources, headed by Bill Moser, was the designer for the layout of the 22,000 sq. ft. chalet. Don Salo and his company designed and supervised the engineering. The Rajala Lumber Company, Deer River, held the contract to clear the hills. Jensen Contracting, Superior, built the chalet.

In May 1974, 12 ski areas in the region filed for an injunction to stop the EDA from making the grant. The lawsuit dragged on during construction, and it was eventually denied by U.S. District Court Judge Gerald W. Heaney.

At that time, the EDA was giving the board lots of input. One suggestion was that they should have no one on the board who knew how to ski. The EDA wanted a year-round facility, so a modern campground, six tennis courts and an outdoor swimming pool were added. For several years, there was an emphasis on summer activities at Spirit Mountain, including an annual renaissance festival. The summer activities were not successful, (except the campground) and were discontinued.

The chalet featured a good-sized, upscale restaurant, featuring a popular Sunday brunch, and a full dinner menu featuring crab legs. A snack bar, rental department, booting area, lounge, and offices completed the facility. The view from the chalet overlooking the St. Louis River was magnificent.

The latest in snowmaking machinery—one of the Midwest's largest—was installed. At that time, Spirit Mountain included 11 ski runs, some of which were lighted for night skiing. In order to get enough water to make snow, a major circular water line was installed from the top of the hill to the bottom. Treated city water, including its fluoridation, was used to make snow. A blurb in the *Readers Digest* said, "Duluth was the only ski hill in America that could get your teeth protected by falling in the snow." Eight round chalets were built as rental units at the top of the mountain.

There was a major worry. There wasn't a flake of snow by December 16. A week before the opening, it started to snow and didn't stop snowing until the middle of January. Everybody blamed (or credited) Spirit Mountain. Gerhard Bartsch and George Hovland had the honor of making the first test run down the mountain, which was a joy. The ski hill opened on December 20, 1974. Governor Wendell Anderson and George Hovland made a downhill run after the ribbon cutting, followed by Hubert and Skip Humphrey. Huge crowds came to ski and many other Duluth and Superior residents came to watch and have lunch and dinner. The staff was working so hard to handle the crowds that something didn't get done—the bank deposits. After nine days, the cashiers' office floor was covered a foot high with money that hadn't been deposited. Outside help was enlisted to make the deposits.

Feasibility studies had estimated totals of 60,000 skiers the first year, 90,000 the second, and 120,000 the third. Spirit Mountain exceeded expectations by showing a profit in the first 43 days of operation with 55,000 visitors. But the first year brought 165,000 skiers and since then, the average year has seen over 200,000 skiers.

Many improvements have been made since the ski area opened, including additional runs and cross-country ski trails, new 3-seat chair lifts, and large additions to the chalet. Spirit Mountain currently provides jobs for 200 people each year.

> The staff was working so hard to handle the crowds that something didn't get done—the bank deposits. After nine days, the cashiers' office floor was covered a foot high with money that hadn't been deposited. Outside help was enlisted to make the deposits.

Ticket sales for skiing started to slow down in the early 80's. In 1984, Larry Hutchinson was hired as general manager and he continued in that position for ten years. He developed a strong, low-cost season ticket program that turned the patronage around and created many more skiers. This program is still in place and has been copied by ski hills all over the

United States. Skiing numbers dramatically increased during this period. In 1996, Rick Certano was named general manager. He continued to aggressively promote season tickets. Currently, $1.1 million of Spirit Mountain's $3.5 million total income is generated from season ticket sales.

The development of Spirit Mountain has had a major impact on Duluth. It helped to extend Duluth's tourist season from a summer season to a year-round tourist destination, bringing in new hotels, restaurants and attractions. Evidence of the economic effect was immediate and clear. Hotel, motel and sales tax revenue spiked within months of the opening.

The Spirit Mountain project succeeded because of the tenacity and imagination of community leaders. Theirs was the key ingredient, and a pattern found in virtually all development in recent decades. Typically, the city furnished support, with proficiency in planning, grantsmanship and legal services. Community leaders provided the knowledge, enterprise, energy and public enthusiasm. ∎

Ben Boo was mayor of Duluth 1967-1975.

22

Grandma's Restaurants in Canal Park

LONELY WAREHOUSE DISTRICT BECOMES DULUTH HOTSPOT

by Brian Daugherty

It was a hot spring night in 1976 and I was looking forward to my first carefree summer after graduating from high school. That dream didn't mesh with the reality I was living at the moment...on my hands and knees pounding flooring for the second floor addition of a new restaurant that had just opened in Duluth. It was called Grandma's Saloon & Grill. One of the owners, Andy Borg, Jr., was right next to me slamming down boards at three times my speed. I watched him closely, trying to pick up what he knew. Who realized I would continue to do that for the next 27 years?

He suddenly got up and walked toward the window while the half-dozen or so of us continued to hammer away. His gaze out the window caught my attention so I stopped working and

"Grandma Brochi's" men at work, circa 1976. Andy Borg (left) and Mick Paulucci (right) wore many hats in the early days of building their Grandma's empire from a warehouse in Canal Park.

walked over to see what he was staring at. It was a sole set of headlights coming down what is now Canal Park Drive. We watched together as it drove by the locally famous Club Saratoga burlesque house, and then passed by the large warehouses, scrap yards, and a towing company.

I could hear Andy softly repeating, "Come on… come on… come on."

The car was apparently making its way to the end of the line where Grandma's Saloon & Grill was now open for business on the first floor. As it neared our parking lot we knew it wasn't going to the new Marine Museum, which was closed for the evening. As the car turned into our lot, Andy dropped his tool set and said, "Let's go, boys." I followed along with another fellow and ran downstairs with Andy to join the other owner of the company, Michael "Mick" Paulucci who was at home behind the bar welcoming the new customers. This was the humble beginning of Grandma's as I remember it.

At the time, Andy was the 24-year-old administrative assistant to the 28-year-old Mick. They both worked for Mick's father, Jeno, at Paulucci Enterprises. Aside from working hard for Jeno, Mick and Andy were involved in a sideline antique business. As a way to link their antiques into Mick's interest in the food business, the two opened Grandma's Saloon & Grill using their warehouse full of antiques, advertising memorabilia and collectibles as décor. To properly present their authentic memorabilia, the guys created the persona of Grandma Rosa Brochi, an Italian immigrant of somewhat dubious reputation. She was never fully dubbed a "Madame." But throughout her travels after arriving in the United States, she gained a wide spread reputation for outstanding hospitality among the Victorian-era working class. This legend seemed quite believable to me when you consider what we discovered as we were gutting that second floor of the original Grandma's on Duluth's waterfront. There were many small rooms throughout, all connected with an alarm system of lights. Maybe Mick really was the long-lost grandson of Grandma Rosa Brochi. Maybe it was his calling to reclaim her ancestry by tracing his grandmother's past travels and accomplishments. It all seemed so possible at the time.

Once the restaurant had been open for a year, its reputation for oversized portions and offbeat atmosphere made it a destination for visitors and locals alike. After being promoted to a server, I would often hear our guests comment on how hard it was to find our restaurant among the junkyards and warehouses. But Andy and Mick knew that someone's junk was another person's jewels, and began to purchase those scrap yards and junk piles. This allowed Grandma's to grow at what seemed like a new addition every year! First, it was the second floor, then a beer garden, followed by outdoor decks. There was always a new promotion or addition going on.

This first year is when we tied ourselves into what seemed like one of the weirdest promotions of all... a 26-mile foot race! The first Grandma's Marathon was in June 1977. One hundred and sixty pioneer runners ran from Two Harbors to our restaurant, finishing right in our beer garden. I remember us employees looking at each other in complete disbelief as these runners continued to celebrate their achievements into the wee hours of the morning. This concept is the same today, but the numbers have changed drastically... both in runners and spectators... 15,000 and 50,000 respectively! Executive Director Scott Keenan was the founder of Grandma's Marathon and continued to nurture its growth as an employee of Grandma's for about ten years.

But in 1986, an act of God literally pulled the marathon out of our hands. A small tornado blew into town directly following the awards ceremony, leaving the marathon celebration spread all over town. What seemed a crisis was a clear sign to Mick and Andy. It was time to let the marathon go...and grow as Scott had so meticulously prepared it to do. The nonprofit entity Grandma's Marathon–Duluth, Inc. was incorporated with Scott still at the helm. This became yet another relationship that I never thought I would be enjoying and learning from for 27 years!

Other investors began catching the vision of Mick and Andy and started making investments in Canal Park as well. The DeWitt Seitz Marketplace opened in 1985, which became the catalyst for specialty retailers, antique dealers, and boutiques of all kinds to follow. The development of Canal Park as an entertainment district had also become part of the City of

Duluth's development plans. They had laid out a long-term investment program for the streets, parking, and other amenities like a Lakewalk, Lake Place Park, and fine details that accentuated Duluth's working waterfront. Together, public and private investment served as a catalyst that was spurring all kinds of exciting developments. Ideas like tour boats, movie theaters, aquariums, a festival park, and expanding our convention center were all concepts that would come to fruition... by the end of this story!

Andy and Mick's creative outlook was catching fire. For the next two decades Canal Park would produce growth every year. For Grandma's, the late '70s and early '80s were busy building beer gardens, hiring bands, and nurturing customers and promotions. This led us to the development of the city's largest outdoor volleyball league converging at our restaurant every summer. This would later spin off another restaurant concept...but we'll get back to that as we reach "the late '80s" segment of the story.

By the mid-'80s, we had expanded our business in other locations, but Canal Park was still exploding with growth. Personally, I had gone from an entry-level dishwashing position and quickly moved through multiple jobs at the restaurant, and was now the general manager. Andy had become the acting president, and Mick the CEO. From what I could tell, in ten years this had already gone further than any of us had imagined. It was then that Mick and Andy leveraged their bet on Canal Park and literally doubled the size and seating capacity of our original Grandma's – Canal Park restaurant. We added over 200 more seats, banquet facilities, and a very funky Duluth gift shop. This newest addition opened as a separate restaurant called Mickey's Grill Steak House.

Mickey's Grill was loved by few and confused many. Our customers insisted on Grandma's food when seated in Mickey's Grill since that was the building they entered (the restaurants shared the same front door). We quickly responded by converting the entire operation to a Grandma's Saloon & Grill menu. Great ideas never die, and many of the delicious entrée ideas for this ill-fated concept were used in other restaurant menus. The signature wild rice specialties for which Grandma's has become famous debuted in Mickey's Grill.

It was now the late '80s, and Grandma's volleyball league had reached a peak of 225 teams. It had become a business within a business. Of course, the guys saw opportunity. Based on what our customers kept telling us, "You need more volleyball courts…" "You need more dining choices…" "You need a dance floor…" they were busy purchasing junk piles and warehouse space for the next idea. In the hospitality business, the customer's always right!

So in 1989, Grandma's conceived another concept. It was to be located directly across the street from the Grandma's Saloon & Grill in Canal Park. Originally designed to house the popular volleyball leagues, it was further enhanced to create a basketball league, a bocce ball league, and a game area for kids and adults alike. For this youthful and athletic clientele, we would also convert the indoor volleyball court into the area's largest dance floor in the evening. Thus was the birth of the 20,000 sq. ft. Grandma's Sports Garden Bar & Grill. This monster of a building was really three buildings combined. And, yes, we were all in there nailing the wood floors down four weeks before it opened. Funny how some things never change. Unfortunately, the week before the building was scheduled to open—which was the week before the 1989 Grandma's Marathon—the Sports Garden was engulfed in a devastating arson fire. Once again, the can-do spirit of Grandma's employees rose to the occasion. An all-out effort took place to have the restaurant cleaned and opened by marathon day. As the doors opened on the eve of the race, there was no trace of a fire in the building… unless you looked at the replica Spitfire hanging from the ceiling. There you'd notice one wing is charred off. That wasn't from a daring raid during WWII. The burned wing serves as a symbol of the effort our staff put into opening Grandma's Sports Garden in time for the big weekend. We do believe in miracles…it's part of our job description.

By the early and mid-'90s, the company was still busy honoring our customers' requests. "The more people we draw down here, the more burgers we can sell," Andy would tell us. By this time, he and Mick had started another company for hotel development in Canal Park. I was promoted to vice president of operations for Grandma's and was anxiously pursuing more "burger" sites. As Mick and Andy opened their first hotel in Canal Park in 1993, the arts and crafts style Comfort Suites, Grandma's had developed its hottest restaurant concept yet. Literally. Angie's Cantina and Grill would introduce tex-mex cooking to the Duluth community. As usual, Andy and Mick went deep when developing this concept—deep into the Southwest to bring back southwestern artifacts and recipes that were sure to blow away our customers. And again, literally, we did. Our first round of recipes included the serrano pepper, measured at 50,000 scoville heat units, and used in the majority of our entrees and fresh salsa. Our customers were speechless, followed by mass consumption of water. We quickly modified the menu with a less heated pepper, the jalapeno, measured at 10,000 scovilles. Even authentic flavor needs to be modified for the Swedish palates up here in Northern Minnesota. We still learn and relearn from every experience, every day. And we keep getting our direction from our customers!

Mick and Andy then surprised everyone and moved forward with a second hotel in Canal Park called the Hampton Inn. The year was 1997 and by now all the major improvements had been made in Canal Park, completely transforming the junk piles and industrial settings that had separated the original Grandma's from the city of Duluth. And as expected, the hotels brought more people to the area setting the stage for yet another restaurant concept that Mick had long dreamed of.

Mick's grandparents are direct descendants from Italy. Bellisio, Italy, to be exact. Mick stays close to his ancestry and has always adored Italian food. There already was Italian influence on much of Grandma's menu.

> Our first round of recipes included the serrano pepper, measured at 50,000 scoville heat units...Our customers were speechless, followed by mass consumption of water.

After all, Grandma Rosa Brochi was his Italian immigrant grandmother...right? Mick had decided it was time to develop a restaurant that was worthy of his heritage. With one small parcel left of their undeveloped land, Mick and Andy invented the fine dining jewel, Bellisio's Italian Restaurant and Wine Bar, in Canal Park. The intimate and classic setting of Bellisio's opened with absolutely no negative feedback or tweaking...it seemed perfect. After 20-plus years in the restaurant business maybe you get one perfect right out of the chute. To this day Bellisio's has become the choice of the Paulucci family when dining in Duluth because of its authentic attention to detail.

So at the turn of the 21st century we see Canal Park, a three-block by six-block area on Duluth's waterfront has been developed into 20 restaurants, nightclubs, and coffee shops, six waterfront hotels, eight major attractions, over 150 antique dealers and specialty retail shops, and enough special events to keep one's schedule busy year-round. Obviously, it's not one developer or project that has caused Canal Park to become the entertainment district it is today. But for me it all started out as a summer job with a couple of guys who had the vision to turn junk into treasure. ■

Over a span of 28 years, Brian Daugherty has also worn a lot of different hats for Grandma's. He currently serves as vice president of operations.

23

Grandma's Marathon

WORLD-CLASS EVENT, SMALL-TOWN HOSPITALITY

by Laura Wright

Duluth is home to many great things—the famous Aerial Lift Bridge, the western tip of the largest freshwater lake in the world, some of the most beautiful scenery in the upper Midwest and the tenth largest marathon in the country, Grandma's Marathon. If it's June, you've probably noticed a certain buzz in the air as this city of 85,000 people prepares for tens of thousands of runners and race fans to arrive during the third weekend of the month. The citizens of Duluth are accustomed to the preparation it takes to host Grandma's Marathon, and rightly so. They've been doing it for the past 26 years.

It all started during the running boom of the mid '70s. A group of local runners, called the North Shore Striders, began planning a marathon from Two Harbors to Canal Park in Duluth. At the time there weren't many races of 26.2 miles or longer, so the Striders, who had organized numerous shorter races, were confident that people would register for the marathon.

There was one major problem however; the group only had $23 in their bank account. It was quite apparent to them that they would have to get a business to sponsor the event, or it wasn't going to happen.

"Back then it was extremely difficult to find sponsorship money as special events were not looked upon by the business community as a strong method of advertising and promotion," explained Scott Keenan, executive director of Grandma's Marathon and former president of the North Shore Striders.

After being turned down by dozens of businesses in the Duluth area, local businessmen Mickey Paulucci and Andy Borg—owners of a new restaurant, Grandma's Saloon and Grill—came to the rescue. "We gave them the title sponsorship and they gave us $600," says Keenan.

Jeff Frey Photography

Scott Keenan is one of the longest-serving race directors of any U.S. marathon. As president of the North Shore Striders, a former Northland running club, Keenan helped plan the first Grandma's Marathon in 1977 for a field of 150 runners. The race has grown dramatically and is now ranked the tenth largest in the nation.

With a budget in place, the inaugural Grandma's Marathon was born. Over 150 people showed up at the starting line on June 25, 1977 including Twig native and 1976 10,000-meter Olympian, Garry Bjorklund. It was Garry's debut marathon, and he won in 2 hours, 21 minutes, 54 seconds, which gave Grandma's Marathon instant recognition in the world of running.

The first race was deemed a success, and entries nearly quadrupled in the second year, with a total of 677 participants. Just as quickly as the field of runners grew, finishing times continued to get faster, with athletes Dick Beardsley and Lorraine Moller both setting course records in 1981 running 2:09:37 and 2:29:36 respectively.

By 1987, Grandma's Saloon and Grill was becoming a well-known restaurant throughout the Midwest, and the marathon was growing into an internationally ranked road race and an annual tradition for the Duluth community. The fast expansion of both entities and the desire of the Twin Ports businesses and individuals to become more involved with Grandma's Marathon led executives of Grandma's Corporation to make the tough decision to yield ownership of the 26.2-mile race.

Determined to keep the event alive, a group of local individuals formed a board of directors and Grandma's Marathon became a self-governed nonprofit organization. While Grandma's Saloon and Grill was no longer the main sponsor, race organizers agreed that the name, which piqued the interest of runners, young and old, should remain the same.

What began as a small race hosted in a little town tucked in the northeast corner of Minnesota has now blossomed into one of the largest multi-race events in the United States. In fact, over 15,000 athletes and tens of thousands of race fans take part in Grandma's Marathon and supporting activities each June.

The growth of this world-class event didn't happen on its own. A mix of an ideal racecourse, community support, organization and expansion of events have been crucial in the development and success of the 26.2-mile race.

THE IDEAL RACECOURSE

June is not the most common month of the year to have a marathon. Often, thoughts of dehydration, drenching sweat and cotton mouth pop into the minds of most runners when thinking of heading out for a run in June. Not in Duluth, however. Cool breezes that roll off Lake Superior keep the city air conditioned for most of the summer.

On race day, temperatures are typically in the mid-40s at the start and low-60s at the finish. The climate, coupled with the gently rolling terrain of the racecourse, has earned Grandma's Marathon the reputation of being fast for elite runners and ideal for first-time marathoners.

"When we started planning Grandma's Marathon, we were confident the Old Scenic Highway 61 would be the perfect course. It's certainly been one of our biggest selling points to this day," says Keenan.

The course is point-to-point, starting just outside of Two Harbors, Minnesota and finishing in Duluth's Canal Park. It features a net downhill drop of 135 feet and very few turns. A hill at mile 22, dubbed "Lemon

Jeff Frey Photography

Grandma's Marathon began in 1977 with a total of 150 runners, and even though the 26.2-mile race now draws over 9,000 participants from around the world, it still maintains a small-town charm.

Drop Hill" (after a restaurant that was once located at the peak) is the only major incline on the course.

"The Grandma's Marathon course is my favorite. I love the fact that it's on a lake and doesn't traverse through long sections of city streets like most major marathons. Duluth is very unique, so even when you do enter town, it's exciting and the crowd support is fantastic," explained Kelly Keeler, a six-time elite participant of the marathon and three-time champion of the Garry Bjorklund Half Marathon.

COMMUNITY SUPPORT

Crowd support, and more specifically community support, has put Grandma's Marathon on the map as one of the most friendly and organized marathons in the nation.

"The citizens of Duluth really come out in force to support this event. They go to extreme measures to make sure it's a special experience for each and every runner—elite or recreational," says Keeler. "You just don't find hospitality like that in a lot of big city marathons."

The race is the only marathon in the top ten that is not hosted in a large metropolitan area, and the community plays a crucial role in the planning and implementation of the weekend. The organization strives to give community ownership of the event and in doing so, it attracts over 4,000 volunteers each year.

"We've heard many times from our participants that the hospitality they experience at our race and in Duluth is second to none," says Keenan. "Our volunteer team assists us in achieving our goal of catering to our runner's needs and being a true runner's race."

Grandma's Marathon has built an experienced team of six full-time staff members, 17 board members, over 200 year-round volunteer coordinators, 100 committee captains and thousands of volunteers. All follow detailed protocols that have made Grandma's Marathon famous for being well organized. "When the race personnel know what they are doing, it shows, and our participants really appreciate it," attributes Keenan.

Since its inception, Grandma's Marathon has generated more than $85 million for the local economy, and currently brings in $8.5 million direct

Jeff Frey Photography

Scene at the finish line on June 16, 2001, the 25th annual Grandma's Marathon. Lyubor Denisova of Russia won the women's division in 2:35:13.

dollars annually to the Twin Ports.

"I can't say enough about the positive impact Grandma's Marathon has had on the city of Duluth," Mayor Gary Doty said. "Each year, thousands of runners, thousands more race fans and the eyes of the running world shift here for one of the nation's premier events. Over time, Grandma's Marathon has evolved into one of the symbols of Duluth."

SOMETHING FOR EVERYONE

Hosting a marathon these days is much more than just putting on a 26.2-mile road race. With thousands of participants and race fans traveling to Duluth from all over the world for Grandma's Marathon, the organization has found it increasingly important to provide them with a variety of activities that last throughout the whole weekend.

By adding the Garry Bjorklund Half Marathon in 1991 and the *SS William A. Irvin* 5K in 1994, participation numbers have increased dramatically.

"We were criticized by many experts when we decided to add shorter races to the event because they felt it would dampen the interest in Grandma's Marathon. They were wrong," Keenan said. "The addition of these races not only expanded the amount of racing opportunities, but also made our event safer. People were finally registering for distances that suited their ability, and this significantly decreased the amount of visits made to our medical tent."

While running is the highlight of Grandma's Marathon, there are plenty of supporting activities surrounding the festive weekend including the SMDC Health and Fitness Expo, Michelina's All-You-Can-Eat Spaghetti Dinner, Whipper Snapper Races for Kids, guest speaker presentations and a huge post-race party featuring live entertainment.

In addition to Grandma's Marathon weekend, the staff and board spend much of the year developing and orchestrating the activities of the Young Athletes Foundation (YAF), a program started by the organization in 1991 to assist the promotion, development and growth of youth athletics in the Twin Ports. The YAF has provided over $100,000 to local youth athletic organizations and has developed opportunities for young athletes through the following programs:

- **Wednesday Night at the Races** – Free races for children held six consecutive Wednesdays in July and August. This YAF activity draws approximately 200 children per night, and emphasizes the importance of exercise and sportsmanship.
- **Running Shoe Program** – Through this program the YAF provides athletic shoes for high school youth participating in cross-country and track. Shoes are awarded on a need basis.
- **Ice Skate Program** – Following the theme of the running shoe program, the YAF provides ice skates for youth at area skating rinks.
- **Grant Program** – The YAF provides money for program support and/or equipment needs on a group or individual basis to local nonprofit youth athletic organizations.

"For over 26 years we have called on the citizens of the Twin Ports to help us, and they have never let us down. The YAF is our vehicle for giving back to our great community in appreciation for all it has done for Grandma's Marathon and supporting events," Keenan said.

KEEPING PACE

Grandma's Marathon has picked up an exciting pace since 1977 and doesn't look to be slowing down. Race officials expect the event to continue to be a major competitor among the nation's most popular road races. In fact, Grandma's Marathon was selected to host the National Women's Half Marathon Championships in 2003 and 2004, another major impact on the Duluth community.

"It's our goal to showcase to the world what a great city Duluth is. We'll continue to strive for excellence and to add more activities and community opportunities each year, so participants and race fans leave Duluth with plans to return, " Keenan said. ∎

Laura Wright is public relations director for Grandma's Marathon.

24

St. Louis County Heritage & Arts Center's Historic Union Depot

FROM DEPOT TO CULTURAL CENTER IN 13 YEARS

by Shirley Bergum

It was 1964 and the Junior League of Duluth was looking for a new project. My husband (Robert Bergum) suggested we find a use for the vacant Soo Line Depot, a stately old terminal that stood proudly on the site now occupied by the Gateway Tower apartment building on Sixth Avenue West.

The league required a formal request for such an undertaking, so I contacted my friend at the St. Louis County Historical Society and asked for such a request. When the response came from their board of directors, it asked the Junior League to "conduct a feasibility study on the use of the Soo Line Depot for some educational or cultural purpose." At that

Thanks to the hard work of the Duluth Junior League and many other organizations and individuals, the elegant old Union Depot became home to arts organizations and museums in 1977.

time, I was on the board of the A.M. Chisholm Children's Museum and also volunteering at the St. Louis County Historical Society, so I was well aware of the limitations they were both experiencing due to cramped quarters. The idea of a joint museum seemed natural. I asked both boards to cooperate. They agreed, but refused to say yes. They would study and consider it.

In the spring of 1966, the brand new State Arts Council gave the Junior League a grant to pay for half of the study. This was the first grant the Arts Council gave to northern Minnesota and the first grant to our project.

By the time the study was completed, the Art Institute and the Duluth Playhouse (formerly the Little Theatre) had been added to the plans. It was apparent that the Soo Line Depot was not large enough. At about that time, the chateauesque French Norman Union Depot—designed by Peabody & Stearns and completed in 1893 for about $600,000—was vacated. The Union Depot on Michigan Street was larger and more architecturally significant, so we picked up our plans, changed buildings and started all over. A big advantage to this location was that we could have active trackage for a railroad museum. Returning to the word "cultural" used in the original request, plans continued to grow as did the committee which started with five Junior League members and a $25 budget and expanded to about 20 members including representatives of the involved organizations, civic groups, as well as civically minded citizens who operated under the name Interim Cultural Center Committee (ICCC). Next, the Civic Ballet and the Duluth Superior Symphony Orchestra joined us, and architectural studies started in earnest.

Negotiations with the Northern Pacific Railroad started in 1968, but hit a snag when they broke off all talks because they were involved in a merger with the Burlington Railroad (CB&Q[1]). However, we kept planning with faith in the future. From 1964 on, I met with civic leaders and organizations throughout the area "selling" the concept of a cultural center in the heart of Duluth. Many listened to me, but some said it would never work, which only made Jean Walker (my good right arm) and me more determined than ever. During this delayed and somewhat discouraging period, Jean and I traveled to five different cultural and art centers, gleaning ideas and recommendations for ours until talks resumed with the newly formed Burlington Northern.

In 1969, the ICCC incorporated under the name Area Cultural Center Corporation (ACCC) and signed an option to purchase the property in June of 1970. We succeeded in getting the building designated a National Historic Landmark and began the very difficult job of drawing up bylaws.

---

[1] Chicago Burlington and Quincy, the old official name of the Burlington.

This proved to be a lesson in patience and diplomacy in order to convince the organizations they could live together without losing their autonomy, and yes, the large areas could indeed be shared. One more problem arose: although the Union Depot was indeed larger than the Soo Line, it was not adequate to house all our plans for the seven organizations involved. Therefore, new plans were drawn for an addition to be built on the western side of the building to house the Duluth Playhouse, Civic Ballet and an auditorium to seat about 300 people.

The ACCC exercised its option in November 1971, and agreed to pay the Burlington Northern, Inc. $87,500 for the old depot and a 400-foot strip of land (which included railroad tracks and two canopies). Fundraising began in earnest. At this time, the Railroad Museum, which had been considered part of the historical exhibits, became a separate organization under the name Lake Superior Museum of Transportation and Industry and work on the track was started. (Today it is one of the largest railroad museums in the United States with active trackage.) This area was the first completed because of a grant from the Economic Development Authority, which required that the grant cover a complete project. While large enough to complete the Rail Museum area, it would not pay for renovation of the Depot.

Although the "official" opening is listed as 1977, by 1975 engines and cars were moved into the Rail Museum and both the Chisholm and Historical Society Museums and offices were moved in and programming in the Great Hall and lower level were taking place. The Art Institute had displays on the balcony and was providing classes. Hammers and saws resounded through the building at what is known as Depot Square, an area on two sides of the Rail Museum depicting life at the turn of the century in Duluth, including an ice cream parlor, theater front, doctor's office, bank, and general store, utilizing a lot of exhibit items from the museums.

The musical "Cabaret" opened the new Playhouse year in the new auditorium in the spring of 1977.[2]

---

[2] The Duluth Playhouse celebrated its 90th anniversary in 2003. It is the oldest continuously operating community theater in Minnesota.

Ownership of the Depot and adjacent property was transferred to St. Louis County and the name changed from Union Depot Center to St. Louis County Heritage & Arts Center. With completion of construction, it was time to look forward. Elizabeth Adams (John) stepped forward to organize the Depot Foundation. In her words: "Now that we have the center, we need to have a foundation to protect it." She set out to raise $1 million and succeeded. Today, the Depot Foundation has an endowment of over $5 million to protect the Depot and assist the organizations housed there.

Our dream for the center was to offer something for everyone through a variety of programs and displays. It never ceased to amaze me how interest in our cultural center continued to grow over all the long years of planning. Our Depot and our success story were featured at a National Symposium on "Reusing Railroad Stations" held in Indianapolis in 1974, which I attended as a panelist. It was an exhilarating experience. I was one of four participants who had been through the launching process; we were introduced as a you-can-do-it-too-if-you-work-hard foursome.

Through the years, volunteers were always there. Junior League members with crowbars and station wagons tore out pieces of the Lyceum Theatre before it was demolished (some were used by the Depot, some not). The company razing the building at my request saved the large stone comedy and tragedy masks from the front, which now adorn the entrance to our auditorium. To save money where we could, board members of the organizations with spouses and friends spent two days tearing out the false ceiling and partitions added through the years and the National Guard came with trucks and hauled away the debris while food was brought in by local businesses. Attorneys and architects donated time and grants came from the Economic Development Authority, Upper Great Lakes Regional Commission, Arts & Humanities, Historical Restoration and area businesses and foundations.

Today, the St. Louis County Heritage & Arts Center is home to the Lake Superior Railroad Museum & the North Shore Scenic Railroad, the Duluth Playhouse, the Duluth Children's Museum, the Duluth Superior Symphony Orchestra, the Duluth Art Institute and the St. Louis County

Historical Society.

Through the years, I served as chairman of the Junior League feasibility study with Jean Walker (Donald), Polly Harlow (Fred), Sue McDonald (Blake), Julia Marshall and Dorothy Congdon (Robert). With the ICCC, I was co-chairman with William Stephenson Sr., Donald Shank, Frank Young and William O'Brien were instrumental in negotiations to acquire the property. The ACCC changed presidents every two years. Frank Young, Robert Rich, Eugene Lambert and Sylvester Laskin served in this capacity. I was secretary those eight years. Next was raising money. I wrote many of the grant applications under instruction from Dr. Robert Heller, Robert Rich and Jack Arnold and with the help of William Moser. When the Depot opened, I was executive secretary and administrative assistant.

I must add that literally hundreds of Duluthians helped over the years through boards and committees to make the center a reality. Many changes have taken place, but the initial dream stays the same. The organizations continue to strive to live together peacefully and cooperatively.

I am grateful to have had the opportunity to play a role over 13 years to work on this project and to see it evolve into the true center of history and culture it is today and I am thankful for all those who are continuing to help it adapt, survive and grow. ∎

Shirley Bergum first served as chair of the Junior League feasibility study for the Depot, next was a co-chair of the ICCC and was secretary of the ACCC for eight years. She became a staff member when the Depot opened.

CHAPTER

25

Barkers Island

MARINA DEVELOPMENT
CREATED WAVES IN SUPERIOR

by Jack Arnold

Barkers Island is a manmade island,
created by dredging the Superior Front Channel to a depth
suitable for freighters to move freely along the bay front
between Duluth and Superior docks. Development of Barkers
Island in the City of Superior actually started in Duluth! The
original plan was to build a marina at Hearding Island, another
dredge spoil deposit along the west shore of Park Point. The
proposal would have provided a marina at nominal public cost,
the City's share to be 10 percent. The Park Point Community
Club opposed this project because of the island's proximity to
residential zoning and because its vegetation provided an
attractive wildlife habitat. Plans failed to win City approval and
were abandoned in the early '70s. While working on this idea I
was also holding discussions regarding economic development

An aerial view of Barkers Island in Superior. The development includes a marina with 420 slips, hotels, restaurants, and tourist attractions.

with the City of Superior and Mayor Bruce Hagen.

Among Duluth people interested in the Hearding Island idea, was marina operator Ed Drill. Several years earlier Ed had considered the Barkers site, and advised us that it deserved another look. Mayor Hagen agreed that the project could foster a whole new image for his city and was worth working on. We started with a general plan to develop something that was more than just a place for boats. Our agency is interested in private sector development and new jobs. With this goal in mind, we envisioned a marina complex with a hotel and restaurant and a park-like area for appropriate activities and investments. Other elected officials and leaders rallied behind the idea because it would encourage new investment, attracting people and bolstering the economy.

There was early resistance from the Wisconsin Department of Natural Resources and Audubon Society who questioned development of the area even though it was not a natural island. We were already talking tentatively to the Radisson Corporation, which showed an interest in the idea and saw the same opportunities the mayor recognized.

> There was early resistance from the Wisconsin Department of Natural Resources and Audubon Society who questioned development of the area even though it was not a natural island.

We were close to a funding plan when another environmental concern appeared: piping plover habitat. Although this shorebird had not been seen on the island for 15 years, the dredge spoil provided a potential home, and the piping plover was an endangered species. To accommodate apprehension about the plover's possible return we were required to replicate the environment that had been created by the original Corps of

Engineers' dredging. This effort cost us more than two years and several million additional dollars. The compromise we reached provided a bird sanctuary duplicating the slope that had attracted the plovers when last seen there in the '60s. This space was set aside to be undisturbed for eight years. If the birds did not return, it could be developed. This area now has valuable homes adding to the city's tax base. The housing value to date is over $6.8 million, with the 27 units paying $200,000 in property taxes.

The marina opened in 1980. The original design featured 360 slips with provision for expansion. To date there are 420 slips. The construction cost was $6 million—$3 million from the EDA, $2 million from the state of Wisconsin, and $1 million from the City. Of the current boat dockage customers, 80% are not residents of the City of Superior, stimulating the local economy with dollars from throughout Wisconsin and Minnesota.

The project is attractive, popular and successful. It has prompted many public and private investments nearby and is now complemented by the handsome new Bong Memorial/World War II Heritage Center. Aside from new business activity and real estate tax benefits, the city receives more than $250,000 annually in fees from the marina operation.

Barkers Island has indeed helped to change the image of Superior to a progressive and business friendly community, and helps provide a welcoming atmosphere along the highway corridor. The current accumulated value of development on and near the island exceeds $14 million. Barkers Island is a model of the result that can be achieved when aggressive local leadership enters into a creative partnership with governmental agencies and the private sector marketplace. ∎

Jack Arnold has served as regional Economic Development Representative for the U.S. Economic Development Administration since 1969. Other EDA project participation in the Duluth area has included the Port Authority Meal Handling Facility, Spirit Mountain Recreation Area, the DECC Northwest Passage, the Duluth Library, Natural Resources Research Institute, Duluth AirPark, and the Duluth incubator for Cirrus Aviation.

26

Miller Hill Development

THE MALL AND THE TROUT STREAM—
FACING UP TO THE PROBLEMS
OF RETAIL GROWTH

by Robert F. Eaton

These are my recollections as an observer and a participant in what has been the development of a major regional shopping area known by most as "the mall." Actually, that description is often used to identify the entire shopping area that now extends from the edge of Duluth Heights into Hermantown.

The mall is also, and originally, Miller Hill Mall, which is owned by Simon Property Group from Indianapolis. Today, J. C. Penney, Sears, Younkers (the old Glass Block), and Barnes & Noble Booksellers are the mall's major stores, with specialty shops (some of which are nationally owned and some are owned locally) and restaurants sharing space within Miller Hill Mall. Other large retail stores, among them Target, Kmart,

Photo by Charles Curtis. Reprinted with permission from the Duluth News Tribune

Early 1990s view of Miller Hill area with Miller Hill Mall parking lot visible at upper left. By 1993, the Ready Mix plant at the right of Miller Trunk Highway would be replaced by Cub Foods and Stone Ridge Center.

Best Buy, Kohl's, Shopko, Menards, Home Depot, supermarkets, restaurants, several auto dealerships and cineplexes are located within a mile radius of the mall itself.

Development of the Miller Hill Mall area has created a regional shopping center that attracts a significant amount of shoppers and sales in excess of $62.6 million to the Duluth metropolitan area.

MILLER CREEK

In the midst of all of this development is a Minnesota designated trout stream, Miller Creek, with a trout population that is believed to be increasing. Residents in Duluth and Hermantown continue to fish (with some success) in various portions of the creek. A cooperative municipal effort by the cities of Duluth and Hermantown is actively promoting the maintenance and improvement of Miller Creek, not only as a trout stream, but also as a place where our natural resources and environment are recognized, protected and available for public enjoyment and use.

> Development of the Miller Hill Mall area has created a regional shopping center that attracts a significant amount of shoppers and sales in excess of $62.6 million.

CONFLICT OF VALUES

In today's world, it does not seem possible that the millions of retail dollars generated by the mall shopping area could possibly come from a place which has such environmental sensitivity, but the fact is the history of the mall shows an early disregard for the environment and a later substantial demand for environmental protection. The balancing of economic development and environmental protection has often been a contentious process. It started without much consideration for Miller Creek, but has led to the municipal respect given the creek by both

Duluth and Hermantown in the form of the Miller Creek Joint Powers Board.

In the early 1960s, Target and its expansive parking lot were built south of Highway 53 and west of where Miller Creek now flows. At that time, however, the Target parking lot was a wetlands through which Miller Creek meandered on its way south to St. Louis Bay. There were no environmental regulations of any significance. The wetlands were filled in and the store and parking lot were constructed.

THE SIMON BROTHERS AND DOWNTOWN DULUTH

Mel and Herb Simon, the founders of what is now known as Simon Property Group were among the first to recognize the significant retail and commercial potential of the area just over the hill from downtown Duluth. In 1963, Herb Simon appeared before the Duluth City Council with a proposal for development of a large commercial and shopping area between Duluth Heights and the Haines Road. The city council was reluctant to provide any support. Herb Simon said that then current retail/commercial trends across the United States strongly favored concentration of shopping opportunities along with plentiful parking.

City councilors, with some support from downtown retail/commercial interests, said such a development would adversely affect the entire city. Surely, the owners/operators of retail/commercial activity in downtown Duluth would develop the necessary improvements (particularly parking) to continue the economic viability of the entire downtown. What was happening in other parts of the country would not happen in Duluth.

Mr. Simon offered a verbal compromise: All requests for development of the Miller Hill area as a commercial/retail area would be withdrawn for one year. During that year, the downtown Duluth business community would be given full opportunity to develop necessary parking and take such other steps as would be required to succeed in their present locations.

If, after that time, the city councilors and administration did not see the significant changes which many believed would be made in response to the proposed Miller Hill development, serious and positive consideration would be given to Herb Simon's development proposal.

From 1964 to 1966, Maurice Labovitz and a number of other downtown retail owners led a strong effort to develop convenient parking and to take other steps which would maintain and improve retail/commercial action in the downtown area. Unfortunately, this was not entirely successful. The one major improvement was the parking ramp at Second Avenue West and Michigan Street. A significant financial interest shared by the major retail/commercial owners and operators apparently did not exist.

The prospect for new economic and tax benefits to the city began to be recognized by the city administration and the Duluth City Council.

The Miller Hill commercial/retail area was completed in 1973. One by one, J. C. Penney, Montgomery Wards and the Glass Block moved their locations from downtown Duluth into the mall, becoming its anchor tenants. These anchors shared Herb Simon's confidence in the development of a much larger regional shopping market. While their downtown locations were closed, they built larger stores at the mall. In turn, the shopping appeal of the mall and its anchor tenants attracted shoppers from an ever-increasing distance.

> ...the value of open space and wetlands was given little attention until national and state laws were passed and regulations to protect the environment were ignited by the National Environmental Policy Act of 1969.

WHAT ABOUT THE ENVIRONMENT?

There was plenty of land, there were not as many cars, and the value of open space and wetlands was given little attention until national and state

Shopping hub of the Northland. Miller Hill Mall, prior to the expansion in
1988. Note Glass Block department store to the left, now Younkers.

laws were passed and regulations to protect the environment were ignited
by the National Environmental Policy Act of 1969.

The value of retail/commercial activity in the Miller Hill Mall area
could not go unnoticed. By this time, there was strong support for and
passage of a Duluth sales tax. The 1% tax was self-imposed pursuant to
popular vote in 1969. Sales at the mall would result in a broader tax base
to support municipal operations. Interest in possible mall expansion
increased. Awareness of the need for protection of the environment,
particularly Miller Creek, increased along with talk of expansion.

Efforts to develop by disturbing additional wetlands north of Miller

Trunk Highway and south of Haines Road were defeated. A major effort to develop a shopping area adjacent to downtown Duluth and our new Arena/Auditorium (Harbor Square) was the subject of extended dispute, which ultimately resulted in loss of financial support for the project.

Opposing forces—some commercial and some environmental—were involved at a high level, along with the municipalities who were affected. Downtown Duluth suffered. Stores closed and offices moved. Sales and activity in the Miller Hill area increased.

THE MALL EXPANDS FOR SEARS

From the very beginning, the Miller Hill Mall was apparently a profitable venture for Mel and Herb Simon. Rumor has it that during much of this period, the mall was among the top five of the Simon properties in sales per square foot.

In 1985, Simon proposed to expand the mall. As expanded, the mall would then provide space for the last large retail business previously located in the downtown area—Sears Roebuck & Co. (By this time, Sears had closed its downtown store and was limited to a catalog ordering operation in the Plaza Shopping Center.)

The proposed expansion was met with considerable opposition and a demand that all environmental and zoning requirements be met before any permits were issued or construction could commence. Public meetings lasted long into the evening. Presentations for and against the expansion were made to the city council, the Planning Commission and the Pollution Control Agency. Letters to the newspapers provided ongoing fuel for the controversy.

One constant factor was present during all of this: both those for and against the expansion understood the procedures required and the ability of the council and public agencies to make the decisions as responsible public servants. There was little effort made to divide or evade responsibility. This type of development work was definitely a contact sport, but those involved were presented with detailed factual information. The accuracy and validity of information as to environmental impact, commercial value, regional market strength and other essential and vital information upon which any expansion would be based was severely tested during the public hearing process. The environmental importance of Miller Creek was recognized, along with the need for monitoring its condition. Earlier and unfortunate elimination of wetlands was recognized. Mel and Herb Simon and their company were required to establish and maintain a drainage system to handle the runoff from the parking area. Snow removal and dumping was to follow specific requirements regarding timing and location of snow dumps, just to name a few of the issues.

In 1988, the expansion to Miller Hill Mall opened with more customers, more cars, more tax dollars and more environmental concern and awareness.

Erosion of the Miller Creek banks was to be reduced or, if possible, eliminated. Fish habitat was to be improved. Shady areas to provide more suitable water temperature were to be protected and expanded.

In the end, however, both the commercial and environmental interests of Duluth were well served as a result of an orderly and well-conducted process.

MORE EXPANSION

Within a year after the Sears expansion, the Simon organization responded to additional market requests from major retailers and grocers. A request for permission to expand the mall building or, as an alternative, to construct a separate larger building to the south of the existing mall building was proposed in 1989. The proposal, which involved substantial expansion to accommodate large grocery and retail operations, was opposed by the adjacent residential property owners.

Not to be overlooked, however, was an increasing opposition to general commercial expansion in the entire Miller Hill area, which was expected to take place as a result of any additional expansion of the Simon property.

Again, extended hearings and public meetings took place. All pertinent information was made available to the public from the very beginning of the process all the way through to the final late evening public voting of the city council.

Here again, the participants all knew and respected the procedures involving environmental permits, as well as zoning, variances and similar requirements under ordinance. While tempers might flare at meetings, the decisions from state and local decision makers were respected. The process was accepted, even by those who might not agree with the final result

This time, the Simon organization did not prevail. Strong consideration was given to environmental issues, but the major concern was the proximity to the adjacent residential area.

Nonetheless, commercial/retail expansion continued in the Miller Hill Mall area. The retail and grocery expansion, which was defeated at Miller Hill Mall, was successfully handled at Stone Ridge Center located easterly and across Miller Trunk Highway/Central Entrance.

Obviously, the economic importance of a strong regional shopping area has to be recognized, along with the fact that such strength and economic interest is a reflection of change taking place in economic and social patterns in a broad regional area.

ANOTHER EXPANSION?

In the early 1990s, the Simon organization proposed an expansion of the mall to include an "unnamed large retail department store" and adjacent small shops.

By this time, there were additional retail, grocery and automotive locations in the Miller Hill Mall area. These were located in both Hermantown and Duluth. Some of them produced an upstream impact on Miller Creek, which fueled opposition to any further expansion of Miller Hill Mall. Of major importance in this third proposed expansion was the possibility that Dayton's would become part of the mall itself. Dayton's, however, did not make any formal commitment.

As before, the city administration and council maintained a sense of unity in agreement upon the process if not upon the result. In the end, the council narrowly approved the proposed expansion.

The opposition to the expansion was sufficiently strong, in this instance, to assemble the necessary support for a public referendum attempting to override the council's action.

The public referendum went in favor of the expansion proposal. A large advertisement in the newspaper indicated Dayton's "interest" in the expansion. After that, however, Dayton's did not commit to a department store in the expansion. As a result, the expansion did not take place.

KOHL'S

Perhaps the most contentious and difficult retail development on Miller Creek (other than those involving Miller Hill Mall) was presented to the City by Kohl's Department Store. The site is upstream from Miller Hill Mall and north of Miller Trunk Highway. West of the site are substantial wetlands. Environmental considerations were predominant.

The environmental community and a few adjacent neighbors were severe critics and opponents of the proposed development. State and federal permits were requested; there were hearings and site visits that lead to approval by the appropriate agencies. Responsibility, in the last analysis, was left with the city ordinances relative to water quality, water resource management and zoning.

A key ingredient was the offer by Kohl's developers to contribute $30,000 to the formation of a municipally sponsored organization that would work with the environmental organizations (both public and private) to develop a program for preservation, protection and development of Miller Creek as a public resource.

The city council, by a close vote, concluded that the proposal made in behalf of Kohl's, met the necessary requirements and authorized the issuance of the required permits.

This project and the process that was followed showed the beginning of the disintegration and a lack of confidence in the decision makers, if not the decision-making process. As of the end of 2003, the permitted location of the Kohl's development is still criticized on the basis that improper attention was given to essential details. This site, however, appears to be well run and in accordance with the permit requirements.

Subsequent to the Stone Ridge Development, the site across Highway 53 from the mall has been developed (the Opus site). The process in place was unchanged, but the apparent public and private mistrust of the process and of the participants in the process showed continued deterioration. After a considerable and lengthy period of public controversy, hearings, site revisions and a public referendum, the appropriate permits were issued and a large retail home improvement store and a restaurant are now in place.

Of additional significance is the Duluth/Hermantown Joint Powers Board with its program to protect and develop Miller Creek by use of funding from private and public sources. To date (Feb. 2004), the Joint Powers Board has obtained potential funding from state and federal sources in excess of $500,000. It is working with the cities of Duluth and Hermantown to obtain conservation easements, to provide clean up for the creek on a periodic basis, to plant trees and shrubs, as well as to construct sediment traps and basins in the creek.

We hope the Joint Powers Board will be able to retain its funding and continue to provide a method and spirit by which Duluth and Hermantown can cooperatively approach the economic, social and environmental issues which affect the residents of the area as well as the economic well-being of Duluth and Hermantown. The Joint Powers Board's future was clouded by a vote of the Hermantown City Council in March 2004 to withdraw from the cooperative arrangement in December 2004.

Procedures for the resolution of public issues such as those I have mentioned, as well as the willingness and ability of those responsible for making public decisions, appear to be subject to severe doubt and, in some instances, opposition. The basic procedures have not changed (except, perhaps, to have become somewhat more complicated). They should not be altered.

Perhaps the difficulty comes from an unwillingness on the part of the individuals responsible for making the public decisions to accept that responsibility as a primary purpose for assuming the office, which gives them that obligation. It still is true that "public service is its own reward" in most instances. A private and personal agenda for political or material gain at the expense of good public decisions should not be acceptable.

Similarly, there should be a willingness on the part of all involved to recognize the rights of one another to have differing opinion on matters which effect the public good. These opinions, in a well-ordered and well-run process, should be freely expressed and without personal rancor or bitterness.

The area known as Miller Hill and Miller Hill Mall has been developed in such a way that not only benefits Duluth and Hermantown but all of northeastern Minnesota. A good process well handled has led to economic benefit for the business owners and developers and the cities of Duluth and Hermantown. The availability of a regional shopping and trade center in the Miller Hill area has provided convenience and benefit for a population extending over 100 miles in every direction. Our Canadian neighbors patronize the mall regularly. The lessons learned in the development of the Miller Hill area should not be forgotten and, perhaps, can provide an example as how interests having a potential strong conflict can resolve their differences without destroying the very things they are trying to protect and promote. ∎

Robert F. Eaton is an attorney with the Brown, Andrew & Signorelli, P.A. law firm. He has represented some of the principal developers in the mall area.

Fond-du-Luth Casino

HERE COMES THE BAND!
DULUTH BECOMES FIRST U.S. CITY
WITH OFF-RESERVATION INDIAN GAMBLING

by Bob Maki

PART I: INDIAN GAMING—OPEN THE DOORS

As the outside attorney retained by the City of
Duluth, I was sometimes affectionately referred to by Mayor
John Fedo as "outhouse counsel." In early 1984, I was finishing
a meeting in the mayor's office with the mayor.

"The Fond du Lac Band, one of the seven bands of the Lake
Superior Chippewa tribe, recognized as a tribal entity by the U.S.
Government through the Bureau of Indian Affairs, has no known
authority to enter into a Joint Development Agreement for
Indian Gaming in the city limits of the City of Duluth," I said.

I continued, "Secondly, there exists the following substantial
legal question: Federal law provides that prohibitory law, such
as criminal laws, apply to bands but regulatory laws which do

A historic meeting in Washington D.C. on Dec. 6, 1985 led to bringing the precedent-setting Fond-du-Luth Casino to downtown Duluth. Left to right, front row: Mayor John Fedo, U.S. Rep. James Oberstar, Fond du Lac Reservation Business Committee Chairman Bill Houle. Back row: Reservation Committee planning official Randy Hella, Business Committee attorneys Henry Buffalo and Jeff Wallace, and City of Duluth Business Developer Jack LaVoy.

not prohibit but only regulate do not apply to Bands. In theory, gaming is not prohibited in Minnesota, as all Catholics in the room know from keno and bingo. The question, Mr. Mayor, is can you push the concept of Catholics pushing keno cards to Duluth authorizing outright gaming in the city..."

"Explain," the mayor interrupted, "How extensive the gaming can be—can we do poker? Blackjack? Dice?"

I silently thanked the Duluth Clinic for blood pressure pills and responded, "Remembering we must address the issue that no legal authority exists for blanket Indian gaming in Minnesota, or in the United States, or Canada, our opinion is that original Indian games are okay—

bingo being allowed for charitable in Minnesota makes it okay for Indian Bands—after that blackjack, poker, and dice constitute outright gambling and no legal authority exists…"

The mayor again interrupted. Putting his feet up on his desk, he said, "I grew up in the West End with Saturday night bingo. So what happens if you adjust the concept and have 52 bingo numbers, deal them out as bingo numbers to no more than seven players, and certain combinations, say three of the same kind are a winner. You know where I am going—can the state shut your bingo game down if you organize it in a different manner?"

I tried again. "Mr. Mayor, you are right—as long as bingo is organized around numbers, that conversion to any game of gambling based on numbers is possible, but that assumes…"

The mayor raised his hand, indicating the meeting was ending, and smiled. "One more question," he said. "Is there any law that you found that somebody could run to a judge, point at, and argue that the law prohibits what the city is doing?"

I knew that the kid who in his early twenties, stood up to Clark Oil on its franchise agreement in the Duluth Heights was more than willing to sit at the table.

He leaned forward so that everybody was looking at him, and said with a slight smile, "Show me exactly where it is prohibited, because I have to explain this to the Band Chairman sitting next to me, who is depending on jobs for his people."

On the way out the door, I asked, "I guess we are on our way to the city council and Washington D.C.?"

> On the way out the door, I asked, "I guess we are on our way to the city council and Washington D.C.?" "It's already on the council agenda," the mayor responded. "I…bought plane tickets…"

"It's already on the council agenda," the mayor responded. "I have a proposal for a Washington D.C. lobbyist and I bought plane tickets to D.C."

With a bold, quick-minded analysis and keen sense of politics, Mayor John Fedo launched the City of Duluth into becoming the first city in the country to do off-reservation gaming.

The letters, memos, legal opinions and documents exist by the box-full with the beginning very positive: "...the joint venture convinces us that it fulfills many of the goals and objectives set forth in the Indian Financing Act of 1974 as well as the Indian Self-Determination Act of 1975, and it is certainly in keeping with the President's statement on Indian Policy published on January 24, 1983," and the end of each U.S. Government document stated: "It has been explained to both parties on numerous occasions that the joint venture arrangement is both novel and unique, and there is no law to state that the commitments made by either party will be enforceable."[1] The joint venture arrangement was the business deal Duluth Mayor John Fedo and Fond du Lac Tribal Chairman Bill Houle sat down and agreed to. At that time a recent case in California held that only a state's prohibitory laws—meaning prohibited to all (Indian and non-Indian)—were illegal, but regulatory laws where certain groups may gamble, much like Minnesota, do not apply on reservation property as only state prohibitory laws apply. The debate in legal circles was how far did this concept go and these two local leaders had the same vision, tenacity and just plain "guts" to test it. When Mayor Fedo and Chairman Houle sat down, staff present immediately knew both thought alike and the only question from either would be, "Tell me how to solve it." Additionally, both had a way of telling staff from both sides that small issues with big racial overtones would not be tolerated. At the third late meeting, Band Chairman Houle, with prompting and support from Fedo, took his historical approach: "You guys gotta understand our language has no word for hour, so meetings are before noon or after noon—that's as close as we get. Don't worry, we don't mind waiting."

---

[1] Written opinion of United States government to all parties in 1984.

Mayor Fedo and Chairman Houle proceeded to the city council and the Band business committee and asked approval of the joint venture— whereby the City and Band would jointly appoint members to a commission; the Band alone would acquire the vacant Sears Building in downtown Duluth and make the building part of the reservation; both parties would set up Indian gaming; the Band would manage the casino and both parties would share in the proceeds. The standard cast of opponents, who claimed openness to the idea but wondered out loud and in writing if their questions might be serious deal killers, had pages of questions. For example, "Will the City, through its ordinances, regulate?" The answer was no, the Sears building will be Indian sovereign land exempt from City regulations. Those opponents, with even graver perplexed looks, immediately had a list of 100 more issues, such as, "Who regulates air emissions? Can cigarettes and liquor be sold? Will they pay taxes? Who are the policeman and the fireman? Will their kitchen be inspected? How about health insurance for employees? Will they pay social security taxes?"

Both Mayor Fedo and Chairman Houle took a unique approach. They said, "Those are good questions, but we are afraid of getting bogged down before we get started. Both the City and Band are desperate for development. Approve the joint commission. Let us go to Washington D.C. and if it works, you will approve the details and we will answer the questions."

The battles in Washington D.C. were no small matter. First, the Band had to acquire the Sears building and the Band boldly gambled by simply buying it before it knew if the reservation status would be granted. The next step was the Federal government accepting the land into Federal "trust status." The Band and the City forced the Federal decision by formally executing a long-term lease of the building to the Gaming Commission and the Band and City executed a development agreement whereby the City would construct a parking ramp and lease the ramp to the Gaming Commission. The uniqueness of a chairman of an Indian tribe and the mayor of a city bringing a completely papered, signed, sealed and delivered business deal to Washington D.C. was impressive, and on June 10, 1985 the Deputy Assistant Secretary for Indian Affairs of the United States Department of Interior wrote to the U.S. Department of Interior Government, "We urge you, in what will undoubtedly be a precedent setting decision, to act on the Band's request favorably."

PART II – CLOSE THE DOORS

As sometimes happens, Federal law gets written and passed by very bright staff that has no idea of what's happening out in the territory. Having no idea the City and Band jointly owned Fond du Luth, the Indian Gaming Regulatory Act (IGRA) passed both Houses of the United States Congress in September 1988 with a requirement that Bands have sole ownership.

When the City of Duluth responded that it had an existing joint venture deal with a Band where it shared ownership, development costs and profits—the answer from Washington D.C. was that the new Federal law prohibited this arrangement. When further discussions with officials proved fruitless, we finally laid it on the line by telling them, "Looks like we have to shut it down, lay off people and destroy the biggest employment opportunity the Band has. What does the new law say about the City having a lien on the building securing the City and if the City forecloses the lien, it destroys the project for both parties?"

Washington D.C. officials responded "We didn't think of that."[2]

Duluth's new mayor, Gary Doty, faced this issue upon taking office.

The mayor had a presentation of the issues made to the city council, and the council again hired me as their outside attorney. The mayor politely said, "I personally do not condone gaming, but the City had a business deal that gives substantial economic benefit to both the Band and the City, and my duty is to enforce the original deal."

The response to the mayor came from Anthony Hope (son of comedian Bob Hope), who was the first head of the National Gaming Commission. He offered that the dispute be mediated at the offices of the new Gaming

---

[2] Senators David Durenberger and Ben Nighthorse Campbell supported the joint venture with a keen sense of fairness in application of Federal law and a vision: if they worked together, so will their constituents.

Commission in Washington D.C.

The meeting room was large and full. When I suggested to Mayor Doty that the Band had two Washington D.C. attorneys, an attorney from Minneapolis, and one from Cloquet—and I was working alone—the mayor's sage advice was, "You can keep up if you think faster." Having worked for Davis Helberg, the long time Port Director and great one-liner, who once informed me "I really want you to handle this lawsuit for the Port Authority against the railroad because nobody has won one in 50 years and we know you won't feel bad when you lose as you lose all the time," I thanked the mayor for his Helbergian line.

The strategy for the City was straightforward: allow the Band full ownership under Federal law, but nothing would prevent the Band from paying a fee, a percentage of gross receipts to the City and independent accounting reports to both parties. The Band had no problem with full accounting, but were good negotiators and brought the mayor to the brink on paying a fee to the City. The Band's legal team wisely spent many days addressing all non-money issues and offered the mayor proposals that worked for each issue, such as employee protections, zoning compliance, liquor compliance and each other issue.

> When I suggested to Mayor Doty that the Band had two Washington D.C. attorneys, an attorney from Minneapolis, and one from Cloquet—and I was working alone—the mayor's sage advice was, "You can keep up if you think faster."

The attorneys for the Band then looked the mayor in the eye and said, "You have been given acceptable answers on all issues raised to date. If you push for a percentage fee and lose, the Band could declare the casino in the middle of your downtown, free of zoning, free of police department—in other words unregulated by the City—or we stop now and you get your controls, but no fee. We will adjourn while you discuss."

The mayor, the administrative assistant Karl Nollenberger and I met in a small room. The mayor asked us if he understood what was being conveyed. The administrative assistant described it as a "precipice"—you take what is being offered without a yearly fee and if you don't you could drop off a cliff as you might lose all City controls. The Mayor then said let's go back to both sides living with the original deal. The deal did not fall apart when the Mayor announced his position. Instead, after more negotiation the Band members and the Mayor departed, leaving the team of attorneys for the Band and myself to work out an ongoing fee to the City for the life of the deal.

The ultimate deal created a compact, giving the Band operational control and the City its yearly fee and other benefits. ∎

Bob Maki is a partner in the Duluth law firm Maki and Overom, Chartered, which served as outside counsel to the City of Duluth in this transaction between the City and the Fond du Lac Band, Lake Superior Chippewa.

CHAPTER

28

Lake Superior Zoological Garden

THE RESTORATION, MODERNIZATION AND EXPANSION OF DULUTH'S ANIMAL KINGDOM

by Basil D. Norton

Frederick A. Meyer was my first mentor. He was the director of the John Ball Zoological Park and he told me that when I got my first zoo as director, to consider staying with it for a long time—perhaps even a lifetime. In 1967, when I first beheld the Fairmont Park Zoo, known to the local people as the Duluth Zoo, I saw a place that had come to a stop in the Depression era for lack of funds and was starting to decay. However, when I witnessed the running waters of the falls cascading down into the valley of the zoo, I also saw the potential it held for future growth and restoration and I fell in love with the lay of the land. Thus began my lifetime of commitment in the spring of 1967.

A ground-shattering groundbreaking ceremony on an elephant kicked off construction of the Australian Connection in 1988. Left to right: Mayor John Fedo, Representative Willard Munger and Zoo Director Basil Norton.

One of the first things I did with the Arrowhead Zoological Society was to sit down with A. Nicol Smith, president, Edward Buchanan, chairman of the Board of Management and the Zoo board of directors to inform them that I would like to create a zoo master plan. I suggested that the first phase would be to develop a Children's Zoo, which they supported. David Shefchik and his brother Thomas used their resources to assist me in the drawings and schematics in 1971. Truthfully, my first efforts were rather primitive, but they stirred interest in the zoo.

One of the first persons interested in a zoo project was Beverly Goldfine, who donated $2,500 for building a much-needed zoo nursery to raise baby tigers that were born shortly before my arrival and were being cared for in my office. This new unit was created in early 1968 and became very popular, raising well over 50 great cats and other zoo creatures.

THE WILL and the WAY

Another contributor was Richard L. Griggs, a banker and a philanthropist. Griggs offered to build a wildlife nature center and his proposal was accepted by both the zoo board and Mayor Ben Boo (1967-1975). It was opened in 1969 as the Richard L. Griggs Wildlife Museum. In 1994, the conversion was started to what it is presently, The Richard L. Griggs Learning Center, the first area to be used exclusively for educational purposes.

Dr. Gordon Levine, president of the Zoo Board of Directors and the newly created Duluth Docent Association, with Phyllis Forbes as its first president, met with the Duluth school administration to see if the children of Duluth would like to work with the zoo on a fund drive, selling buttons for one of the new exhibits within the children's complex. My wife Ruth co-coordinated the button campaign through phone calls and my family bagged buttons for distribution. Thirty schools agreed to participate. With the enthusiastic efforts of these children, $18,000 was raised and in 1976 our prairie dog exhibit was opened. These children, now adults, can be proud of their first civic endeavor. It was and is still one of the most popular exhibits.

Representative Willard Munger (1954-1999) sat on the Arrowhead Zoological Board holding a lifetime membership and seat on its board of directors. He was one of the primary driving forces in the Minnesota State Legislature in rebuilding the Duluth zoo. His first effort to this end was to push forward a bill in the House of Representatives to acquire funds to build the new Children's Contact Building. The cost was

The establishment of the children's zoo barn in 1968 was only the beginning of many improvements and additions at the zoo.

$160,000, with half being matched by the City of Duluth tax dollars. In the previous year, we had lost out on receiving this money by one vote, but with hard work and the dedication of the Duluth delegation, Mayor Robert Beaudin (1975-1980) and the zoo board of directors, we snared the desired appropriation. The Children's Contact Building was dedicated in 1978. Two years later, there was an addition to the Children's Contact Building known as the Nocturnal House, which opened in 1981, along with many outside exhibits that were completed that summer. The total cost of the complete Children's Zoo with outside exhibits and plaza was approximately a quarter of a million dollars funded by the City of Duluth and the Minnesota State Legislature.

The 1980s were a time of rapid growth at the zoo. John A. Fedo (1980-1992) was elected mayor and he took great personal interest in the progress of the zoo. However, the zoo applied for accreditation with the AZA (American Zoo and Aquarium Association) and in 1984 the zoo learned that it would have to correct some of its most pressing problems to gain the accreditation. Mayor Fedo asked for a list of corrections needed and recommended to the city council a $200,000 resolution to update the zoo. It was granted. Gerry Johnson, the city architect, put together and coordinated the improvements. This brought us into compliance with the guidelines set by the AZA. In September of 1985, we were proud to be listed with many of the most prestigious zoos in the country. Between 1985 and 2000, we have been accredited two more times (accreditation is required every five years).

After consulting with the zoo board, Mayor Fedo gave them permission to hire a professional zoo architectural firm whose duty it was to create a new master plan, adding all the existing buildings from the prior years as well as the newly created buildings. The only buildings not in the plans were the small animal shelters, which were dilapidated and later razed. Zoo Plan of Wichita, Kansas was hired to oversee this new development with Gerry Johnson. By 1988, the name of the Duluth Zoological Gardens was changed to the Lake Superior Zoological Gardens to reflect a more regional concept, encompassing a greater arena of interest, both economically and politically.

In 1989, the old bear dens were renovated and the Australian Connection was completed, along with Lions Pride. In early 1992, the renovation of the Main Building began. This would include primate and tiger exhibits, administration offices, a café food service, a gift shop and a temporary animal medical treatment center. The Snow Leopard Exhibit, the Children's Zoo Contact Barn, the Prairie Dog Exhibit upgrade and the dedication of the Basil Norton Library for zoo research were completed and dedicated 1993 and 1994 under the auspices of Mayor Gary L. Doty. It is during this ten-year period under the firm leadership of President Stephen Lewis, director of the zoo board, that all these projects came to fruition.

Polar Shores was completed in 1990, and opened to the public on December 31 with a big bash that became an annual event known as the

Zoo Year's Eve Celebration, sponsored by Target Stores and the City of Duluth. Polar Shores is one of the more popular exhibits even to this day, featuring the polar bears Bubba and Berlin.

Several residents of the zoo have attained fame. Mr. Magoo was an Indian mongoose that was smuggled into the country. When the government ordered his destruction, President John F. Kennedy gave him a presidential pardon and Mr. Magoo lived out his life at the zoo until his death in 1968. Certainly, Bessie, the Asian elephant, was extremely beloved by the residents of this region. Fozzie was a Kodiak bear whose size was his asset: he would charge the glass and give zoo visitors a surge of excitement. Along with this same type of wild entertainment was Max, an Anubis baboon. He liked to make a person's day by throwing his excrement on them if he could, causing many onlookers to run quickly away, screaming.

> Mr. Magoo was an Indian mongoose that was smuggled into the country. When the government ordered his destruction, President John F. Kennedy gave him a presidential pardon.

These animals plus many more brought the people into the new buildings. They wanted to see the changes, but they also wanted to visit old friends and favorites or something new. It wasn't just about tourism. It was also community involvement. The people who came to be entertained also found that signs depicting the animal's natural history, by the many talks from dedicated zoo docents and by the enrichment programs, which were designed to keep the animals active and healthy, were educating them.

The 1993 AZA Regional Central Zoo Conference was the most important event that put the Lake Superior Zoological Garden on scale with the larger zoos. Mr. Robert Walker, executive director of the AZA, said, "Your Polar Exhibit is one of the better ones I have seen and the water clarity is exceptional." The conference opened up the reality of having a National Zoological Conference in the future. It was through the dedicated efforts of Richard Laine, Assistant Zoo Director, Julene Boe, Duluth Public Information Coordinator and the Lake Superior Docent Association volunteers that this conference was so successful. Mr. Laine and Ms. Boe were no longer employed at the zoo, but graciously lent their time and talents to the effort along with so many other dedicated people.

In 1963, the yearly attendance was 68,983 and by the end of 1994, it had increased to over 147,500 people. In 1994, according to the executive administrator of the Zoo Society, Sam Maida, the attendance was up 25 percent from the year before and the response from many businesses was wonderful. With the dedication of the Bert Onsgard Room, in honor of the zoo founder and director, other events included: The Pioneer Bank Day, Easter Egg Hunt, Subway's Zoofest, Spirit Valley Parade, Christmas Parade, Purina's Big Cat Weekend, First Bank's Winter Festival Snow Sculpturing Contest, Boo at the Zoo, the West Duluth/Duluth Centennial and much more.

With all this active participation, the future of the zoo is now secure. However, one more facility was desperately needed and that was a medical/commissary building, which was in every master plan created. In 2000 ground was broken and dedicated to one of Duluth's most honored and respected men, Willard Munger. The facility is formally known at The Willard Munger Animal Care Center, a fitting tribute to one who cared about this institution enough to devote his political career to environmental causes as well as the zoo's progress. I am pleased to have known this man for he also was a mentor to me from the first time I met him. In later years before I retired, he kept asking me, "Basil, why are you leaving? You have so much to offer." I never really left. The zoo's welfare is still with me as it shall ever be.

My mentor Fred Meyer was right. It was a commitment—a long one. However, he didn't tell me how lucky a zoo director was in his profession. All aspects of zoo life were mine (1967-1994) from its day-to-day events, its ups and downs and its growth and progress. President Robert Sederberg, Jr. (in the late 1970s) once told the Arrowhead Zoological Board that once a project was underway, I was already thinking of the next great project. That may be true, but I had a wonderful journey from the dreams drafted on paper to the actual creation of the buildings and to filling them with creatures both great and small.

I was a person who awoke every day and could take that little boy inside of me to visit the zoo—and get paid for it. ∎

Basil D. Norton served as zoologist and general curator of Lincoln Park Zoological Garden 1961-1967, and as director of the Lake Superior Zoological Garden 1967-1994.

29

Duluth-Superior Area Community Foundation

GROUNDWORK WAS LAID IN THE '80S TO PROMOTE PRIVATE GIVING FOR THE PUBLIC GOOD

by Kay Slack

In the early 1980s Duluth was cycling through one of the low points in its economic history. We had a declining population, high unemployment rates, and significant wealth leaving the area. This had a depressing effect on the United Way's ability to raise funds sufficient to support the community's nonprofit organizations that were struggling to meet increasing service needs.

After attending a national United Way conference, Duluth's United Way Director Jay Hess and I realized that we were not alone in this predicament. Looking at solutions found useful in other communities, we became aware of the tremendous resource community foundations were in many cities. Was it time to start such a foundation in Duluth?

We visited public and private foundation executives in the Twin Cities with only one suggesting we "go for it." Others suggested times were bad. We surveyed leadership in our community and learned it had been tried unsuccessfully twice before. The idea was not warmly received, but we minimized the opinions of the naysayers and persisted. Jay, and I as chair of the United Way board, nagged the trustees until they agreed to set up a feasibility committee. We never looked back.

In 1981, eight "Can-Do" folks on the committee quickly raised the $25,000 for a formal feasibility study that was required by foundations that might grant us start up funds. Our first support came in a three-year administrative grant from the Blandin Foundation. At the time, large private foundations were strongly supporting the start up or revitalization of community foundations on the premise that charitable decisions could be best made in the local community. Community foundations could also attract and hold charitable funds not accessible to private foundations. To achieve credibility among donors, it was believed at least a $1 million endowment was necessary. To achieve critical mass where the trust would build on itself, a goal of $3 million was set.

The Bush Foundation believed in our effort to the extent that they made a $750,000 challenge grant in 1983. At the time, it was the largest grant by a private foundation to a community foundation on record and a great vote of confidence on which to build. Thus, we lobbied the gatekeepers of community wealth—bank trust departments, accounting firms, estate planners, attorneys, major businesses, family foundations and individuals able to share their wealth. No longer did community foundations have to wait passively for wills to be executed but had an incentive to match outside dollars to create their endowments. The concept of a Duluth Community Foundation became a reality.

The committee hired part-time staff to assist us with mountains of data collection and applications for grants as well as the housekeeping chores of mission statements, bylaws, and incorporation in 1982. Part-time staff member Bula Hess became full time and much of the credit for getting the organization off to a good start goes to her exceptional ability to build relationships and solicit advice from those with wisdom and experience statewide and nationally. Much credit is also due Richard Burns, our volunteer attorney, who kept us legal and mindful of the big picture at all times.

One of our advisors, aware of our demographics, suggested it was important that Superior also become part of our service area. Bula Hess, a former director of the United Way of Superior, made overtures to leadership across the harbor, resulting in Robert Banks, Joel Gates, and Robert Gee joining the community foundation's board. We promptly became the Duluth-Superior Area Community Foundation and incorporated again in 1983. As a result of the area concept, the first private trust turned over to us was the Douglas County Disaster Fund that helped earn a pro-rata share of the Bush Foundation challenge grant.

Our first grant-making funds came from the initiative of James Claypool who had connections to an out-of-state company. While not part of our permanent endowment, funds from the St. Mary's Parish Land Co., based in Denver, Colorado, gave us much valuable publicity and an immediate demonstration of the community foundation's ability to attract funds from outside the area.

The big picture as outlined in our first Bush Foundation challenge grant application described the community foundation as a way to respond to the changing needs of the Iron Range whose economies were in decline with unemployment between 20% and 80%; to break down rivalries between Duluth and Superior; to introduce a broadened sense of community; to bridge the gap between the public and private sector; to respond to area wide issues; and attract outside dollars to the region. We met that challenge grant and, as they say, the rest is history. In 1990, Holly Sampson joined the staff as president and kept the growth spiral going. Under her leadership, the Community Foundation has grown from $5 million to over $33 million. During 2002 alone, grants and scholarships totaled over $2.2 million. Financial support was given to 126 nonprofit organizations and 367 individuals were awarded scholarships. The Community Foundation serves seven counties in northeastern Minnesota and two counties in northwestern Wisconsin. Affiliate funds have been established in Two Harbors, Bayfield and Grand Marais.

The generosity and stewardship of the founding trustees and their successors has kept the Community Foundation on the fast track of development. Fulfilling a current $1.5 million Bush Foundation challenge grant will likely push the endowment over $35 million. That's a resource available forever (and with great promise for continued growth) to address changing community needs unmet by public funds or annual private giving.

This book is about community leadership and project development. So, what can we learn about how these project leaders touched our area in such a significant way? They saw a need, conceived a possible solution, found successful models, and created their own version. They moved quietly and persistently on their beliefs and vision for the Duluth area. The effort was strengthened, not discouraged by doubters whose respectful feedback was part of the process. They were flexible and adaptive as their learning curve increased. We hope their story will encourage others to "go for it." ∎

Long active in service to her community, Kay Slack was president of the incorporating trustees of the Duluth Superior Area Community Foundation. A retired nurse, UMD Student Health Center coordinator and psychology instructor, she was the only grandmother earning her MA at UMD in 1986.

CHAPTER

30

UMD's Natural Resources Research Institute

RESOURCE-BASED INITIATIVE DEVOTES APPLIED RESEARCH TO JOB CREATION AND ENVIRONMENTAL RESPONSIBILITY

by Michael Lalich

The mid- to late-1970s and early-1980s were particularly difficult times for Minnesota's natural resource based industries, particularly for the taconite mining industry. In the face of a domestic steel crisis, shipments of iron ore from Northeastern Minnesota's eight taconite plants plummeted. Growth in the taconite industry, which had begun in the 1950s, ended and employment in this critical base industry dropped from about 16,000 to 3,000. About 2,000 supply companies on the Iron Range, in Duluth and elsewhere in the state were critically impacted.

Perhaps not as dramatically as the taconite industry, the forest products industry was similarly disturbed by the difficult

The SAGE building was donated to UMD for NRRI
in the early 1980s. It was built in the 1950s by the U.S.
Air Force to house the Semi-Automatic Ground
Environment (SAGE) system—the latest in real-time,
computer-based command and control for air defense
purposes. Today, it is the home of an institute that is
breaking new ground in economic development and
environmental stewardship.

economy. Northeastern Minnesota's logging and pulp and paper companies, in particular, were affected. Then, as now, natural resource industries accounted for the major portion of northeastern Minnesota's economy.

In the face of these challenging times, civic, business, government, higher education and labor leaders began to focus on initiatives that might help the economy. With a strong belief in its long-term value, U.S. Eighth District Court of Appeals Judge Gerald Heaney became a prime advocate for research. In his 1982 gubernatorial campaign, Rudy Perpich proposed that a center be established to do research on such resources as peat, biomass, forest products, water and minerals. Judge Heaney didn't let the governor forget his promise. After his election Governor Perpich established a number of economic recovery commissions. Two of these dealt directly with northeastern Minnesota. One was the Minerals Development Commission, chaired by Jack DeLuca, President of Abe W. Mathews Engineering Co. in Hibbing. The second, on forestry, was chaired by Harold Zigmund, president of Blandin Paper Company in Grand Rapids.

As the concept of a research center focused on natural resources was considered, there was vigorous and sometimes acrimonious discussion over issues, including:

- Whether or not the University of Minnesota's Mineral Resources Research Center (MRRC) and School of Forestry should be given improved funding and moved to Duluth.
- A debate as to whether or not factors would prohibit high quality research from being done at a greater Minnesota location like Duluth.
- Would the SAGE Building, vacated by closure of the U.S. Air Force base, be a suitable cost-effective location or would it be better to hold out for a new building on the University of Minnesota Duluth (UMD) campus?

A report from Governor Perpich's Minerals Development Commission, dated February 15, 1983, made a preliminary recommendation that a Natural Resource Institute be established as a division of the University of Minnesota, Duluth. The report indicated that "the activities of the Institute are not envisioned to be in basic research (e.g., theory-oriented), but primarily to focus on using technology derived from basic research." It called "for a transfer of the present MRRC program from the Twin Cities campuses of the University to Duluth." The School of Forestry was, however, recommended to "remain at the Twin Cities campus." The report included a preliminary evaluation of costs associated with remodeling the SAGE Building by Duluth architects Thomas & Vecchi.

"A Proposal to Establish A Natural Resources Research Institute at the University of Minnesota, Duluth" was submitted to the Minnesota State Legislature under the seal of the regents of the University of Minnesota in April. The proposal affirmed the applied nature of research at the new institute, noted that its work would be separate and distinct from the MRRC, and recommended the SAGE building as an adaptable site. The proposal called for the institute to be divided into four major divisions: (1) minerals, (2) biomass, (3) water, and (4) energy. The regents' proposal listed the members of the Minerals Development Commission, the Duluth High Tech Task Force and Duluth Future Task Force as endorsees of the institute.

The simple notation of first year funding of $1,650,000 and second year funding of $2,250,000 for the Natural Resources Research Institute in the *Laws of Minnesota for 1983* marks the establishment of the institute. It does not, however, begin to reflect the intense effort required by a diverse group of supporters for the institute to actually fight the political and logistical battles required.

At the state level, Governor Perpich's support was unwavering. He asked former State Representative Mike Jaros to assist NRRI during its formative stages. Support of regional legislators was essential. Besides the strong regional endorsement, two influential Twin Cities-based legislators, Senator Michael Freeman and Representative James Rice, provided key leadership.

The U.S. Department of Defense transferred ownership of the SAGE Building to the University, and the U.S. Economic Development Administration provided matching monies of $1.8 million for renovation.

Congressman James Oberstar, who became a long-term supporter of NRRI, and Senators Rudy Boschwitz and David Durenberger were instrumental in the building transfer and funding process. UMD Economics Professor Dr. Jerrold Peterson was named acting coordinator of the institute and he began to hire temporary employees. An advisory board, with UMD Dean of the College of Sciences and Engineering George (Rip) Rapp as chair, was established. Individual members of the advisory board, some of whom are still active 20 years later, have provided essential guidance and support.

In August 1983, UMD Provost Robert Heller, an ardent promoter of NRRI, envisioned NRRI doing between $5 and $10 million per year in research and employing up to 150 staff members in 5 years.

Dr. Michael Lalich, with a background in industrial research and development, was hired in 1984 as the first permanent director of the institute and began the task of development by conducting national searches for associate directors for each of the four divisions. Successful candidates included: Dr. Thys Johnson, a native Duluthian and Department Head of Mining at the Colorado School of Mines; Dr. Robert Naiman, a scientist at the Woods Hole Oceanographic Institute and Director of a Research Station in Quebec; Dr. Eugene Shull, Associate Director of the Penn State Combustion Laboratory; and Dr. Roy Adams, a senior research scientist at the Michigan Technological University Institute of Wood Research.

Early attention was given to additional tasks including development of a vision and research agenda, establishing a positive culture and work environment at the institute, and developing an organizational structure and the business systems to support the institute. Ernest Breton, a consultant, assisted with the research vision and agenda, and Pamela Wilson focused on the business systems.

The once controversial SAGE building was transformed to contain functional and cost-effective office, laboratory and pilot plant space over a period of several years. Members of the D.E. Stanius Architectural firm design team, including Ken Johnson, design architect, and Ron Stanius, project manager, were recognized for their award-winning design along with Johnson-Wilson Builders, Hedenberg Construction, and others who made the design a reality.

Many people from the community, UMD, industry, and agencies, contributed countless hours working on committees to conduct national searches for outstanding scientists and to assist with the SAGE building renovation process. It was clear that Minnesotans, and particularly those in northeastern Minnesota are highly dependent on natural resources from an economic perspective, but also that there is a keen sense of awareness of resource management issues and the environment. In short, Minnesotans link natural resources to their quality of life. With this in mind, and in the spirit of its founders, NRRI adopted the mission to "foster economic development of Minnesota's natural resources in an environmentally sensitive manner to promote private sector employment."

Three goals have helped institute staff focus their activities through the years:

- Assisting entrepreneurs and businesses with near-term economic development.
- Conducting applied research and development to develop products, processes and services that will be of future benefit to Minnesota.
- Improving the knowledge base with regard to natural resources to assist resource managers to make sound economic and environmental decisions.

THE INSTITUTE TODAY

Today, with about $16 million in annual budget activity, NRRI functions with a staff of 200. With grant and contract research from industry, and state and federal agencies, NRRI is UMD's principal research arm. After excluding the major research efforts of the University of Minnesota in the Twin Cities, the institute has more research activity than the remaining university and state college campuses combined.

With assistance from key supporters, such as Chancellor Kathryn Martin and former Regent Tom Reagan, NRRI has emerged as a model within the University of Minnesota for university-industry interaction. Thanks to its success in competing nationally for grants from agencies, such as the National Science Foundation and the U.S. Environmental Protection Agency, the institute also has the university's largest research effort on water and the environment.

Many of the research directions, originally outlined in the early documents in support of the institute have proven to be productive areas for research. They continue to define NRRI's research agenda. Applied research to help provide the taconite industry with more efficient processing and to improve pellet quality has been a mainstay of the NRRI since its inception. Helping the forest products industry to develop value-added products has been a primary objective. Other early objectives have proven to be more elusive. The idea that companies could be recruited to Duluth on the basis of their interest in abundant fresh water proved to be ill-conceived as was the initiative to burn peat and wood for energy.

Challenges and opportunities related to these issues of research direction contributed to reorganization of the institute from the four original divisions to its current structure based on three centers:

- The Center for Applied Research and Technology Development was developed under the guidance of Dr. Thys Johnson and is more recently managed by Dr. Donald Fosnacht. Primarily, it includes elements of the original minerals and biomass divisions and does research on minerals, forestry and forest products, peat and peat products, and environmental clean-up. The center recently added a rapid prototyping capability that is one of a kind for universities in the United States.
- The Center for Water and the Environment evolved from the water division under the direction of Duluth native Dr. Gerald Niemi. This center's strengths include ecosystem studies on

forests, wetlands, streams and lakes in addition to a leading effort in the area of computational chemistry.

- The UMD Center for Economic Development is a joint program of NRRI, the School of Business and Economics, and the College of Science and Engineering. An early effort by NRRI focused on developing business support to scientists and industry collaborators to help them determine the economic viability of technical efforts. These services, provided by the NRRI Business Group, were combined with programs offered by the School of Business and Economics and later on with the College of Science and Engineering to provide "one-stop shopping" at UMD for clients needing business assistance. Former Dean David Vose and Dr. Kjell Knudsen, the center's first director, facilitated the effort.

As it has grown many events have helped to define and shape the NRRI. Several are worthy of particular note:

- In 1986, NRRI began a long-term relationship with United States Steel Corporation to manage its Coleraine laboratory. The laboratory, which has now been transferred to University ownership, is one of the premier mineral processing laboratories in the nation. With a staff of 25, NRRI is conducting numerous projects at any given time in support of improving the efficiency of taconite processing and the quality of pellets. On a regular basis, these projects reach the stage of commercial implementation.

- NRRI signed an affiliation agreement with the Greater Minnesota Corporation in the mid-1980s. The agreement continued under Minnesota Technology, Inc. until several years ago. Under this relationship, matching funds for 15 to 25 projects with entrepreneurs and industry collaborators were provided annually. The program was unique in that it helped the institute realize its goal of near-term economic development.

- A grant by the National Science Foundation to establish a geographic information system (GIS) laboratory at NRRI, one of only several such centers the agency sponsored in the country, has proven to be an extremely important tool for the Center for Water and the Environment. The standard available visualization and spacial modeling techniques, along with state-of-the-art procedures developed in the GIS lab, have proven to be useful in a majority of Center projects. Thus, the advanced GIS laboratory has helped to provide NRRI an advantage in the very competitive environment for procuring federally sponsored research grants and contracts.

In 20 years of operation NRRI has had the good fortune to have the resources, and support of a wide range of collaborators, necessary to allow it to mature and gain experience as an applied research and development organization. The infrastructure it has developed in terms of a team of outstanding scientists, supported by excellent laboratories and equipment, represents an excellent base, which should serve the region well into the future. ∎

Dr. Michael J. Lalich has served as director of the Natural Resources Research Institute since 1984. Before coming to Duluth, Lalich was director of research and development at Foote Mineral Company in Exton, Pennsylvania. He was inducted into the Academy of Materials Science and Engineering at Michigan Tech in 2000, and received the Distinguished Service Award by the University of Wisconsin College of Engineering in 1998.

NRRI'S ORIGINAL BOARD MEMBERS

(CM=Charter Member)

Rodger Arndt (CM)
University of Minnesota
(Hydraulic Laboratory)

Matthew Banovetz
Reserve Mining Company

John N. Berklich
Hibbing Taconite

Margaret B. Davis
University of Minnesota (Biology)

Jack DeLuca (CM)
Abe W. Mathews Engineering Co.

Rondi Erickson
Bay West, Inc.

Charles Fairhurst (CM)
University of Minnesota (Metallurgy)

Alfred France (CM)
Lake Superior Industrial Bureau

Judge Gerald W. Heaney (CM)
U.S. Circuit Court of Appeals

Clayton LeFevere (CM)
LeFevere, Lefleur, Kennedy,
O'Brien and Drawz

Norbert Jaworski (CM)
U.S. EPA Freshwater
Research Laboratory

Richard Lichty (CM)
University of Minnesota Duluth
(Economics)

Chris Makai
First Bank Duluth West

Jack Malcolm
Mining Consultant

Ralph W. Marsden (CM)

Glenn B. Morey
University of Minnesota
(Geological Survey)

Donald McNaught
Minnesota Sea Grant Institute

Penelope Morton (CM)
University of Minnesota Duluth
(Geology)

Clifford W. Niemi (CM)
U.S. Steel Corporation

Gerald Ostroski
Minnesota Power

Douglas Pratt (CM)
University of Minnesota (Botany)

George R. Rapp, Jr. (CM)
University of Minnesota Duluth
(Science & Engineering)

Thomas J. Smrekar
Potlatch Corporation

Gilman D. Veith
U.S. EPA Research Lab, Duluth

Charles Westin
Northeastern Minnesota
Development Association

Harold Zigmund

CHAPTER

31

The University of Minnesota School of Medicine, Duluth

EFFECTIVE TREATMENT FOR
A REGIONAL HEALTH CARE SYSTEM
IN NEED OF FAMILY PHYSICIANS

by James G. Boulger

In the late 1960s, it was apparent that Minnesota—and the rest of the nation—was facing a growing crisis in the accessibility of medical care. Studies by the Hill Family Foundation, the Carnegie Foundation and the federal and state governments clearly documented the need for additional training of physicians, and particularly the need for more family physicians. Since the end of World War II, the profession of medicine had become much more specialized and the number of medical school graduates choosing general or family practice had markedly decreased. In Minnesota, there

UMD's laboratory school on the Old Main campus served as the first home for the University of Minnesota School of Medicine, Duluth.

The University of Minnesota School of Medicine, Duluth has helped to strengthen northeastern Minnesota's leadership in healthcare. The school is consistently ranked as one of the top five medical schools in the country for the proportion of graduates selecting family practice as a specialty and for graduates practicing medicine in smaller and rural communities.

were tremendous shortages of family and other physicians in rural and small communities. At that time, the University of Minnesota Twin Cities was home for the only medical education program in the state, graduating approximately 130 physicians annually.

The efforts of the Duluth business and educational community in response to the House and Senate legislative studies on medical education were not the only efforts. Groups in St. Paul and Rochester also were interested in the establishment of medical schools in those communities. The St. Paul group had been working on a proposal since 1966. In addition to meeting the educational needs of the state, the economic impact of a new medical school was projected to be quite large over the years. The presence of a medical school would lead to growth within the health care industry and the various community areas that support medicine.

In Duluth, the initial efforts were led by Dr. Sam Boyer, a cardiologist, and Dr. Robert Heller (then assistant to Provost Raymond Darland) at the University of Minnesota Duluth. Following agreement that Duluth was the best site for a new medical school, they began to meet with representatives of the medical, business and educational communities. Within Duluth, there was immediate support from the leadership of the business sector, primarily Erwin Goldfine, Warren Moore and H. E. "Wes" Westmoreland, who led the developmental and early fundraising efforts. The medical community was ably represented by Dr. Boyer, Dr. Charles Bagley, Dr. Cy Brown, Dr. Robert Goldish, Dr. John Thomas and Dr. Gordon Strewler. At the

> Groups in St. Paul and Rochester also were interested in the establishment of medical schools in those communities. The St. Paul group had been working on a proposal since 1966.

University, the efforts of Dr. Darland, Dr. Heller and Dr. Ted Odlaug (head of the Biology Department) were very productive.

Following a long series of studies and political efforts (led at the Minnesota legislature by Rep. Al France and by Jim Oberstar, who was then aide to Rep. John Blatnik at the federal level), the legislature—to the joy of the Duluth contingent—allocated funds to the University for the "establishment of a separate basic sciences program as a part of an additional medical curriculum in the State of Minnesota." $340,000 was allocated for the initial biennium, to begin the school at UMD and do the initial hiring of the dean and faculty.

Dean Robert E. Carter was appointed in the summer of 1970 and immediately began recruitment of the faculty and staff of the new school. Curricular efforts were designed to best select and educate students who were interested in rural and small community family practice. On September 20, 1972, the University of Minnesota School of Medicine, Duluth opened its doors to the first class of 24 students, 23 of whom graduated from the University of Minnesota in 1976 following their transfer to the Twin Cities campus.

From that first class, four members practiced in the area (Dr. Lee Cohen, a family physician in Two Harbors; Dr. Alan Johns, internist at the SMDC and School of Medicine; Dr. Jon Stephenson, a family doctor in Superior; and Dr. Roger Waage who practiced with the Rudie group downtown for years, then became the associate director of the family practice residency here in Duluth).

The school began on the "Old Main" campus where it was housed in the Lab School for the first seven years. In 1978, the students and faculty moved to a newly constructed facility on the UMD campus; this $8 million building was funded by the federal government (80%) and the state (20%). Federal funds were obtained after an intensive lobbying effort by the business and medical communities; Dr. Art Aufderheide, then acting dean, Jeno Paulucci, Dr. Bob Heller, Dr. John Thomas and Dr. Cy Brown met with Rep. Jim Oberstar and Vice President Walter Mondale to develop the strategies that were successful in gaining the federal funds. In 1998, a $3 million addition was completed, which provided more instructional and laboratory space.

Since its inception, the University of Minnesota School of Medicine, Duluth has consistently led the nation in the proportion of graduates selecting family medicine as a specialty (52% for all students graduating from the school's inception to 2003) and practicing in smaller and rural communities (55% in non-urban communities with populations smaller than 20,000). The school is consistently ranked in the top five nationally in rural health.

The Duluth health community has changed markedly in the past 35 years, and so has the University of Minnesota School of Medicine, Duluth. Each entering class is now comprised of 53 new students; tuition/fees per year was $973 in 1972 (now, it is more than $25,000 per year for Minnesota residents). The annual operating budget is nearly $16.5 million— approximately $10 million from the State of Minnesota; approximately $3 million per year is obtained from federal grants. More than 300 Minnesota and Wisconsin physicians have clinical faculty appointments at the school. The school's Family

> The school's Family Practice Preceptorship Program has been recognized as the nation's premier rural training program for medical students.

Practice Preceptorship Program has been recognized as the nation's premier rural training program for medical students. The faculty is quite competitive and successful in obtaining external funds for support of their research.

But what, in addition to the financial benefits that accrue to Duluth and the region, do we get in return for all of the support that we have received from the community? There are 976 School of Medicine Duluth graduates in practice, 59.3% that are in Minnesota (71% in Minnesota and Wisconsin). In the Duluth area (Duluth / Superior / Two Harbors /

Hermantown / Proctor / Cloquet), 102 doctors who started medical school in Duluth are currently in practice. An additional 23 family doctors trained at the residency (but who did not go to UMD) are also in practice in our area—so 125 doctors are here who very likely would not be if the school had not opened in 1972. In the Arrowhead region of Minnesota, more than 200 physicians who are graduates of our program practice.

The mission of the University of Minnesota School of Medicine Duluth is the same as when we began:

To educate students who will practice family medicine and other primary care specialties in rural Minnesota and American Indian communities, to provide high quality academic and clinical education programs for professional, graduate and undergraduate students, and to create distinguished research programs that advance knowledge in the health sciences, including rural and American Indian health issues.

The University of Minnesota School of Medicine, Duluth has, and will continue to, achieve this mission, and the people of Duluth, our region and state are well served by the school's presence. We are cognizant of the fact that we do not live in isolation in academia and that we owe a great deal of our remarkable success to the people of the region. Without the early efforts of many, many people in the business, education and medical sectors, the University of Minnesota School of Medicine, Duluth would not have been successful. ∎

Dr. James G. Boulger is associate professor in the Departments of Behavioral Sciences and Family Medicine at the University of Minnesota School of Medicine, Duluth. He is also the Director of Alumni Relations, Director of Family Practice Preceptorship Program and Director, Center for Rural Mental Health Studies. He was appointed to the faculty of the University of Minnesota School of Medicine, Duluth in 1973, and was associate dean of the school for 16 years.

CHAPTER

32

Sprucing up Enger Park

HOW A NEGLECTED PARK BECAME THE SITE OF A PRIZED CITY GARDEN

by Helen Lind

Duluth's Enger Park on Duluth's western hilltop is presided over by the imposing 80-ft. granite B. J. Enger Memorial Tower. When Bert J. Enger gave the Duluth Parks Department $50,000, the City purchased the tract of land that would become the 400-acre park and golf course.

Bert Enger was a Norwegian immigrant who first worked as a lumberjack in Wisconsin, and later came to Duluth where he and a partner started Enger & Olson, a retail furniture company. Enger, who never married, became known in Duluth as a philanthropist. When he died in 1931, he left a legacy of $185,000, some of which was used to pay for the construction of the tower that we enjoy today.

Enger Park opened in 1934, although work on the tower didn't begin until 1937. The tower was dedicated in 1939 at ceremonies attended by Crown Prince Olav and Crown

Gardens of peace and beauty. The Peace Bell, presented to Duluth as a gift from our Sister City of Ohara, Japan in 1994, holds a place of honor in Enger Park.

Princess Martha of Norway, as well as hundreds of proud Duluthians. Although it was never intended as a lighthouse, the tower is lighted, and continues to serve as a comforting beacon to ships on Lake Superior[1].

Enger Park immediately proved popular, but over the next 45 years, it fell into disrepair. When John Fedo became mayor in 1980, he saw a city depressed not only monetarily, but also spiritually. The parks were rundown, and one of the first things he did as mayor was to declare a "Citywide – City Pride" campaign to spruce up city parks.

Young people enrolled in the Painters' Union pre-apprenticeship program were enlisted to sandblast the graffiti-covered granite exterior of

[1] The beacon was extinguished during World War II, and was relit in 1953. The green beacon light continues to be maintained by the Duluth Parks and Recreation Department.

Enger Tower and to apply a sealer to protect the stone. Pre-apprentice members of the Cement Finishers Union laid new concrete walks. The campaign was also supported by the Duluth Vocational-Technical Institute, with financial support from the Duluth Private Industry Council and Mayor's Manpower Planning Council—about $3,500.

The City's plans for Enger Park included adapting walkways for handicapped accessibility; sandblasting and restoring the pavilion; and adding new picnic tables, more concrete walkways and tree plantings. The City also discussed plans to limit night-time access and to police the park more closely—a response to the late-night vandalism that continued to present a challenge to maintaining the park.

Flower gardens were also on the list, and that's where I enter into the story.

In 1983, when I had been working for the City as a part-time gardener, Ray Carson, the director of Parks and Recreation, asked me to go up to Enger Tower to inspect a sidewalk that had just been installed. What I found there was appalling—scrub oak and broken glass. I reported this to Mr. Carson and he suggested that I build a rock garden in the parking lot circle.

During the summer I thought about this, but I had visualized a garden following the contour of the land rather than on a flat plain. I also envisioned offering an opportunity to teens to help me.

By the end of the summer nothing had been done and Mr. Carson kept hinting about the rock garden, so with my crew of summer youth (ages 15-18), we started "grubbing" out in front of the stone pavilion. At the end of the season, it was all clear and bare with the natural rock exposed. My next-door neighbor gave me some crocus bulbs to plant so that I would have something to look forward to (they are still there).

The following spring, I received a donation of 20 hostas, and that was the basis of the garden. The City forestry crew trimmed up the oaks to permit more light, and we planted perennials and built pathways through the rock garden. Since that first spring, many hundreds of hostas and perennials have been added. Each year the garden was expanded and now includes a woodland garden, an alpine garden and even a Japanese garden.

In 1994, Enger Park became home to the Japanese-American Peace Bell, presented to Duluth as a gift from our Sister City, Ohara, Japan. The story of the Peace Bell is a moving tribute to the friendship between our two cities that formed after World War II. The original bell, an ancient Buddhist temple bell, was sacrificed by Ohara for the war effort and came to be found by an American who brought it to Duluth as a war trophy. It was installed for display in Duluth's City Hall until a Japanese citizen began working for its return to Ohara in 1954. Mayor George D. Johnson arranged to have the bell returned that same year, and in gratitude, Ohara renamed the bell "American-Japanese Peace Bell" and installed it in a public park. The replica in Enger Park dates from 1692.

The ambiance of Enger Park continues to be a peaceful, beautiful place with a view of the lake over the knoll as an added bonus. John Fedo was a great inspiration to me to "go out and do it!" I also have to give credit to Ray Carson who had faith in me to tackle this project with only a crew of kids.

Most of the credit goes to my crew who eagerly jumped into the project with only hand trowels and a "go get 'um" attitude. They taught me just as much as I taught them. To work side-by-side kneeling next to each other weeding and cultivating the garden gave me a great insight into a diverse group of people. Many former crew members who are now adults have returned with their families to visit Enger Park, still filled with pride at what they accomplished. ∎

Helen Lind worked as a gardener for Duluth Parks and Recreation Department 1982-1997. She was appointed permanent City Gardener in 1992.

CHAPTER

33

The Paper Chase

DULUTH'S ODYSSEY
IN PURSUIT OF A PAPER MILL

by Jack H. LaVoy

As you top the crest of Thompson Hill for the descent into Duluth, it is hard to imagine that magnificent view without billows of steam rising from a large, sleek manufacturing facility at the foot of the hill—for our West Duluth paper mill and nearby recycling plant seem to have been there forever.

Less than 20 years ago, the 92-plus acre site that is home to what are now the two Stora Enso plants, was a mix of 69 residential units and six commercial properties which included a contaminated state Superfund site. Bordered by the freeway, junkyards, bulk shipping facilities, and a mothballed, outdated steam electric generating facility on the bay, the site seemed an unlikely candidate for large-scale industrial development.

The effort to attract a new paper mill to Duluth began in 1976 when community leaders first learned that the Blandin

Grandmaison Studios

April 26, 1986, LSPI groundbreaking. From left: Murray Harpole, Mayor John Fedo, Governor Rudy Perpich, Ron Kelly, Jack Rowe, Arend Sandbulte, and D. Eugene Nugent. Several groundbreaking photos were taken so that all key players in the campaign could be acknowledged. If you recall being among those photographed, you are probably right.

Paper Company was considering an expansion of its papermaking operations in Grand Rapids, Minnesota.

The economy of the region was relatively strong everywhere but in Duluth. To the north, sizeable investments were continuing to be made, increasing and upgrading taconite production capacity across the Iron Range. And, in the smaller communities dependent upon forest products, demand for paper and wood products remained strong, so strong in fact that national business indicators demonstrated that investments in additional papermaking capacity for coated business papers could be justified nationwide. In response to those indicators Blandin Paper Company had begun making its plans.

When word spread of Blandin's strategy, Duluth's leaders began to wonder if the company might instead be enticed to expand at a new, freestanding facility in Duluth. The person best suited to ask that question, at that time, was Robert Babich, executive director of the Northeastern Minnesota Development Association (NEMDA).

Babich had a special edge in pushing the question. He and the CEO of Blandin Paper, Myles Reif, were married to sisters. Reif agreed to examine options for a Duluth site.

It was at that time that I first became involved with the Duluth paper mill project as part of a task force set up by Mayor Robert Beaudin to work with Blandin. As various sites were assessed across the city, one had an advantage— a site in West Duluth adjacent to the mothballed M.L. Hibbard Steam Electric Station.

The unexpected death of Myles Reif in the midst of this process interrupted its momentum and created an air of uncertainty over its long-term potential. Harold Zigmund, who succeeded Reif as Blandin CEO,

> At the top of Thompson Hill someone purchased a billboard that said, "Would the last one out of town, please turn off the lights?"

eventually leant his full support to the Duluth effort. Then a change in the federal tax code, forbidding nonprofit foundations from owning profit-making operations, forced the Blandin Foundation to dispose of the Grand Rapids paper mill, which had been under the foundation's ownership. They sold the plant to a Canadian company, British Columbia Forest Products. This, in turn, triggered an antitrust investigation by the United States Securities and Exchange Commission that delayed and ultimately killed the Duluth project.

Economic conditions in Duluth continued to deteriorate. The Duluth Air Base closed in 1981, with the elimination of 1,600 jobs. Jeno's, Inc. moved its food processing operations to Ohio, for a loss of another 2,500 jobs. And, Zalk Josephs, American Hoist & Derrick, Clyde Iron and

National Iron each significantly cut back or closed facilities as well. At the top of Thompson Hill someone purchased a billboard that said, "Would the last one out of town, please turn off the lights?" The *Minneapolis Tribune's* Sunday magazine featured a cover story entitled, "Duluth: The Tale of a Dying City."

Air Base re-use efforts succeeded in bringing a minimum security federal prison camp to town, as well as adding another fighter wing to the Duluth Air Guard base, and in securing legislative approval for the creation of a University of Minnesota-operated Natural Resources Research Institute (NRRI) in the former NORAD command center. During the same session that the legislature approved the NRRI, it also approved an engineering school at UMD. This initiative would hold the key to the future of the Duluth paper mill project.

Why the engineering school? Like many UMD projects, the effort to establish an engineering school had to be forced upon the central administration of the University of Minnesota by tremendous pressure from the outside—strong and vocal public support at home coupled with intense legislative pressure by our regional legislative leaders. The local support came from a group of regional engineers who were pulled together to form the Northeastern Minnesota Engineering Education Curriculum Council (NMEECC). NMEECC consisted of engineering executives from, among others, Hibbing Electronics, Potlatch Corp., Reserve Mining Company and, most importantly, Minnesota Power.

At the encouragement of Jack Rowe, Minnesota Power's CEO, the doors at 30 West Superior Street flung wide open to permit a flood of engineers to join together in championing the cause. Among them were Dick Swenson and John Johnson who served as special projects managers for the company, and Robert Marchetti, the company's senior vice president.

To help with the legislative effort in St. Paul, John Johnson was assigned to work with me at the capitol full-time. With Bob Marchetti serving as chairman of our NMEECC citizens advocacy group, he also became a frequent visitor to the capitol. The three of us worked closely together, determined to overcome opposition to our efforts by the university's central administration.

Thanks to the determination of our St. Paul delegation, particularly Senator Sam Solon, the project gained vital support and sufficient momentum to convince the university that it deserved to be implemented. It was approved with enough money to establish two engineering programs initially at the Duluth campus, with the potential for future growth.

After the legislature adjourned, Bob Marchetti asked me now that we had the engineering school project under our belts, what should Minnesota Power and the City of Duluth start working together on next?

I told Bob about the earlier efforts to attract Blandin Paper Company. I told him about an article in the *Wall Street Journal* and a similar one in *Business Week* that indicated how demand for high-quality printing papers was exceeding supply to a point where as many as ten new paper machines could possibly be built in the United States over the next several years. "Why don't we try to have one of those built in Duluth?" I asked. Bob said, "Let's do it!"

Our first focus was on Blandin, then owned by Fletcher Challenge, a worldwide forest products company headquartered in New Zealand.

...demand for high-quality printing papers was exceeding supply to a point where as many as ten new paper machines could possibly be built in the United States over the next several years. "Why don't we try to have one of those built in Duluth?"

We had developed a modest public financial incentive package and some updated visuals as to how a paper mill might be developed in West Duluth near the M.L. Hibbard plant. Mayor John Fedo, John LaForge,

Jack Rowe, and I made a trip to Grand Rapids to make a presentation to Al Wallace, Blandin's new CEO, who had recently arrived from Canada. Although Wallace had not been a part of Blandin's earlier Duluth efforts, he was polite, receptive and intrigued by the earlier interest his predecessors had shown in a Duluth mill. In about one month, we received a letter commending us on our efforts and turning us down. No thank you, but you do have "many tremendous advantages for a paper mill."

About a month later, we learned that Governor Perpich was going to host the president of St. Regis Paper Company for breakfast at the governor's residence to discuss expansion plans. We made a strong appeal to the governor to make our case. He agreed to provide the St. Regis CEO with a copy of our proposal—but only after they had concluded the company's agenda.

That meeting did not go well. There had been some difficult discussions between the St. Regis' executive team and representatives from the Minnesota Pollution Control Agency over issues that both sides apparently found stressful.

As the meeting broke up, Governor Perpich dutifully handed his departing guests the book containing the Duluth paper mill proposal with a request that they look it over. Considering the overall negative tenor of the meeting, it was not a great start.

To cover our bet, I asked Terry Serie, state government affairs manager for St. Regis, if he could help us. He suggested that I make three copies of the proposal and leave them at the office of Senator Jim Pehler, who, in 1984, represented the St. Cloud and Sartell region where St. Regis operated.

Within little over a month, a planeload of St. Regis executives came to Duluth to look us over in March of 1984.

We entered into an odyssey of learning on what it takes to put a paper mill project together. They taught us about the paper business and what it would take to operate competitively in our city. They learned from us about financial incentives we could muster and how they might pay the costs of site assembly and infrastructure development. We checked everything out—the Lakewood pumping station, the Western Lake

Superior Sanitary District (WLSSD), water main diameters and water pump flowage capacity, landfill issues, environmental concerns and every possible other consideration.

We were not the only community under consideration by St. Regis. We were competing with expansion options at their plants in Bucksport, Maine, and Deferiet, New York. It was this competition that finally focused us on the one item in which we were not competitive—the ability to provide steam at a competitive cost.

Retrofitting the Minnesota Power M.L. Hibbard Steam Electric Station and operating it as a private utility, separate from the paper company, was too expensive in comparison to expanding steam capacity at their existing plants. The only way those costs could be cut would be to use tax increment financing and tax exempt steam utility bonds, and the only way that could be done was if the facility was under public ownership.

I shared my concerns with Bob Marchetti who suggested I call Arend "Sandy" Sandbulte, president and COO of Minnesota Power. I explained to him the challenge and potential deal breaker of the steam issue. I asked if his company would consider donating the necessary boilers, equipment and easements to the city so that a publicly owned steam district could be formed similar to the one operating in downtown Duluth. That could be the key to using public resources to make the changes needed to retrofit the mothballed plant to make it more economically efficient and environmentally compatible.

Sandbulte soon said we could work something out. We totally revamped the steam issue to reflect the new circumstances and came up with costs that beat our competition. The project had been saved.

That August our project team of city officials, sanitary district personnel, fiber resource experts and Minnesota Power executives met with the group from St. Regis. We held a final review of the project in anticipation of having it presented to the company's board of directors in September.

About 10:30 in the morning the telephone rang. It was for James Browersock, St. Regis senior vice president and leader of its project team.

He was informed that the international news mogul, Rupert Murdock, had announced his intent to make a hostile takeover of St. Regis. This news ruined the mood of the meeting as discussion was diverted to "poison pills," "golden parachutes," and anti-takeover defenses.

Within two months the company merged with Champion International and ceased to exist, while in the process consuming most of its project money in one-time merger costs. We never saw them again.

The loss of St. Regis nearly dealt the deathblow to Duluth's paper mill efforts. While the process had validated Duluth as a paper mill site, the loss of St. Regis taxed the patience and commitment of some city leaders. In that atmosphere I picked up my seven-year-old copy of *Post's Pulp and Paper Directory* and began calling every paper company in the United States and Canada that produced lightweight coated paper, and made a pitch to take a look at Duluth. Two agreed to do so. One was a company called Repap, from Montreal, and the other was Pentair.

After hosting visits by executives from both companies, everyone's favorite was Pentair. They were based in St. Paul, and the character and culture of their executive staff seemed to make a good fit with the executives from Minnesota Power who were working on the project at that time.

After evaluating our proposal and comparing it to an expansion Pentair had considered at its paper mill in Niagara, Wisconsin, the Pentair leadership concluded that the Duluth project was more competitive. However, Pentair did not have enough financial strength to handle such a capital-intensive project on their own. They would need a partner and they encouraged us to help find one.

In November of 1984, we went to Thunder Bay to pitch the Pentair partnership idea to the management team of the Canadian Pacific Forest Products Company that operated a large paper mill there. Next we tried Norske Skog over much of the winter, through a Norwegian forest products consultant we met via the Minnesota World Trade Office.

Then, in the spring, a carload of Japanese business people showed up at our office in City Hall to express their interest in possibly participating in a Duluth paper mill project. They were from Mitsubishi.

The Mitsubishi team informed us that they made paper machinery, built and ran paper mills, and financed projects—any one or all of which they might possibly be interested in doing in consort with Pentair, in Duluth. It was March 1985—nine years since those first conversations with Blandin.

Over the past few months I had been entreating Bob Marchetti to try to interest Minnesota Power into becoming a partner with Pentair. After all, the company's efforts at diversification had led it to own a telephone company in Wisconsin and water utilities in Florida, so why not half ownership in a paper mill in Duluth? I'd ask the question and each time, Bob would come back with an answer from his superiors that basically said, "We know about utilities, Bob, not paper. Go find yourself a paper maker." Perhaps now, in Mitsubishi, we had our winning prospect.

I didn't know it at the time, but Bob Marchetti's efforts were causing some renewed thinking within Minnesota Power as they got to know more about Pentair and better understand the project's potential. Prior to a meeting of our city team, Mitsubishi and Minnesota Power at Pentair, Jack Rowe sent one of his associates down to Pentair to learn more about them. In the meantime, I resigned from my position with the City of Duluth effective June 15. This was going to be my last meeting on a Duluth paper mill project—either it would work and someone else could take over, or it would die, once and for all.

On the morning of May 19, we assembled in the Pentair Board Room: top executives from Minnesota Power, Pentair, a delegation from Mitsubishi, Mayor John Fedo and myself. The morning's discussion centered on a detailed and professional presentation made by Ron Kelly who outlined Pentair's perspective on a new "greenfield" paper mill in Duluth.

Unlike previous efforts, this new plant would not produce lightweight coated publication grade papers, but instead would make a relatively new paper grade, "supercalendered" paper, or SCA as it was known in the trade. It was a grade that was widely produced in Europe, and because of its growing acceptance in the United States, it was a product under consideration by at least three other North American-based companies. If a decision was made to proceed, it would have to be done on a "fast track" basis in order to beat out any potential competition.

By late morning, it became clear that Mitsubishi's corporate structure with its hierarchical nature and strong control from headquarters in Japan, was not compatible with the "fast track" requirements Pentair advocated. As the presentations began to wind down and the meeting was about to break up, Jack Rowe, Sandy Sandbulte and Bob Marchetti asked to meet privately with Pentair's chairman Murray Harpole, its president, D. Eugene Nugent and Ron Kelly.

At lunch Harpole sat next to me and asked me several questions. He said he heard that I was leaving my position with the City of Duluth in mid-June, which I confirmed. He then told me that it looked like they would be proceeding with the project in partnership with Minnesota Power and he felt it would be important to have me involved. The following day, I was working at the state capitol on city legislative issues when Bob Marchetti left me a message at Senator Sam Solon's office. He told me it appeared the project would move forward, and that Mr. Sandbulte had asked him to inquire about whether I would be interested in continuing to work on the project, only this time for the private sector.

On July 1, 1985, I opened an office at Minnesota Power as an independent consultant. I was to work with Ron Kelly and others on coordinating a $3.5 million study to determine the feasibility of developing a state-of-the-art, world-class greenfield paper mill in West Duluth. It was basically the St. Regis project, but only bigger, better, with different owners and a different grade of paper.

The feasibility study supported moving forward.

By mid-October it appeared that all systems were "go," save one. The area that was to be assembled for redevelopment included an abandoned scrap metal yard that was polluted with lead and polychlorinated biphenyls or PCBs. All liability and responsibility for the pollutants would transfer to any entity that would assume ownership of the site.

Neither company was willing to accept that responsibility. We explored several other site locations and project options, but none had the merits of the initial site if it were not for this dark cloud of liability.

Our only hope was to appeal to Governor Rudy Perpich for some type of state intervention. In order to make that appeal, we enlisted the help of Representatives Willard Munger and Mike Jaros as well as Senator Sam Solon. We met in the Governor's office and outlined the issue. The state agreed to hold any new owners harmless from any liability. It became the state's number one Superfund site to be cleaned up, free of the contaminants, on a fast track.

The only other bump in the road was a disagreement with Jeno Paulucci over the value of his former Chun King building on part of the site. It would be several years and an extended lawsuit before that issue became resolved.

Ground was broken on April 26, 1986, and the start-up of paper production began on November 4, 1987, setting a world record for the design, completion and start-up of a greenfield paper mill.

The community spirit that burst forth following the announcement of the feasibility study result evolved into an over-all sense of community pride that Duluth could give birth to such a well-respected, world-class facility. There was a particular sense of gratitude to Minnesota Power for taking such a bold step, coupled with a respect for Pentair as a quality corporate addition to Duluth's business fabric.

In early 1988, the *Minneapolis Star Tribune* wrote a new cover story in its Sunday magazine. This time it was entitled, "Duluth: The City That Refused To Die."

By 1992, business was humming and despite some uncertainties in other aspects of the international paper industry's marketplace, the outlook for supercalendered paper seemed strong. Pressure was rising however among some key customers for the availability of a recycled content product, particularly from Target stores, one of LSPI's larger customers. Other regional paper makers were feeling similar pressures, but none to a great enough extent to permit any one company to justify the construction of a dedicated paper recycling facility. As a result, a unique relationship was developed that led to the construction of a sister facility next to the Lake Superior Paper Industries (LSPI) plant, Superior Recycled Fiber Industries (SRFI), which opened in 1993.

Unlike the paper mill that was a joint venture between Minnesota Power and Pentair, SRFI was developed entirely by a Minnesota Power subsidiary, Synertec, Inc. in cooperation with LSPI, and included a unique customer/partnership relationship that involved other paper companies like Blandin Paper Company, Canadian Pacific Forest Products, Ltd, in Dryden, Ontario; Consolidated Papers, Inc. in Wisconsin Rapids, and Potlatch Corporation in Cloquet.

In 1995, LSPI and SRFI were sold to Wisconsin-based Consolidated Papers, Inc. In 2000, the entire operations of Consolidated Papers were sold to Finnish-based Stora Enso. While change has had its impact on the operations, the legacy of the project to the community of Duluth cannot be ignored and will remain as benefits to its economy for decades to come. ∎

Jack LaVoy, Director of Marketing, Communications and External Affairs of the Iron Range Resources and Rehabilitation Agency, represented part of Duluth in the Minnesota legislature, 1971-1975, was employed in economic development by the Duluth Port Authority and the City of Duluth, 1974-1985, and was a vice-president of Lake Superior Paper Industries, 1985-1996.

34

Interstate 35 Extension

HOW A CONTROVERSIAL FREEWAY PROJECT
BECAME THE RAINBOW
AT THE END OF THE HIGHWAY

by John Bray

Duluth's 2.3-mile I-35 extension project spanned 30 years—one of the most controversial...and most lauded...transportation projects in U.S. history.

Besides completing the final leg of the 1,600 mile-long freeway that ends at the Mexican border, the freeway extension project also bulldozed its way through the careers of six Duluth mayors and three district engineers of the Minnesota Department of Transportation (Mn/DOT).

The project ran headlong up against an amazing degree of controversy, public hostility and across-the-board community opposition of the highest order. Ultimately, involvement by community members radically reconfigured the project to make it one of the best designs throughout the entire 44,000-mile interstate system. It is truly the rainbow at the end of the

Mn/DOT

The story of how the last stretch of Duluth's freeway was completed is *almost* as dramatic as how its creative and unique use of tunnels, parks and pedestrian walkways continue to enhance visitors' and residents' experience of the city and Lake Superior.

highway.

This $250 million project remains the largest single transportation undertaking in the history of Minnesota. In fact, Duluth is one of only five communities around the world that have designed and built highway projects on a similar scale (the others being Florence, Italy; Barcelona, Spain; Seattle, Washington and Boston, Massachusetts).

To understand the I-35 freeway extension project, you need to place it in its historical context. The U.S. freeway system that we depend upon today was originally envisioned in 1956 by President Dwight D. Eisenhower as a national defense initiative to connect all major urban centers coast-to-coast with a four-lane, divided, controlled access highway network capable of serving the needs of military mobilization. The Minnesota Highway Department announced the route of a freeway through West Duluth to 10th Avenue East in 1958, with construction estimated to take ten years, at a cost of $45 million. As was typical of these times, little or no social or aesthetic impacts were considered in the first plans for I-35 in Duluth.[1]

Plans for the Duluth freeway called for it to be elevated using pillar construction, and to parallel downtown's Michigan Street, requiring removal of all buildings along the south side of the street. Although there was some opposition to removing buildings downtown, Duluth Mayor Eugene Lambert hailed the freeway plan as a "face-lifter and a solution to Duluth's downtown traffic problems." Work began in 1964 between Thompson Hill and 32nd Avenue West. Approximately 700 homes were razed or moved in West Duluth, and about 250 homes were taken from the neighborhood between 30th Avenue West and 20th Avenue West below Superior Street. The pressure was on to keep the pillar design intact through the downtown area as well.

By 1958, the Duluth Joint Highway Committee recommended extending the freeway from 10th to 27th Avenue East and then to follow

---

[1] The construction of another portion of Minnesota's I-35 freeway paved the way for controversy to our south. Just before the 1962 gubernatorial election, DFL politicians claimed the Hinckley-area stretch of I-35 was substandard, and blamed it on Gov. Elmer L. Anderson. Elmer Anderson subsequently lost the 1962 election to Karl Rolvaag by 91 votes.

the Duluth Missabe and Iron Range Railway corridor through eastern Duluth—all the way to 68th Avenue East.

Controversy about the freeway's endpoint and how the construction would impact downtown Duluth began to surface. A grassroots Duluth organization, Citizens for Integrating Highways and the Environment (CIHE) formed in 1970. Its members advocated a complete re-analysis of alternative solutions to transportation problems east of Mesaba Avenue. The founder of CIHE was local landscape architect Kent Worley, a visionary who would design virtually all of I-35's awesome waterfront amenities.

Meanwhile, the West Duluth stretch of freeway was steadily nearing completion...and coming closer to the outskirts of downtown. By November 1971, the western portion was complete, ending at Mesaba Avenue.

In August 1972, a new citizens' group rose up, calling themselves "Stop the Freeway Action Group," proposing that the freeway end at Mesaba Avenue. In October 1973, Jim Gustafson presided at a public hearing in the Duluth Auditorium on freeway issues, attended by 1,100 citizens. Much of the discussion centered on whether to terminate the freeway at 10th, 26th or 68th Avenues East. Although the Duluth City Council had given its unanimous approval to the freeway route as planned, ending at 10th Avenue East in 1960, citizens continued to debate the issue. Some felt that the freeway might divide Duluth's downtown district and the Lake Superior waterfront. Although Duluth's waterfront area consisted primarily of abandoned warehouses and a busy railroad yard, these citizens saw the Lake Superior shoreline as a major asset. They were concerned that I-35 would obscure views of the lake, thereby ending hopes of ever reconnecting the shoreline to the downtown area. Others were concerned that the historic brewery district, located in the proposed path for I-35, would also have to be demolished.

In December 1975, newly elected Mayor Robert Beaudin appointed an "I-35 Citizens Advisory Panel"—a diverse panel composed of both opponents and proponents of the initial freeway extension concept to study and make their recommendations. He convinced the state and federal government to put a hold on the project, scrap their initial design plans for the freeway project, and start over with a clean slate. The I-35 Citizens Advisory Panel was empowered to work with government officials to fully integrate the design of the freeway into the urban environment of the City of Duluth. The mayor charged the committee to ensure that any eventual extension of I-35 would unfold into a renewal opportunity for our city's urban core, be the catalyst for the renaissance of our downtown central business district and be the stimulus to reconfigure our city's linkages to Lake Superior.

The panel included: Lauren Larsen, chair; Joy Williams, vice-chair; Bill Abalan, Dave Allison, Rondi Erickson, Harold Frederick, Mary Olin, John Peyton, Rod Wibbens, Tom Gruesen, Earl Liljegren, Myrtle Marshall, Cliff Olson, Bob Seitz and Donna Ekberg.

The I-35 Citizens Advisory Panel and its partners from the Minnesota Highway Department (now Mn/DOT), the Federal Highway Administration and the City of Duluth, worked tirelessly for nearly three years. In 1976, the panel voted 11-2 in support of an "inland" freeway route (much as it is today) by tunneling to the north side of Superior St. and continuing through Leif Erikson Park.

In 1977, approval was given for federal interstate money to finance a freeway to end at 68th Avenue East, and discussions began on how that money might be used if the freeway were ended closer to downtown. Eventually, during the administration of Mayor John Fedo, the $74 million of federal money—originally earmarked to construct I-35 between 26th and 68th Avenues East and blending into the Highway 61 expressway on the east side of the city—financed city and state projects, including the reconstruction, bricking and streetscaping downtown streets; building four downtown skywalks; rebuilding Haines, Arrowhead and Martin roads; and making DTA transit improvements.

The question as to where to end the freeway was put to a referendum vote in 1980. Duluth residents cast 21,107 votes to terminate I-35 at 26th Avenue East, and 16,404 votes to terminate it at 10th Avenue East. The Duluth City Council later also voted in favor of ending the freeway at 26th, but in 1984, it reversed itself, voting 6-3 to stop I-35 at 10th instead of 26th Avenue East, an action Mayor John Fedo vetoed. A city council majority overrode his veto, but in 1984 a bill requiring the state to extend the freeway to 26th Avenue East (overturning the city council decision) was approved by the Legislature and signed into law by Governor Rudy Perpich. The freeway would end at 26th Avenue East.

Many issues had to be worked out to implement the innovative design. Architectural Resources, Inc., where Kent Worley was a principal, was hired as a consultant for a multiple-use study of the areas through which the freeway would pass. Mn/DOT worked with eight major consultants to design the freeway extension, including Bennett, Ringrose, Wolsfeld, Jarvis & Gardner, Minneapolis; Architectural Resources, Inc., Duluth; DeLeuw, Cather & Company, Chicago; Bakke, Koop, Ballou & McFarlin, Minneapolis; Sverdrup Corporation, Seattle; Larsen, Harvala, Berquist, Duluth; Edwards & Kelcey, Minneapolis; and Thomas & Vecchi AIA Architects, Duluth.

First, the busy railroad yard on the waterfront had to be moved. Financed by the Federal Highway Administration and the Minnesota Department of Transportation at $45 million, it took ten years for the five independent railroads—Duluth, Winnipeg & Pacific (DWP); Burlington Northern (BN); Duluth, Missabe & Iron Range (DMIR); Chicago North Western (CNW); and the Soo Line—to move their switching yards to Superior. The complex task was made even more complicated by the need to coordinate efforts with many government agencies and jurisdictions. The project involved shippers, unions, property owners and local jurisdictions, and approval or rulings were required from at least 23 public agencies. In November 1984, the move was finally completed. A federal railroad administration official later called it "one of the best urban rail consolidation projects in the country." Although there were many players in this complex project, attorney Harold Frederick deserves special recognition.

Digging of the tunnels began in 1983. The final design featured three tunnels: the Brewery Historic District Tunnel, the Jay Cooke Plaza tunnel and the Rose Garden Tunnel.

Endion Station (a railroad passenger depot listed on the National

Register of Historic Places) lay directly in the path the freeway. It was moved 15 blocks from 15th Avenue East to its present location adjacent to Duluth's downtown Lakewalk near Lake Avenue and First Avenue East. The fragile 4,000-ton brick and sandstone building was moved via city streets at a cost of $370,000.

The Rose Garden in Leif Erikson Park was torn up and eventually reconstructed after the tunnels were built at a cost of $3.8 million. Because of the disruption to the many community groups that relied on the park for their activities, Mayor Fedo and Mn/DOT District Engineer John Sandahl requested additional money from the federal government. The city received $616,000, which was used for replanting the Rose Garden, maintenance and other expenses.

On October 28, 1992, the I-35 extension officially opened to traffic. Besides the completed freeway, Duluth gained many new amenities and preserved and enhanced existing amenities, thanks to the innovative design and construction of the I-35 extension. Lake Place Park, a 2.5-acre park, was built atop a cut-and-cover tunnel, linking the lakeshore to downtown Duluth. The Lakewalk—a favorite place to stroll for tourists and residents—follows the rebuilt shoreline. The Minnesota Slip drawbridge offers access to Canal Park. A new lake trout spawning reef is located off-shore near the Fitger's complex. A 580-foot mosaic Image Wall—an award-winning creation of Kent Worley and Mark Marino—is displayed on the lake side of the Lake Place Park tunnel, depicting lakefront, marine and ship images in ceramic tiles. Other new park areas, also designed by Worley, include Lake Place, just north of where Endion Station is now located and Jay Cooke Plaza Park, which offers a panoramic view of Lake Superior. Walkers enjoy new pedestrian bridges in Leif Erikson Park. And the Fitger Brewery, the October House and the Hartley Building have all been preserved for posterity.

It has been our honor at District 1 of the Minnesota Department of Transportation to receive three Federal Highway Administration's "Excellence in Highway Design" awards in 1992, 1994, and 1998 for aspects of this epic project.

Beyond any doubt, the Duluth I-35 experience stands as the epitome of one of our nation's most astonishing examples of urban transportation design ingenuity, which became the spark for the spectacular rebirth of Duluth. Because of I-35, our reinvigorated downtown and its breathtaking waterfront now welcome millions of visitors each year who come to savor the ever changing coastal moods of Lake Superior, silhouetted by our city's enchanting, vibrant and diverse urban landscape.

This final segment of I-35 is a magical thread that connects Duluth's downtown to Lake Superior. But even more, the I-35 extension project is a spectacular legacy to citizen involvement, community empowerment of the highest order and a magnificent showcase of what can happen when governments form true partnerships with their customers. In a very real sense, the Duluth I-35 extension project was one of the early inspirations for what we now call "context sensitive design," and it still serves as a model of the magic that can be achieved when public works stays clearly focused on their customers. ▮

John Bray is special assistant to the district engineer for the Minnesota Department of Transportation District 1. In 1996, Bray was one of the founders of the Northshore Inline Marathon and currently is chair of its board of directors. The Northshore Inline Marathon, which takes place every September on a course between Duluth and Two Harbors, has grown to become the largest inline marathon in the U.S., and is the second largest inline marathon in the world.

CHAPTER

35

Lake Place

A CREATIVE DESIGN SOLUTION
LED TO A POPULAR PEDESTRIAN
OASIS OVER FREEWAY

by Kent G. Worley

The proximity of a proposed freeway to Lake Superior represented one of the most critical challenges of the entire Interstate 35 corridor within the City of Duluth. The freeway's alignment between downtown and lakefront areas demanded unique design solutions to protect environmental resources, link major downtown land use areas and improve pedestrian access to the long-neglected lakefront—and I had the opportunity to serve as project landscape architect.

After a long public involvement process that identified the negative impacts of a freeway between the downtown and the lakefront, the design team proposed a 3-acre, $10 million park structure over the freeway as a design concept to address these negative impacts. The negative impacts included the following:

From above, it's easy to see why Lake Place is called a bridge that connects people to the lake front.

1. The freeway and placement of protective walls along the lakeshore would have created visual, as well as, physical barriers between commercial/residential areas and Lake Superior.
2. Freeway alignment would have eliminated any significant potential for lakefront open space in the vicinity.
3. Severe weather conditions off Lake Superior would cause hazardous roadway icing.

Mn/DOT

4. Proximity of the highway to downtown and the lakefront would have created severely negative impacts of noise, lighting, air quality and accessibility.

5. Long-range community goals to unify and strengthen the core downtown would have been forfeited.

The citizens of Duluth and State/Federal Departments of Transportation recognized these potential impacts, and we moved forward in addressing

Ken Worley

The rainbow at the end of the freeway. Lake Place is a sunny spot for Duluthians and visitors to enjoy spectacular views of Lake Superior. It's also frequently visited by city planners and urban designers from around the world who come to study the many creative and attractive solutions used to squeeze a freeway between our downtown and our Lake.

them. The design team included Minnesota Department of Transportation (Mn/DOT) administration and staff, the City of Duluth and several consulting civil, structural, mechanical and electrical engineers. My role was as urban design lead, and included conceptual through final design services for architectural and site components of Lake Place.

Defining the needs and programming the extent and levels of improvement for the facility were my initial challenges. This early conceptual work and extensive project justification became the basis to obtain federal, state and city funding commitments involving a wide range of design opportunities—all focusing on design solutions to "integrate" the highway and city in linking the public with Lake Superior.

Lake Place, completed in 1990, incorporates two major elements. First, a wall was constructed between the roadway and the lake. A covering deck was then built over the highway to provide protection from Lake Superior over-spray and wind-driven debris. Second, and most important, the deck of the protective structure was planned as a multiple-use outdoor area in conjunction with the development of lakefront trail systems. These multiple-use concepts for Lake Place and the urban highway corridor have created harmonious transportation, recreation, open space, and quality environment—far exceeding visions of client-city-citizen expectations. They also resulted in community reinvestment and renewal of once marginal lakefront property. This unique oasis for travelers and residents not only protects, but becomes a gateway for the most valuable natural resource of the region—Lake Superior.

Design concepts insured that the freeway would not visually or physically separate the lakeshore from the city. The two-block-long Lake Place park structure forms one of four highway tunnels within the corridor. Although a "tunnel" in name, Lake Place was envisioned as a pedestrian "bridge" connecting people and places, and once it was completed, acceptance has been enthusiastic as citizens could finally see, and physically reach their lake.

A 580-ft. long ceramic tile Image Wall mural on the outside highway wall, facing lake-level use areas, was designed and assembled in collaboration with Duluthians Mark and Sandra Marino. Consistent with community waterfront themes, the wall depicts historic marine images and provides an additional highlight for lakefront trail visitors. Lake Place continues to accomplish one of its goals with new adjacent improvements, development and attractions; several adjacent downtown blocks will see eventual renewal as direct result of this multiple-use highway improvement.

A comprehensive Mn/DOT/Federal Highway Works Administration undertaking, the urban Interstate 35 resulted in several individual multiple-use improvements with Lake Place as the focus. These were designed as a system, and share continuity of design philosophy, design vocabulary of materials, colors, textures, native vegetation, site lighting and subtle messages of environmental awareness. Public acceptance is best illustrated by observing response through public use and enjoyment of these rediscovered resources. I recently heard the comment, "With these improvements, there is a new spirit in Duluth!"

The downtown Duluth interstate issues with their 20-year environmental stalemate illustrates the crucial importance for landscape architects to state their case and initiate leadership to attain "something better." Lake Place, and other highway corridor multiple-use improvements are living examples of a larger context of human and community opportunities which need to be managed through a process of inventory, analysis and solution. ∎

Kent Worley is a Duluth-based landscape architect who spearheaded the design and development of Lake Place. His design work included identifying Duluth's unique lakefront opportunities and encouraging citizen involvement to prevent major downtown and lakefront highway separation. He provided conceptual through final design services for architectural and site components of Lake Place, Lakewalk and all site components of the downtown Interstate 35 construction 1981-1994.

CHAPTER

36

Oneota Industrial Park & West Duluth Redevelopment

HOW THE ARRIVAL OF INTERSTATE 35 TRIGGERED BIG LAND USE CHANGES

by Bill Majewski

Like many projects in Duluth between 1950 and 2000, Oneota Industrial Park had beginnings related to the extension of I-35 into western Duluth. As plans were being drawn for the route of the freeway toward the heart of the city, thought was being given to what kinds of changes might occur adjacent the roadway.

A study done in the early 1960s by Mark Flaherty, then a senior planner in the City Planning Department, entitled "Highways, Opportunities, and Land Use Controls" covered the West Duluth neighborhood but focused on the Oneota area. That 1963 plan began the general layout of the future land uses and access to and from the freeway. At the time, this area was a mixture of residential, industrial and vacant land.

Two major ravines with small streams bisected it and because of the deep ravines not all streets in the area were continuous. This initial study was funded by the Bureau of Public Roads (now Federal Highway Administration). Its purpose was to identify and study opportunities adjacent to the freeway where land use controls would direct material changes in the land use mix as a result of the new limited access highway. It also provided some framework for future considerations of development/redevelopment scenarios to other adjacent parcels not directly connected to the roadway. A few of the recommendations from this report were:

1. That 40th and 46th Avenues West serve as a split diamond intersection for access to the freeway, opening the way for commercial/industrial land conversion.

2. That the freeway be depressed in this area to allow for the local streets to remain connected at grade and that these streets connect to other industrial sites in the area.

3. That the I-35 intersections provide the backbone for local street connections to area streets and roads.

I-35 was under construction down Thompson Hill and through the West Duluth neighborhood in the early 1960s. Apparently as part of the need to find sites to dispose of excess earth material excavated from the construction the freeway, the contractor, Johnson Bros. of Litchfield, acquired three blocks of privately owned land between 43rd and 46th Avenues West on the north side of the right-of-way for the freeway. This property was vacant ravine-crossed land. The freeway is depressed in this section and the material taken out had to be disposed of somewhere. This proved to be a beneficial decision; the land served first as a convenient inexpensive disposal site for the contractor and secondly, the filled site was later suitable for industrial development when the project was completed.

In June 1969, a report titled "A General Neighborhood Renewal Plan and Industrial Development Opportunities for West Duluth" prepared for the Duluth City Council and the Housing and Redevelopment Authority of Duluth by Harland Bartholomew and Associates, was released. This report covered the area between the ore docks and the zoo and included some general recommendations for conversion of portions of this area for industrial purposes. It laid the basis for current and future redevelopment activities and made the case for potential public funding for some of the redevelopment of the area. Its recommendations were consistent with the earlier study prepared by Flaherty.

In October 1969, Midwest Planning and Research, Inc. prepared a report for Johnson Bros. titled "Oneota Center Development Concept Study." This study focused on the area between 39th and 48th Avenues West and included some suggestions for the "after-use" of the land the contractor had acquired and filled during the construction of I-35. It picked up on the information outlined in the earlier Planning Commission report prepared by Flaherty and begins to define more specifically how the Oneota Industrial Park between 39th and 48th Avenues West on the upper side of the freeway might be configured in parcels and the desirable arrangement of land uses.

In 1973, the HRA applied for over $600,000 from HUD to begin land acquisition. The city council approved this application for acquiring and relocating the 14 residences in the 44th to 46th Avenue West portion of the site. City Councilor Leo McDonnell sponsored the resolution of approval for this project. In the next several years the residents were relocated from the area, clearing the way for final plans. Five years later, in July 1978, Barton-Aschman Associates prepared a detailed "Oneota Industrial Park Development Plan" for the City of Duluth. A Technical Advisory Committee for the Oneota Industrial Park had been formed to guide the redevelopment of the area. This report was the model that the eventual plat and rezoning was based on. The I-P zoning district was added to the City Zoning Code. The new code included standards not found elsewhere in the code. These included provisions for aesthetic purposes as well as safety due to exposure to the freeway. Among these were exterior building materials, landscaping requirements, site drainage plans, setbacks and screening controls for outdoor storage as well as standards for off-street parking.

By 1979, the City Planning Commission approved a plat prepared by Salo Engineering for the area between 40th and 46th Avenue West as an industrial park. This area was better known as Oneota, since it did not include the areas either to the east of 40th Avenue West or west of 46th Avenue West. Superior Street was vacated between 41st and 46th Avenues West to make the parcels larger for industrial park purposes. This meant the relocation of utilities to the new major street alignment. All the overhead utility lines were put underground to improve the appearance of the industrial park.

Bombardier, Briggs Trucking, Crane, Northland-Lakehead-Twin Ports-Arrowhead, the City Tool House, Mack Truck, Perkins, Glenndenning Trucking and AMPI (American Milk Producers Incorporated) were already in the area. Once the plat was established, it did not take long for applications to be filed for development in the area. Johnson-Wilson Constructors, Twin Ports Heating and Supply Co., Williams Welding, and Viking Industrial Center were among the early applicants.

Mack Truck was located on 40th Avenue West and owned several land parcels. Some of this land consisted of a willow ravine south of the railroad tracks with a small stream in it behind their main building on what was platted as 41st Avenue West. Further downstream this ravine had been filled as a part of the freeway construction and the stream had been put into a pipe. City staff worked with Mack Truck to identify land parcels that might make their operations more efficient and worked out an arrangement to trade land. The purpose of this was to enable the City to place a storm sewer pipe in the ravine and fill the area to make useable land. Eventually the area was filled with demolition debris hauled to the site by various contractors. In later years Mack Truck moved their entire operations to the Truck Center on Central Avenue. That area had been the focus of the major redevelopment to accommodate large over-the-road trucks coming in and out of the Twin Ports. The site is now owned and used by the City for one of its major tool house facilities. One portion of the site that was filled is now occupied by mini-storage buildings.

During this same period changes were occurring in the West Duluth Business Area, now commonly referred to as Spirit Valley. The Western Area Business and Civic Club and other neighborhood community clubs were working on a plan for the business area in the vicinity of Central Avenue and Grand Avenue. Several iterations of plans were developed after 1970, when Mayor Bob Beaudin encouraged the formation of a non-profit group in the area to work with the city to secure federal funding for some of the improvements needed to keep the commercial area vital. Dr. Joseph Balach, a dentist in the business area was the first president of the Spirit Valley Citizens Neighborhood Development Association (SVCNDA). That initiated the creation and review of several plans— some by the City and some by consultants such as Aguar Jyring Whiteman Moser, Inc. One of the major impediments to doing anything creative in the business area was that railroad tracks bisected the area on the southeast side of Grand Avenue and there was concern that the business district was too split up to be successful. This was the first major project for the new organization. Although it was not easy, the tracks were acquired and removed and a new plan for the mall area was prepared by Dave Sebok of the City Planning and Development Department. That set the stage for redevelopment that saw removal of 20 homes and 15 businesses to make room for mall construction where Kmart now operates.

This organization was different from most civic bodies. Rather than meet once per month, they met each week for lunch. These sessions were focused and results-oriented with the idea of keeping on top of progress and what should be done next. These sessions included anyone from the area who was interested. City staff, consultants and others working on current projects were strongly encouraged to be present to participate in these discussions. If progress was not satisfactory, the principals of the organization were not bashful about making contact with superiors to find out why "things were not getting done." Dr. Balach was joined in those early years by Drs. Jim Westman, and Bill Zimbinski, Helen Lind, Jeanne Koneczny, Charlie Bell, Jim Aird, Vern Johnson, Joanne Carroll and Tim

Leland. Bill Spehar and Roy Holt from Gary-New Duluth were early and regular members of this group as well.

While not directly involved in the details of the Oneota Industrial Park as a group, some of these individuals also participated in these efforts. Their primary focus was dealing with getting the railroad out of the business area and replatting those lands for redevelopment.

While the final details were being put on the initial area, progress was started on the second activity area referred to as Oneota I, the area west of 46th Avenue West. There were 25 residences located here in a several block area near where the relocated US Highway 2 Bong Bridge would connect to 46th Avenue West and I-35. The old highway connection to Wisconsin had been located further west/south on Grassy Point over the Arrowhead Bridge that had become antiquated. With the construction of I-35, it needed to have a more modern connection to the Interstate Highway system. The engineers for the new bridge connection at 46th had projected vehicle noise levels above acceptable national and state standards for most of the residences found here. This opened a funding source for acquisition and relocation of a significant portion of the residents of the area. The Duluth Housing and Redevelopment Authority was hired to coordinate preparation of appraisals of the property to be acquired and proceed with making offers for the acquisition and relocation work needed. While it was painful at the time for owners and their families to be leaving, after some concessions by the city council to provide additional benefits all of those moved out of the area were relocated into more modern and up-to-date homes elsewhere in the neighborhood, nearby neighborhoods or elsewhere in the city or suburbs.

By 1984, all of the residents had been bought out and relocated. Community development funding was used to purchase those properties located outside or beyond the noise limits. Had they been left, the few homes would have been totally isolated in a predominantly industrial area. The logic was that there realistically were not enough homes left to be a considered a viable neighborhood anymore. That same year a Tax Increment District was designated for the whole Oneota Area to help finance some of the needed improvements to stimulate development.

This phase made way for Collalillo Drive to connect into the West Duluth Business Area. With that, all the necessary utilities were rerouted into the proper right-of-ways for service to all parcels and the publicly owned land could be packaged and sold for redevelopment purposes. At the same time some of the old railroad spurs routed through the area were removed to make parcelization of the land easier. It did not take long and additional development began to locate in the second section of the industrial park. The last remaining parcel was developed for the new campus of the Duluth Business University from its former downtown location.

Oneota II, the area to the east of 40th Avenue West has had the most recent attention and efforts are still underway to redevelop it. This is not a wholesale attack like the first two areas but rather a piecemeal approach. Residences are not being approached for acquisition. Businesses rather have been the focus. A preliminary plan has been drawn for the area to show how the parcels should be laid out within a future street pattern. At some point in the future, the circulation system will be revamped. In the meantime, parcel layout and configurations are being made to not pre-empt the future construction of the new streets and roads. While some businesses have moved out of the area, others have moved on to new facilities. An example of this is when Wickland Collision Center moved out and the Fastenal Company moved in.

In the early 1980s further redevelopment of the West Duluth area continued with the establishment of the Lake Superior Paper Industries plant by Minnesota Power and Pentair Corp. at the site of the former Chun King plant and a scrap yard. This multimillion dollar project created the need for preparation of the "West Duluth Plan—Opportunities for Change." SVCNDA's next challenge became how to balance the need for industrial/commercial development areas and still protect the residential fabric of the neighborhood. I-35, the West Duluth Business Area and the Lake Superior Paper plant projects had required the acquisition and relocation of hundreds of residences. In many cases, relocation sites were not found in the neighborhood. Much to the credit of the SVCNDA, the implementation of many of the recommendations of the plan prepared in 1988 were accomplished within a relatively few years after the plan was adopted by the city council. The area was designated as a Tax Increment Financing (TIF) district, which assisted with the financing of many of the projects. This was one of the more successful TIF districts in the city.

While some of the redevelopment in the West Duluth area was agency driven, the success of many of the projects can be attributed to the dedicated tenacity of the business interests and the residents of the area who banded together to see to it that the projects fit the area and would not detract from their neighborhood, and more importantly were accomplished in a timely fashion.

A final footnote to the assembly of much of this material is that when Mark Flaherty completed the 1963 study "Highways, Opportunities and Land Use Controls," Mn/DOT felt comfortable enough to allow him to continue at the local level with the formation of a staff to undertake the Duluth-Superior Metropolitan Area Planning and Transportation Study. That effort began in 1964 and continued until 1968. During that time the office established the Head of the Lakes Council of Governments headquartered in the Duluth City Hall. Eventually that division spun off into a fully independent organization that is now ARDC (Arrowhead Regional Development Commission) which has a Metropolitan Interstate Committee that attends to metropolitan transportation planning issues on a continuous basis. ∎

As a city planner, Bill Majewski worked on the acquisition of the industrial park lands for the area between 40th and 49th Avenues West, coordinating funding requests and Mn/DOT contracts, and providing city guidance to the HRA staff that was handling the property appraisal, acquisition and relocation activities. He also worked with the SVCNDA mainly in the preparation of the 1988 plan and for several years following its adoption. He retired from the City of Duluth Planning Department in 2001.

CHAPTER

37

Northwest Airlines Maintenance Base

A GOOD PROPOSAL AND PERSONAL RELATIONSHIPS LEAD TO A SUCCESSFUL PROJECT

by John A. Fedo

I've always felt that a successful economic development project started with a good business opportunity and concluded with a good business opportunity and a personal relationship.

This was very true with the success of the City of Duluth in locating a new A-320 Airbus Maintenance base in the city.

To begin at the beginning: in 1988, Duluth was experiencing the first results of a very intensive local economic development effort that was paying dividends. A series of projects were being completed or constructed that would create a new image and thousands of new jobs for Duluth. Only a few years earlier, Duluth had the dubious distinction of being cited with other

After intensive lobbying, legislation to bring the Northwest Airlines A-320 Base to Duluth passed in 1991. Attending the official signing of the bill were: (left to right) Alfred Checchi of Northwest Airlines, Congressman Jim Oberstar, Duluth Mayor John Fedo, Governor Arne Carlson. Standing behind the governor are St. Louis County Commissioner Gary Doty and Hermantown Mayor Wally Loberg.

rust belt cities as one of the "ten most distressed cities in the country." A national recession, the closure of a U.S. Air Base, the downturn of the northeastern Minnesota mining industry, the loss of several major employers including Jeno's Inc., local double digit unemployment and the abandonment of its core downtown by major retailers heading for the suburbs left Duluth gasping and struggling for survival.

A new approach and diversification had the city on a new course. With the successful location of a new state convention center, construction of a new $450 million paper plant, a new waterfront and a freeway project that would ultimately generate $350 million worth of direct and indirect construction in the downtown corridor, Duluth had a strategy that was directed to the future and a change of both substance and image.

The change was one of major consequences. It set the stage for further economic expansion.

In 1988, Northwest Airlines Chairman Steve Rothmeier stated

Milwaukee, Memphis, Detroit, Nashville, Miami, Denver and Minneapolis-St. Paul were all listed as potential sites. Duluth wasn't on anybody's list.

that the company was looking for a location for a new maintenance facility to service a series of new A-320 Airbus planes. Rothmeier's personal choice was Milwaukee, Wisconsin despite the fact that Northwest's headquarters was in Minnesota. The issue of his site preference became moot, however, when Northwest Airlines was acquired by a new ownership group headed by Alfred Checchi, Gary Wilson and Fred Mahlik.

The maintenance base siting, however, was still a priority for the new owners of Northwest and a site location was a headline story in most major cities across the country that fit the airline's profile. Milwaukee, Memphis, Detroit, Nashville, Miami, Denver and Minneapolis-St. Paul were all listed as potential sites. Duluth wasn't on anybody's list.

However, Hal Greenwood, a frequent Duluth visitor and the chair of the Metropolitan Airports Commission felt that Duluth fit the parameters of the airline's site needs. When I quizzed him, he gave me several contact names at Northwest to pursue. We enlisted the assistance of several partners in this effort. Some of the first were the Duluth Chamber of Commerce and its director David Cordeau; Thomas Micheletti, vice president of public affairs for Minnesota Power; and Duluth industrialist Jeno Paulucci; as well as a team of city employees headed up by planning and economic development director David Sebok and finance director David Talbot.

This core group was the beginning of a very large community effort that extended beyond Duluth's borders to surrounding communities including a group of local officials on the Iron Range.

Our plan was a simple, straightforward one—to put together a factual presentation on the merits of a Duluth location that Northwest could not ignore, and then get that presentation in front of the decision makers. At first, it seemed simple.

We began with a list of assets that included the Duluth Airport and former Duluth Airbase, extremely sophisticated landing and weather detection equipment, the longest airstrip in the State of Minnesota, minimal air traffic conflicts, free land available adjacent to runways, a lower cost of living for employees relocating to our area, and a creative financing package. We added another strategy, calling for an engine repair facility to be part of the project. We proposed that the engine repair facility could be located at the Hibbing Airport industrial park, thereby sharing the benefit with the Iron Range. This strategy expanded our base of support.

Tom Micheletti and I went to meet with a group of mayors and local officials in Virginia, asking for their support and assistance, and we saw our team expand again. The next step was to contact Governor Rudy Perpich and present our proposal. His first reaction after hearing our detailed proposal was, while it made sense, the existing employees at Northwest would be unwilling to relocate to Duluth. However, he became convinced Duluth was the best site when we presented him with an employee survey that indicated they were fairly enthusiastic about the relocation possibility. Our team now had a statewide leader who could help open doors because of his bias for northeastern Minnesota.

The team moved on to Washington and a meeting with our Congressman, Jim Oberstar. The governor, Tom Micheletti and I met with Jim in his office. His concerns were less about competition with the rest of the country than with Minneapolis/St. Paul. As the highest-ranking Democrat on the House Transportation Committee with a special focus on air transportation issues, he did not want to see the two largest airports in Minnesota squaring off against each other. We all agreed and said that we would try to work out an amicable solution and still pursue the project.

On a parallel track we were continuing to work our way up the chain of command at Northwest. We had help from the local Northwest representative in identifying who and how we could get specific access to present our proposal. This was critical help! We finally had an opportunity to make a presentation in Northwest's Eagan, Minnesota headquarters. We had assembled a very large and detailed presentation package and the presentation went extremely well. Our effort paid off and we began to be acknowledged in the media as a viable contender for the site location.

Our next effort was to gather and expand our local working team. On a Saturday morning in March 1990, we invited approximately 75 local community, business, education, medical and union leaders to the Holiday Inn to seek their pledge of time and resources to the project.

Next, we prepared and presented a full competitive proposal outlining the advantages of a Duluth site. This was done in the context of both the business proposal and the strengths of our community including our quality of life, schools, etc. The city staff members who prepared the package did a phenomenal job. We collected information with help from throughout the community and assembled one of the finest presentation packages I've ever seen. It was both graphically and business-wise just superb! There were formal competitive presentations at Northwest headquarters by all competing communities.

THE PERSONAL RELATIONSHIPS

The new ownership group presented another opportunity to offer the best case on behalf of Duluth. Alfred Checchi was a very high-profile personality and he was making a number of personal appearances on behalf of the new Northwest leadership. Duluth has an annual Hall of Fame dinner to honor outstanding citizen contributions by individuals over a lifetime and it was suggested that Alfred Checchi should be invited as the guest speaker. It was a perfect opportunity to present our community and to develop a personal contact.

When Checchi arrived in Duluth, I had a chance to take him on a tour of the city in a helicopter and explain our community's offer "up close and personal." This was very effective. Before the dinner, I presented the City's package directly to Checchi in a meeting in the mayor's office and Jeno Paulucci took the opportunity to also strike up a personal relationship at that time. Checchi did a marvelous job at the dinner and he and his wife were charming and very much at ease in the public setting. They were an immediate hit in the community.

Over the course of the next several months Jeno and I both separately and together took every available opportunity to contact Al Checchi to persuade him about the merits of our site. In October of 1990, Jeno, as one of the founding members of the Italian American Foundation, asked Al to speak at the annual dinner in Washington D.C. Again, Checchi was a hit. We were closing in on the selection of Duluth on two fronts: the business side and the personal side.

In November of 1990, Arne Carlson was elected governor and we immediately made a pitch to him on the Duluth site. Congressman Jim Oberstar organized a meeting at the Duluth Airport with the governor and our team representatives. The governor had been briefed in advance and he was quickly up to speed and was a very strong proponent. He also helped us sort out the conflict between the Metropolitan Airports Commission St. Paul-Minneapolis site and Duluth.

At the governor's recommendation, a bill was being prepared to be introduced in the 1991 legislature that would finance, through a State of Minnesota loan guarantee, the construction of the A-320 maintenance facility in Duluth and an engine repair facility in Hibbing. It was decided that Duluth was the State of Minnesota site based on a negotiated package that included $350 million bonds to build Duluth ($250 million) and Hibbing ($100 million) facilities. The rest of the competition from other states began to either fall away or were eliminated by Northwest until we found ourselves standing alone as the site.

At this time, I was in Washington D.C. to attend a mayor's conference, and Al Checchi happened to be there as well. We met for breakfast at the Hay Addams Hotel where he was staying. He wanted to make a commitment to the Duluth site but wondered what the possibility was for the Minnesota Legislature to finance the $350 million base construction and also refinance $320 million in Northwest debt in exchange for an absolute guarantee to continue its gate presence at the Minneapolis/St. Paul Airport and other improvements in their Minneapolis/St. Paul operation. My first reaction was surprise at the proposal but realizing that the bases were going to be tied to the refinance proposal, offered several suggestions on how we might introduce the concept without being blown out of the water by opponents.

From that point on and for the next six months we were on a dead run through the State legislative process. Our City of Duluth staff and lobbyists, chamber staff, the governor's staff, Department of Revenue, NWA staff and lobbyists outlined who were supporters and opponents, developed strategy, gave testimony, did interviews, fended off misinformation and criticism right down to the day of the final House and Senate votes. Senators Roger Moe, Doug Johnson and Sam Solon had done a magnificent job, but on Saturday afternoon we were getting rumors that Attorney General Skip Humphrey was working behind the scenes and knew State Auditor Mark Dayton was publicly questioning the package. The vote was scheduled in both houses on the following Monday morning and we had 36 hours to finish with a full court press and hope the votes we knew were there didn't slip away. We called on labor. I called Fred Salo, President of the Duluth Building Trades and also called the Steel Workers on the Iron Range. We were able to put together several full buses that left Duluth and the Range at 4:30 a.m. Monday. They met flight and mechanics union members from the Twin Cities at 8:30 a.m. at the capitol, and began to make the rounds of legislative offices, Humphrey's office and Dayton's office. We then posted everyone outside both chambers, lobbied and waited.

It worked: the bill passed and NWA A-320 Base was coming to Duluth.

There were provisions in the bill that demanded that a specific number of jobs (250-450) be created over a ramp-up period in order for NWA to receive tax credits and other benefits. During the 1992 legislative session, the due diligence required in the bill was completed and the State Dept. of Revenue authorized issuance of the bonds for construction and refinance but the engine maintenance facility in Hibbing became a Reservation Center in Chisholm that now employs 575.

This project is a testament to a community that would not be denied and the fact that it is both the deal and the personal relationships that create a successful project. ∎

John A. Fedo was mayor of Duluth 1980-1992. John and Lori now live at Side Lake, north of Hibbing, Minn. John is an economic development consultant and Lori is executive director of the Hibbing Chamber of Commerce.

CHAPTER

38

Cirrus Design Corporation

A BOLD NEW AIRPLANE DESIGN
TAKES FLIGHT IN DULUTH

by Kate Andrews

During the early '80s, amid the throes of devastating decline in the general aviation industry, two brothers barely out of college were diligently plotting their course to aviation greatness. Cirrus Design Corporation began when these two young men glanced upward at a blue sky sporting cirrus clouds over Baraboo, Wisconsin, and in a gutted dairy barn the brothers' dream took flight.

To Alan and Dale Klapmeier, the idea of starting a company would not be considered unusual, as their parents were also entrepreneurs. What was unusual was their decision to enter an industry known for not taking kindly to young upstarts. This was not a deterrent for the Klapmeiers, perhaps due to their youthful enthusiasm. To Alan and Dale it was quite simple; bring to market a "modern" airplane, with fundamental changes in interior design, safety and ease of operation.

Cirrus Design

Cirrus Design founders Dale (with sunglasses) and Alan Klapmeier, during the
Cirrus Owners and Pilots Association - Minnesota Migration in June of 2003.
Over 80 Cirrus aircraft flew in from all over the U.S. for the occasion.

The first aircraft designed by Cirrus Design was a kit plane called the
VK30. When introduced at EAA AirVenture in 1987, the futuristic
looking aircraft with the propeller on the tail drew large crowds. The
innovativeness of the VK30 also attracted a handful of bright, creative and
talented engineers and an equally dedicated mechanical support staff into
thinking that a renovated dairy barn in Baraboo was a fine place to work.

The VK30 program gained popularity and momentum, but the
company was outgrowing the confined spaces of the barn and Baraboo
airport. With the practice of the VK30 under their belts, the Klapmeiers
determined it was now time for them to do what they had envisioned all
along; design, FAA certify and manufacture a new "generation" of general
aviation aircraft. But they would have to move.

The magnitude and potential of such a project dazzled various Midwest communities and their local economic development authorities. On the other hand, here were two young men who had never done this before, in an industry that had a history of failure. Grand Forks, North Dakota had agreed to provide the necessary finance package for the company to relocate within their community. As the closing day grew closer, uncertainty set in with Grand Forks and the deal began to unravel. New suitors needed to be found and fast, as time was flying and Cirrus Design Corp. needed a home.

Duluth Mayor Gary Doty was extremely interested in growing the economic base for the city. Job growth was sorely needed in Duluth with businesses closing or moving away because of consolidation. Mayor Doty was contacted by Cirrus and informed that the Grand Forks deal had collapsed. What was bad news for the Klapmeiers became very good news for Mayor Doty and the City of Duluth.

Mayor Doty "got it"—he understood the Klapmeiers' vision and Duluth was the perfect fit. Cirrus was a young and growing company, offering a high-end product and good jobs within a new industry that could spur other growth. The mayor swung into action and quickly amassed a team to develop the incentives necessary for Cirrus to locate in Duluth. Much to the amazement of everyone on both sides, the deal was struck, and signed in an unheard-of short period of time. The "air-conditioned city" was now home to Cirrus Design Corporation.

The first phase of development commenced in 1993, with the construction of a 32,000 square foot building to house the company's headquarters and their research and development facility. Upon its completion on January 1, 1994, 32 employees who had as much grit and determination as the Klapmeiers moved into the new structure, and began

> Mayor Doty "got it"—he understood the Klapmeiers' vision and Duluth was the perfect fit.

working on the first prototype aircraft that would obtain a Type Certificate, the SR20.

The SR20 prototype was developed over the course of the next year with great excitement and anticipation of its maiden flight. And fly it did with great success. So encouraged by the flight test results with the first aircraft, a second, more refined prototype was added to the flight test program. Things were looking up for the new company and they needed more space.

Phase Two of development initiated in 1996 included breaking ground for a new facility in Grand Forks, North Dakota, encompassing 67,500 square-feet of manufacturing space and expansion of the of the Duluth facility by an additional 114,000 sq. ft. The time had come to officially submit the application for the FAA FAR Part 23 Type Certification. Two more aircraft were required to complete the certification process. Now Cirrus Design had to learn to become a manufacturing company.

A Type Certification for a general aviation aircraft is so costly and time consuming that it is rarely done. Alan and Dale believed so strongly in their mission to revitalize general aviation and the importance of that success, it never occurred to them they wouldn't succeed. Time was moving on, however, and a development project that would be costly in time and money commenced—the innovative device that would make Cirrus aircraft like no other when it comes to safety. This safety system became known as the Cirrus Airframe Parachute System (CAPS). All Cirrus airplanes would carry the system designed to lower the entire aircraft to the ground in case of pilot or aircraft incapacity. Even the FAA would wonder about this. Time was ticking: it was the end of 1997 and the first "production prototype" was preparing for its maiden flight and the second "production prototype" was on the line. Things could be worse after all; certification was getting closer to reality.

In the meantime, the word was out in the industry that Cirrus was successfully making their way to certification and the SR20 would be the plane to own. Everything that had been missing in traditionally designed

Continued on page 270

How we convinced Cirrus to pick Duluth

by Gary Doty

The mayor of Grand Forks, ND, could easily be writing this column about how his city attracted Cirrus Design's headquarters to town. In 1993, Cirrus founders Alan and Dale Klapmeier were in the very last stages of negotiations to build their aviation facility in Grand Forks.

But then we in Duluth got wind of this opportunity—granted, it was late in the game when we heard of it—and we decided that with everything we had to offer, we weren't going to take no for an answer.

Duluth's pitch began with me calling Bill King, a Cirrus leader I remembered vaguely from his days as a city manager in Waconia, Minn. Perhaps as a courtesy to a former government colleague, King arranged a visit between the Klapmeiers and me.

I went to their home in Baraboo, Wis., and told them there's no reason to go anywhere else. I said Duluth has the workforce, the airport and the desire to make Cirrus succeed. Maybe because they thought I must have been exaggerating, they agreed to take a tour of our city.

That's when I told a whole lot of community leaders that I needed their help, and I needed it right away before Cirrus chose Grand Forks. Everyone dove in.

Dale flew into town and we had a helicopter waiting for him, courtesy of Minnesota Power. It was a perfect, sunny, blue-sky day as we showed off our beautiful city from the air.

We landed in the DECC parking lot and walked inside to a lunch with an impressive group of business and labor leaders. They're the ones who really sold the city—as they always do when we're trying to attract businesses to town—each telling stories of how Duluth's stable and productive workforce was a big reason for their success.

From that day on, we literally had non-stop, daily contact with Cirrus to get them to move here. The city's business development staff put together a potential package in record time. City support included staged tax increment financing, preparation of the 14-acre site, 1200 Fund loans, and SBA loan guarantees. The City also pledged to endorse applications for financing by the Northeast Minnesota Initiative Fund, Minnesota Power Revolving Loan Fund, and Northeast Ventures. The State of Minnesota also assembled a program of grants and loans with City encouragement.

I took Cirrus on as my own personal project. This was the kind of high-tech development Duluth needed, and I could feel we had a real chance. I let them know

Continued on page 271

aircraft seemed to be present in the SR20 and orders were amassing. Some who paid the down payment to reserve a position did so knowing they may not ever receive a plane—such was the excitement incurred by the gutsy Cirrus Team.

The down payments for aircraft did not cover the growing costs being incurred. As the manufacturing of an airframe made of composite materials had never been done before, Cirrus needed to certify all of the composite components required to actually manufacture the aircraft.

In October of 1998, at a cost of $40 million, 3 1/2 years, and with 142 employees on the payroll, Cirrus Design received the FAA Type Certification. Now the company needed to produce them and at what cost? An additional $35 million was ultimately required to simply get the first production aircraft off the production line. But they sold like hotcakes. Hundreds of orders were now in back log and those who had taken delivery of a SR20 were extolling the virtues of the wonderful new aircraft. From the outside, Cirrus appeared a huge success, though reality painted a much different picture.

> The financial industry did little to help this brainchild... "Business suits" from big cities would come and go with promises of funding that none of them would keep.

Since this particular type of aircraft had never been manufactured before, chances were slim that someone could be found quickly to help Alan and Dale ramp up. It is not that Cirrus was doing badly in the production arena; it was that Cirrus was not doing it quickly enough. Orders continued to accumulate in backlog, but the massive project had eaten away, bit by bit any monies that had been raised up to that point. Time and time again, various recourses were tapped to keep the company afloat. Grants, loans, another round of stock offered, and frustrated but faithful customers became shareholders. A

CIRRUS TO PICK DULUTH
Continued from page 269

second model aircraft, with increased performance and increased profit margins, was needed to take the burden off the company. The SR22 was born.

In the meantime, the new millennium was approaching and general aviation was enjoying a comeback. Sales of new and used aircraft were up, more students were enrolled in flight schools and the Cirrus SR22 moved through certification relatively well. Actually, compared to the SR20, it seemed seamless. New orders for the new model rolled in and the SR22 was heralded as "latest and greatest" in the industry. Now to learn how to build them!

The financial industry did little to help this brainchild. Alan had taken on the responsibility to raise the funds and "dot-com's" were all the rage. "Business suits" from big cities would come and go with promises of funding that none of them would keep. Never ones to waiver or give up, and with the responsibility for over 600 employees, Alan and Dale made payroll their priority, and payroll was met on time. The waiting list of customers grew to 400, an enviable position for any company in the general aviation industry. However, the tremendous burden of certification and ramp up had taken a toll and the company faced lay-offs. Eventually, the Klapmeiers would have to make a decision to stop production of the SR20, and only produce the higher profit margin model, the SR 22. The search for financing continued, and albeit slowly, Cirrus aircraft rolled off the production line, customers loved them, and new

I was here to address any challenges they had, including visiting Washington, D.C., with them a couple of times.

My relationship with Alan and Dale quickly progressed from strictly business to also become a friendship. One thing that made this high-stakes project such a pleasure is that the Klapmeiers are regular people who simply had a dream. They didn't have someone else negotiating for them. They were always forthright and honest. They never kept anything from me, and conversely I never kept anything from them.

When they told us that we'd convinced them—that they were bringing the future of aviation to Duluth—we let out a cheer all around the city. Then we got back to working hard to ensure we delivered what we said we would. We— hundreds of people in the community—kept our promises just as the people of Cirrus are keeping theirs.

Gary Doty
Mayor of Duluth, 1991-2003

orders continued.

Finally in the fall of 2001, Crescent Capital, an Atlanta Georgia investment company, committed $101 million to secure Cirrus' future. With this new partnership, Cirrus was able to ramp-up production to its current production level of two aircraft every business day. Another building phase was completed in October 2002, when a 63,000 plus sq. ft. expansion called Cirrus Customer Center opened for business.

Internationally, Cirrus Design, headquartered in Duluth, Minnesota, is now the second largest manufacturer of general aviation, four-place, single-engine aircraft in the world. Cirrus Airframe Parachute System proved its worth when in October of 2002 a SR22 pilot became the first person in a certified aircraft to be saved by a parachute system. As of August 2003, there are over 1,000 Cirrus aircraft owners located all over the world, with both Cirrus models receiving numerous international awards and recognitions. Worldwide, the Cirrus SR22 was the single most popular aircraft sold throughout all of 2002.

Today, there are over 820 people employed by Cirrus, with more than 600 in Duluth alone. The company produced 478 airplanes in 2003, with anticipated sales revenues of just over $125 million. At a time when lay-offs are commonplace in the aviation industry since September 11, 2001, Cirrus continues to hire, sell and produce. The industry now looks to Cirrus for leadership in the research and development of general aviation technology.

Alan and Dale Klapmeier continue to be the ever-vigilant guardians of a vision that took flight. What they knew intuitively is now being validated with success that is rarely achieved—and only by those who dare. ∎

Kate Dougherty Andrews, communication manager for Cirrus Design Corporation, has been with the company since 1998.

CHAPTER

39

Soft Center

TEAMWORK BUILDS DOWNTOWN TECHNOLOGY CAMPUS INSPIRED BY SWEDISH MODEL

by Kjell R. Knudsen

In 1991, Ernst and Young did a study for a consortium of Arrowhead region economic development interests. The study suggested that one target of 21st Century manufacturing jobs would be "industrial controls."

Upon doing some preliminary research, it was discovered that industrial controls actually referred to computer software (a new industry at the time), with great potential due to its annual growth rate of 20%.

By 1994, an area business development organization called TEAM Duluth first attempted to recruit software businesses to the area using the abandoned US West Building, as a magnet in a project called the Duluth Technology Center. The Duluth Technology Center was operated by the University of Minnesota Duluth through its Center for Economic

Development, with assistance from Minnesota Technology Inc., a statewide technology organization. Lake Superior College was also involved in the Duluth Technology Center with its Flexlab program.

In 1995, one of Duluth's sister cities, Vaxjo, Sweden, invited the Duluth Area Chamber of Commerce to send a delegation to Vaxjo to talk about business opportunities.

For years, Duluth and Vaxjo had been doing educational and cultural exchanges. Now Vaxjo wanted to look at the possibility of doing some international economic development.

The delegation from Duluth consisted of Mark Mansfield, president of the Chamber of Commerce, Jim Roberts of Minnesota Power, Andy McDonough of the Duluth Seaway Port Authority, Greg Fox of the University of Minnesota and chair of the Chamber's board of directors and Mike McNamara.

Following the group's arrival in Vaxjo, the delegation was surprised to find that the sister city was about ten years ahead of Duluth in technology development and had approximately 100 software companies.

The hosts in Vaxjo suggested that the delegation travel to two small cities, Ronneby and Karlskona, as part of their itinerary.

Located on the Baltic seacoast about 80 miles south of Vaxjo, Ronneby and Karlskona are, ironically, referred to as the Twin Ports, like Duluth and Superior.

In Ronneby, the delegation found one of the premiere information technology projects in Europe, "Soft Center," an ultra-modern campus with more than 100 companies co-located with 1,800 software students. The director of Soft Center explained that their Twin Ports, like ours, had been dependent on a heavy industrial base, but, ten years earlier their largest company, a foundry, had closed.

After two years of unsuccessfully trying to bring in other heavy industry, the community leaders decided to take a bold move into the future and began the work to create a software industry.

The Soft Center development was everything that Duluth had hoped its Technology Center would become. The delegation asked Soft Center if they would mentor Duluth in its pursuits toward software technology development.

Perhaps because of the strong ethnic ties between Minnesota and Sweden, they agreed and sent the delegation home with considerable information.

The next year, representatives from the Duluth Seaway Port Authority, Duluth Area Chamber of Commerce and TEAM Duluth traveled to Sweden with Governor Arne Carlson's delegation celebrating the Golden Jubilee of the Swedish migration to America. Again, Soft Center, which had continued to grow, adding companies and students, was visited.

That fall, a delegation from Soft Center traveled to Duluth and an official partnership agreement linking the Duluth Technology Center and Soft Center Ronneby was signed.

The major break came the following summer when Mayor Gary Doty, after hearing so much about the project, traveled to Soft Center Ronneby and asked the Swedes if they would consider franchising the Soft Center concept in Duluth.

After nine months of negotiations, Duluth, with the help of the State of Minnesota, entered into an agreement to build a Soft Center.

During the same time frame, the University of Minnesota Duluth (UMD) was exploring the possibility of creating a technology park. The university developed the concept for the Duluth Technology Village to be located on the block directly east of Lake Avenue and north of Superior Street in downtown Duluth.

Eventually the two ideas converged and the Soft Center project was considered as the anchor tenant for the Duluth Technology Village.

The Duluth Economic Development Authority (DEDA), one of the TEAM Duluth partners, advertised for a developer and after receiving several proposals selected A & L Development, a local developer aggressive in Duluth's commercial development market.

A plan for a tax increment district that included the acquisition and demolition of several blighted properties on the site was developed. On September 9, 1998 ground was broken and the building was completed in the spring of 2000. By the summer of that year, two educational facilities had relocated in the building, UMD's Center for Economic Development and Lake Superior College's Technology Center. In addition, seven technology companies, including Applied Interventions, eSystems21, Scan Health, United Health Care, AppRight, Knight-Ridder.com and Saturn systems had located in the building.

A&L Development and Salomon, Smith Barney had also moved in. DEDA had signaled its intention to lease 10,000 square feet to house Soft Center offices, an interactive classroom and an incubator.

In 1999 Soft Center Duluth was presented with the prestigious Global Bangemann IT Challenge Award for its office campus in the Best New Business Structure category. The award was presented by the King of Sweden on June 9, 1999 in a ceremony at Nobel Hall in Stockholm. In 2000, the project received the Techne Award in the Partnership Category by Minnesota Technology Inc. and the Minnesota High Technology Association.

The Soft Center Duluth/Duluth Technology Village project has not been without its difficulties. Soft Center has gone through several changes in management and board members, there has been and continue to be funding challenges, and the crisis in the technology sector of the economy has had its impact. However, the Duluth Technology Village is today host to a substantial number of technology-based companies and three educational institutions have facilities in the building including UMD, Lake Superior College and University of Wisconsin Superior. It may be true that the project has not yet fulfilled all of the hopes and expectations the community had for it, but we continue to believe it has had a positive impact on the community and that the last chapter has yet to be written. ∎

Dr. Kjell Knudsen is dean of the University of Minnesota Duluth Labovitz School of Business & Economics.

40

Great Lakes Aquarium

REVEALING THE SECRETS AND MAGIC OF FRESH WATER AND THE GREATEST LAKE

by Donn Larson

Our region has many economic and environmental assets—forests, minerals, parks, abundant water, recreation, education, health and cultural resources, but the most magnetic and valuable of all is Lake Superior. More than any other single factor, it is Lake Superior that attracts people and supports our economy.

We who make the headwaters our home, and all who visit, share a fascination with this greatest lake. Regardless of your view about the extent and appropriateness of development in the watershed, there is clearly one thing about Lake Superior that is *under*developed: our knowledge of its importance and many secrets. The Great Lakes Aquarium is dedicated to "capturing the wonder and excitement of Lake Superior, inspiring responsibility for the world's largest lakes and fresh

Great Lakes Aquarium opened in the summer of 2000. Located on the site where a ship chandlery once stood, and later home to the Flame restaurant, the architectural style of the aquarium echoes the industrial style of buildings once common along Duluth's historic waterfront.

water and creating an understanding of their value": this is our aquarium's mission, and commitment. How did we win such an important institution for our community?

In the 1960s, physical and economic reform began to change Duluth's central business district and waterfront. The deteriorating western gateway to downtown and vestiges of commerce and rail transportation around Fifth Avenue West were leveled in an ambitious, federally financed urban renewal program. This opened space for redevelopment, inspired the siting of a new arena and auditorium and stirred up fresh ideas for the highest and best renewal opportunities, now at the terminus of a new freeway from the south. People who loved the lake began to feel that it was no longer right for the waterfront to be our back door.

Julia and Caroline Marshall, Duluth philanthropists with ideas and resolve, sowed the seeds that eventually sprouted and grew to become the

Great Lakes Aquarium

Lake Superior, up close and personal. Great Lakes Aquarium's largest tank is part of the Isle Royale exhibit, which can be viewed from two levels. Visitors come face-to-face with the ancient sturgeon, our local "dinosaur" and Lake Superior's largest resident.

Aquarium. In 1977 the Marshall sisters were key players in forming the Bayfront Park Development Association, a private, non-profit citizens' group. With the sisters' large contribution, augmented by gifts and vouchers from many Duluth families and businesses, the Association bought 15 acres from Marvin Meierhoff for $800,000. In 1984 the group purchased the Flame restaurant building, originally a waterfront ship chandlery, from Ben Overman, Iz Crystal, Prof Davis, George Berman and Louie King. By 1986 Bayfront was the debt-free owner of land needed to pursue the sisters' dream. Julia and Caroline's vision for a magical place that would introduce people to the lake was becoming clear.

During the late '70s and early '80s, the Association contracted with its first employee, Robert Reichert. The group won a federal grant to develop sketch plans and began to talk about a place for interpreting the Northland's special natural assets. I remember Don Shank, president of the DM&IR, promoting ideas for "Minnesota Center" on the lunch club circuit. In 1984 boosters of this concept merged their ideas with a group of lake advocates who imagined a place for the public to learn about Lake Superior. They were stimulated by the success of exhibits at the New England Aquarium. Also, Shank and UMD Chancellor Robert Heller had been inspired by a visit to the National Aquarium at Baltimore. Lake Superior Center was named and taking shape.

In 1985, supported by the Duluth Improvement Trust (a small group of advisors chosen by the Marshall sisters to assist with their philanthropy), the Association hired Bob Bruce, a member of the Duluth City Planning staff, as executive director. Development of Bayfront now began with new vigor, and attention turned to Lake Superior Center in earnest. Deaton Museum Services of Minneapolis, ultimately the Aquarium's principal exhibit contractor, submitted preliminary ideas for making our lake a *lens* to focus on all the world's fresh water. During this period we also looked at other sites, but eventually came back to the two-acre parcel at the Flame building, which became our temporary home.

In 1989 we incorporated as a private nonprofit corporation, chose a founding board of directors composed of educators, environmental activists and business people, and announced our intention to build Lake Superior Center as a joint public and private effort. Nick Smith was our founding chair. Throughout our seminal years, Nick held fast to a course that would fulfill Julia and Caroline's wishes. At the outset, we explored ways to promote international stewardship of fresh water, setting up a sister lake relationship with Lake Baikal in Russia. We sought but failed to win a $20 million grant from the U.S. Environmental Protection Agency.

We began practicing our educational purpose in 1991, with Superior Lakewatch, a lake-wide network for testing and recording water clarity. The Center began networking with other environmental education places and programs. Soon, with help from the Blandin Foundation, we reached out to schools with a traveling curriculum and invited classes to our preview exhibits at the Flame building. We also recruited an expert panel to review qualifications of architectural firms. They picked Holt Hinshaw Architects, San Francisco, from a national field of 40 candidates.

In April 1992 the Minnesota legislature granted us $2 million in the state bonding bill for design and engineering work. The Lake Superior Center Authority, a public corporation previously created by the legislature to build but not operate the Center, received this money. Governor Arne Carlson appointed directors[1] to the Authority in June of that year, and in November, we elected a new chair, Arend Sandbulte. Sandy, CEO of Minnesota Power, would prove our premise that we needed a person of his influence as we entered a period of serious fundraising.

The citizens of Duluth became major stakeholders in January 1993, when Mayor Gary Doty announced "at least" $5 million in support. This helped our appeal for further private and public contributions and allowed the board to authorize Holt Hinshaw to continue design work. Nevertheless, we were still far short of our need and dismayed when we again missed out on a federal grant. Flooding on the Mississippi and other needs more pressing than environmental education overwhelmed the U.S. Army Corps of Engineers' budget, where we'd hoped to find $8 million.

Those were stressful times, but we managed to stay afloat with a $4 million appropriation from the legislature in 1994 and a $144,000 pledge for program development from the Blandin Foundation. Corporate and private gifts were growing now, too. Leadership pledges from Minnesota Power, US Bank, Lakehead Pipe Line Company and others helped us reach over $3 million in private contributions and loans with favorable terms. To operate more efficiently we combined our two governing units, the state-appointed authority and non-profit board[2]. Late in 1995 Bob Bruce resigned to accept a post at Northland College after guiding us through six formative years. One of his final tasks was to set up a plan for changing architects as the design-development stage was winding down. We picked Hammel Green & Abrahamson (HGA) of Minneapolis. The two firms cooperated well to make the transition go smoothly. HGA was a finalist in our initial search, had studied the project's objectives, was

[1] Original appointees were Cindy Hayden, Rod Sando, Tom Spence, Cindy Jepson and Robert Carlson.
[2] The State Authority and the non-profit board separated again in 2001.

closer to the action and agreed to retain Holt Hinshaw's exterior "Duluth vernacular" design, which reflected shapes from our historic industrial waterfront and Lake Superior colors taken from Craig Blacklock photography.

While we scoured the nation for a new executive director, Amy Wiedman and Bob Scott filled in to help with lobbying and administrative responsibilities. By late summer of '96 our search committee completed its interviews and recommended David Lonsdale, deputy director of Chicago's Shedd Aquarium, to join the project and build a fresh water aquarium with unique appeal. David had just completed work on a major expansion of the Shedd and was ready for a new challenge. We will always be indebted to him for the integrity of our exhibits.

A funding milestone was reached in 1996, too. Intensive lobbying and support by key members of the Duluth legislative delegation brought another $10 million pledge from the state. We were still about $4 million short of our goal. The shortfall was reduced by changing or deferring some of our plans and realizing that we would either need to raise more money, accept some debt or both. The reality, however, was that the state's pledge would not be released until we could prove we had enough money to finish the project. And further, a frivolous lawsuit, escalating prices, a shortage of structural steel and other factors were relentlessly delaying a start and upping the ante.

In 1997 HGA completed the building design. We began to call ourselves the Great Lakes Aquarium at Lake Superior Center. The clouds of uncertainty parted when the City of Duluth and the Duluth Economic Development Authority (DEDA) assembled a $10 million package of grants and loans, partly underwritten by US Bank. On June 29, Mayor Gary Doty swung the wrecking ball to start demolition of the Flame building. We moved our offices to the UMD limnology lab at the Lester River, and leased space as a holding area for live exhibits. Ann Glumac succeeded Arend Sandbulte as chair in November 1998. Duluth contractor Johnson-Wilson Constructors, teamed with Adolphson & Peterson of Minneapolis, began site preparation and pile driving in January 1999. After nearly ten years as students of planning and fundraising, we felt like this was graduation day. Commencement, however, is beginning, not completion. It would not be until mid-summer of 2000, that the unique new $33 million landmark on Duluth's waterfront would be dedicated and open, realizing the vision of Julia and Caroline Marshall and all who supported their desire for a special public place celebrating Lake Superior.

In September 2000, the Board selected Ann Glumac as president, allowing David Lonsdale to devote full time to science and education. Long-standing director John Anderson succeeded Ann as chair in this reorganization.

I'll have to accept the risk of omitting many important people, but would like this account to include a few more names of those whose high standards and perseverance were especially important to completion of the project: Chuck Koosman, our project manager; Denny Krenner, director of operations; Andrew Slade, education director; and Kay Nierengarten, financial deputy.

The aquarium was scheduled to open around Memorial Day in 2000. Due to an unexpected construction delay related to problems with concrete work on our centerpiece Isle Royale tank, we did not open until July 29, with the loss of much of the main visitor season and corresponding substantial loss of revenue. Further, a claim by the contractor for extra work on the Isle Royale tank required use of operating income to resolve the claim. These setbacks cast a cloud over operations and, regardless of how popular we were with visitors and citizens, there was a collective anxiety about how we could get everything in trim. Exercising its contractual responsibility, the City of Duluth took control of the Aquarium in October 2002. Among many further cutbacks, the City set a reduced winter schedule. Facing uncertainty about the facility's future, Ann Glumac chose to resign. Jon Driscoll became full-time director as a loaned executive from the Duluth-based hospitality company, Zenith Management Corporation. Zenith's Monnie Goldfine and attorney Harold Frederick contributed countless hours of advice and support during this stressful reorganization.

The quality of our aquarium and its validity are reflected daily in visitor interviews, teachers' responses, and membership renewals. Our community's leaders in government, environmental stewardship and the visitor industry have been steadfast in their support. In the fall of 2002 Mayor Doty appointed a task force of highly qualified and objective citizens to help us realize the aquarium's potential. It was chaired by Marti Buscaglia, publisher of the *Duluth News Tribune*. The task force's two main findings: the aquarium must be debt-free in order to succeed, and should seek a management contract with experienced aquarium operators. Ultimately, Ripley's Entertainment Corporation was chosen. During the transition year, 2003, Todd Torvinen and Cindy Hayden accepted stints as board chair. In its first summer season Ripley brought a wealth of operating knowledge to the aquarium. They kept their promise to maintain a strong education program, streamlined operations, substantially reduced costs, while emphasizing entertainment values. As peak summer tourism began to subside in the fall 2003, the Duluth Convention and Visitors Bureau released statistics on Duluth's visitor season. The Great Lakes Aquarium was the #1 paid attraction in Duluth.

To meet the task force's first recommendation, early in 2004 the Duluth City Council voted to forgive the aquarium's DEDA bond debt. This not only required no new tax commitment, it enabled laying out a plan for management, maintenance and the addition of new exhibits. Many people worked tirelessly on putting together this essential fresh start.

The aquarium was not the first Duluth venture to experience a rocky start-up. Several others featured in this book had early problems that needed attention and adjustment. Wouldn't it be disappointing if Duluth's leaders stopped taking risks? Be kind of boring, too. ∎

Donn Larson was a charter member of the Lake Superior Center Board. He served nine years and became the Aquarium's first Director Emeritus in 1998.

CHAPTER

41

Canal Park and Downtown Waterfront

OUR URBAN LAKESHORE
IS NO LONGER OUR BACK DOOR

by Jerry Kimball

The modern renaissance of American waterfronts from obsolete industrial areas to places that often define the identity of American communities was born in Baltimore's Harborplace and Boston's Faneuil Hall Marketplace in the early 1980s. Duluth was not far behind and was among the first cities to realize the quality of life and economic benefits of redefining its urban waterfront.

As head of the City's physical planning division, I had a unique opportunity for a city planner—to plan and coordinate implementation of Duluth's downtown waterfront project. This large-scale rehabilitation occurred mainly between 1985 and 1992 and extended from Interstate 35 to the water's edge, and from Bayfront Park to Leif Erikson Park. The heart of this area is Canal Park.

Before the Lakewalk, 1984, the Lake Superior shoreline where the hotels are today on Canal Park Drive.

Waterfront renaissance. Today, Duluthians and visitors from around the world enjoy the lakefront and its many parks and public spaces. "I love to walk the Lakewalk and overhear local folks talk about it," writes Jerry Kimball. "They sometimes...proudly describe how it was accomplished...it's music to my ears."

The City's decision in late 1984 to make our downtown waterfront the top planning and development priority was shaped by a 1983 citizen planning commission that sponsored a series of visioning forums called "Future City, Duluth Tomorrow." The *Downtown Waterfront Plan and Strategy* was published in early '86 and was 90% implemented by 1993.

THE FOUNDATION

The downtown waterfront project of the 1980s was successful because of a solid base of earlier work. The 1960s, '70s and early '80s produced an amazing display of civic activism that planted many vibrant seeds.

However, perhaps the earliest effort at change in this area occurred in the mid-1950s with the St. Croix redevelopment project, which was Duluth's first federal urban renewal program. It cleared many blighted structures east of what is now called Canal Park Drive and replaced them with light industrial uses and a motel. One of the leaders in this effort was Art King, who was a long-time member of the citizen Housing and Redevelopment Board (1948-'68). Art was a true local patriot and gave thousands of hours to his community. He was on many local boards and the King Manor housing complex is named for him.

Jeno Paulucci and others had steered the community to a consensus on the location for a new entertainment and sports venue. The Arena/Auditorium (now the Duluth Entertainment and Convention Center) opened in 1966.

Retired Corps of Engineer administrator Ralph Knowlton, Julia and Caroline Marshall, Bill Van Evera and others had a vision to offer visitors and Duluthians more reasons to love this city. The Canal Park Visitors Center opened in 1973. These citizens saw opportunity in capitalizing on the thousands of locals and visitors who were already watching the great ships of industry slowly, quietly but powerfully moving through the Duluth ship canal.

C. Patrick Labadie came to Duluth to direct the new museum and served the city and Corps of Engineers for 28 years. Although the book you are reading shows many examples of the spirit of private citizens driving the processes and projects that have built Duluth, it is important to recognize that public employees often are driven by much more than their professional responsibilities. Ralph Knowlton and Patrick Labadie are examples of this. It was always clear that their love for Duluth even after retirement drove them to want others to better understand the importance and uniqueness of our maritime history. It would be well for public administrators to seek employees who have such a devotion.[1]

Mick Paulucci and Andy Borg, Jr. had opened Grandma's Saloon and Grill in 1976 and along with their promotional attachment to Grandma's Marathon the next year, they emphatically introduced more Midwest visitors to Duluth's Canal Park. To this day they continue to add value to the Canal Park experience with their ongoing investments.

In 1979 Monnie and Erv Goldfine had purchased the excursion boat business that is now called the Vista Fleet. Rumor has it that it is not a major moneymaker, but that the brothers' community spirit always kept it going. Ted Gozanski, Hyman Kaner and Jimmy Oreck had operated the tour boats from 1959 to 1968 at the foot of 5th Avenue West next to the revered Flame Restaurant and understood visitors' deep interest in the activities and character of a working world port.

Another major foundation piece for the downtown waterfront project was the design compromise consensus that was reached for the freeway extension after decades of controversy. The citizens who so fervently fought original freeway plans were vilified by some as naysayers and praised by others who knew the design would have blocked access to the water. The controversy produced a much better, though delayed, freeway that provides water access never dreamed before. People like Julia and Caroline Marshall and many others made this possible with their contributions for detailed design refinement.

THE SUCCESS INDICATORS

The 1985 to 1992 Downtown Waterfront project enjoys several indicators of success.

One of the best ways to measure success of a large urban effort is the

---

[1] An excellent book has recently been published on the dynamics of Duluth's planning history (as well as those of four other American cities), covering impacts by citizen planning commissioners and community leaders as well as city planners. *Making Places Special—Stories of Real Places Made Better by Planning* by Gene Bunnell is published by the American Planning Association.

response from locals. Has it developed pride to the degree that most residents would say they have a better place in which to live—perhaps even a great place to live? I believe it is clear that Duluthians became more self confident and prideful after the waterfront improvements. I still love to walk the Lakewalk and overhear local folks talk about it. Often the Lakewalk is the first place they take visitors and they sometime seem to proudly describe how it was accomplished. It's music to my ears.

This local pride is a measurement of our individuality, the packaging of our unique local identity which is defined by our natural features, perhaps mostly by our waterfront.

Also important is our image from outside the city. With more people exploring our town the outside image has improved, and that has translated to increased investments and jobs. Examples are the Karpeles Manuscript Library Museum, United Health Group and Cirrus Design, each of which identified Duluth's waterfront and other preservation efforts as among the reasons they invested here.

I believe the Duluth downtown waterfront project helped uncover a love affair with Lake Superior. We have given much more attention to the lake, and she is paying us back. In 1990, Duluth jumped 30 places to number 21 out of 300 cities in *Money Magazine's* "Best Places to Live" survey, and in 1992 they ranked us number 14.

In 1993 the city of Duluth was awarded the international Waterfront Center's prestigious top honor award for excellence in waterfront development. In earlier years the center's awards were for major single construction projects, whereas Duluth was cited for consistency of quality and the totality of projects. In 1994 we were awarded the League of Minnesota Cities' First Place Achievement Award for the Canal Park streetscape development.

During those years (1985 to 1992) I sometimes felt that I and two of my staff, Bill Majewski and Jill Fisher, were spending too much time on the waterfront project. (I probably spent 70% of my time on this activity.) As the head of the city's physical planning function, I may have neglected other parts of the city, including zoning and other planning issues. However, I believed then as I do now that it was a good strategic decision.

Our local economy also improved, with dramatic changes in important indicators. From December 1991 to December 1994 there was a 90% increase in gross sales in Canal Park. The number of large conventions in Duluth increased from 12 in 1988 to 42 in 1997, in part due to the type of waterfront features that convention planners look for.

THE PLANNING PROCESS

The Downtown Waterfront project enjoyed both political and general citizen support—a factor not always evident in a city having so many citizens with passionate love of what already exists. I believe there was some luck with good alignment of stars. There were many highly committed advocates resulting from a planning process that stressed meaningful citizen involvement.

In 1983 the planning commission, chaired by Roy Holt, sponsored a citywide visioning program of six monthly forums. They included nationally known experts on urban issues. People such as author William H. Whyte, urban law expert Robert Freilich, journalist Neal R. Peirce and futurist Luther Gerlach presented ideas that were then discussed by participants. A broad based consensus emerged—that it was important to concentrate much more planning effort on the waterfront.

John Fedo was mayor of Duluth during this time. If John was sold on a project he feverishly pursued it. And he was effective in getting things done. John would go to mayors' conferences around the country bringing back ideas he thought would be helpful. David Sebok, Duluth's director of Planning and Development and my boss, had a background in planning and design and was skilled at packaging complicated funding resources that enabled the many construction projects to proceed.

Mayor Fedo authorized my travel to a number of cities in the U.S. and Canada that had redeveloped their waterfronts, to study what they had done and to try to learn from their successes and mistakes. Along the way, I took hundreds of photos which helped spur imagination and stimulate public interest in our project.

Our main consultants were from New York City: Buckhurst, Fish, Hutton and Katz and Pei Property Development Corporation (headed by the son of world renowned architect, I. M. Pei). They were steeped in economics and property development as well as urban design, architecture and facilitating public discussion. A key to their success was their understanding of the concept of doing a plan "with us" instead of "for us."

BFHK helped us organize four major citywide public "planning events" which consisted of roundtable discussions and brainstorming sessions. Average attendance was 130 citizens. People trusted this process, thereby resulting in supportive citizen ownership for both the plan and its implementation.

Another trust builder was the establishment of the Waterfront Contact Group that represented sixteen private and public organizations having specific interests in the waterfront to review the work of the consultants and to offer advice.

THE PRINCIPLES

It is much easier to create a plan than to implement it. It is also no fun to see it not implemented. So, the citizen-generated plan called for being true to our strengths with authentic interpretation of what constitutes our uniqueness. We wanted an action-oriented strategy with lots of energy and variety—a steady stream of improvements that would keep the interest vital.

We were aware of many creative features at other city's waterfronts, but we concentrated on what would work best in Duluth. We wanted change, but only if it nurtured our uniqueness. We wanted quality, which we addressed through attention to design detail and concentration on our historic industrial and maritime image. Specific design details often go unnoticed, but they are critical to an overall sense of quality. One example is our adding a wash of lighting over the walls of the canal's north pier lighthouse. Although outside the scope of the Canal Park Drive streetscape project, we included it anyway. Nobody noticed it, probably thinking it was always there. All the better.

A local architect, Larry Turbes, was hired to draw suggested storefront design ideas that complimented the area's original architectural spirit. A low-cost loan program was established by the City to assist in storefront improvements. Larry was also hired to work hand-in-hand with the engineers designing the Minnesota Slip Bridge to assure its beauty. Special state legislation was created to allow for the adoption of a mixed-use design review district citizen board. This enables a wide range of uses, while reviewing designs for compatibility with our historic character. Not all property owners approved of these controls, but most may now be happy that the area did not suffer from the blighting garishness sometimes seen where development is not coordinated.

Rob Link is a property owner who showed a keen sense of design quality that, I believe, spread to others. Mick Paulucci and Andy Borg of Grandma's Restaurant also provided leadership with good spirited designs in their several Canal Park projects, notably with fun, quality graphic signs.

The goals of the plan also called for an emphasis on local services and products, as well as a major commitment to public art. Although expansion of tourism was a major goal, a more important one was to give Duluthians more reasons to be proud of living here. It is gratifying to see today that the majority of businesses in the area do not carry national franchise logos but, rather, are local businesses with unique offerings. This makes Duluth stand out against a national backdrop of cities that have patinas of sameness.

Finally, we tried to remember that the star of the show is the lake. Therefore, access to that lake and emphasis on both historic and working vessels are of prime importance.

PUBLIC INVESTMENTS

After publication of the plan in 1986, several improvements were implemented:

In 1986:
- The SS *William A. Irvin*, a 600-foot ore boat was purchased, renovated and opened as a floating museum and testimonial to our shipping culture ($140,000 acquisition, $250,000 renovation).
- The city obtained a lease, cleared the scrap yard and built a 230-car parking lot north of Grandma's Restaurant.
- Minnesota Slip bulkhead was repaired ($400,000).

- Endion Station (400-ton historic railroad depot) was moved one mile to the corner of the lake and used for Visitor and Convention Bureau offices (using freeway funds).

In 1987:

- The city established a contract for public activities and events at Bayfront Festival Park. Sixteen formal events were held in 1987, growing to 78 events in 1992.
- The federal Corps of Engineers completed a $12 million reconstruction of the ship canal piers including widening of public walkways.
- The state legislature approved special Duluth legislation for waterfront design review zoning and the city adopted the ordinance in 1990. A citizen design review board was appointed and reviewed 112 applications by September 1992.

In 1988:

- The first section (1/2 mile) of the Downtown Lakewalk was completed (ship canal to corner of the lake). By 1994, the Lakewalk along with Baywalk and Lakewalk East extended a total of 4 miles. The Lakewalk utilized freeway tunnel rock to clean and secure the shore and extend public shore land depth.
- Canal Park Pilot House, from a former ore boat, was donated to the city and installed as a storm-watch pavilion and gift shop.

In 1989:

- The city established a low-interest loan program for building-front renovation design and reconstruction subsidies oriented to historic renovation.
- A parking lot was constructed at Bayfront Park.

In 1990:

- Lake Place Image Wall was completed—a 580 ft. by 12 ft. mosaic wall (the largest in the country) utilizing computer interpretations of photos of historic local shipping scenes.

- The new $18 million State Convention Center opened, funded by the state of Minnesota.
- A 55 ft. high Entry Tower was constructed using brick and stone typical of old waterfront buildings, with the purpose of drawing the attention of people from the freeway just as the lighthouse guides ships to the harbor. It also provides a counterpoint to the Aerial Lift Bridge.

In 1991:
- Lake Avenue was reconstructed, including decorative streetlights.
- Major utility reconstruction took place, including complete new storm water sewers, the placement of overhead power lines underground and new water and gas mains.
- The Canal Park Streetscape project was completed, a $9.4 million improvement including widening and paving of sidewalks, installation of street furniture, public art, landscape materials and extensive other amenities as well. (A generous 5% of the budget was spent for public art.)
- The Buchanan Street boardwalk was constructed to connect the Lakewalk and the DECC.
- The Minnesota Slip Pedestrian Drawbridge is constructed, connecting Canal Park with the Bayfront area and DECC ($722,000). During the first eight months of 1992, 450,000 pedestrians crossed the bridge.
- Lake Place, a 2 1/2 acre, $10 million park is constructed over Interstate 35, effectively connecting downtown proper with the waterfront. (Federal and state highway money.)

In 1992:
Eleven major public outdoor art pieces, mostly bronzes, were installed.

In 1993:
- Two more major sculpture pieces were added to Lake Place's International Sculpture Garden (Japan and Sweden).

PRIVATE INVESTMENT

Meanwhile, Duluthians accelerated their investing, piggybacking the public investments.

In 1987:

- The Bayfront Park Development Association (mostly the Marshall sisters) contributed half of the $700,000 for construction of Bayfront Festival Park. They also contributed valuable land for the park. On eleven acres, it included a 500-foot boardwalk and stage with a tensile structure covering.
- The historic Aerial Lift Bridge was permanently lighted with a $30,000 grant from the Rotary Club of Duluth.
- Bill Meierhoff constructed additional docks for the consolidation of the growing charter fishing fleet in Minnesota Slip (4 boats in 1986, 48 in 1990).
- Grandma's Saloon and Grill doubled in size.
- Local farmers established an outdoor market.

In 1988:

- St. Croix Station was restored by Rob Link. It is used as a police station for a reinstituted horse patrol. Also, two private companies operate seven horse-drawn carriages.
- Vista Star, a dinner cruiser was added to the Goldfine's excursion fleet.
- Several private businesses were opened in restored warehouses, including "Sports Garden," a unique family-oriented sports court, restaurant and entertainment complex.

In 1989:

- The private Waterfront Plaza Marina was opened in Minnesota Slip.

In 1990:

- Playfront Park, a 10,000 sq. ft. playground was constructed over a four-day period by 2,000 citizen volunteers.
- Several new businesses opened, including five restaurants (and, by 1997, three new hotels).

In 1991:

- The Vietnam Veterans Memorial is completed, paid for by veterans' organizations, local contractors and building trade unions.
- The non-profit North Shore Scenic Railroad excursion train initiated daily operations.
- Major civic projects need three ingredients for success: vision, leadership and public support. The 1985 to 1992 Downtown Waterfront project enjoyed each of these requisites:

The vision was a community one, a consensus formed by intense participation by many Duluthians in the 1983 *Future City—Duluth Tomorrow* public forums and the 1985 citywide public planning "events" which were honestly structured with round table "give and take" discussion groups.

The leadership was mostly provided by Mayor John Fedo who, though irritating some with his aggressiveness, was effective in channeling successful projects, finding resources to pay for them and causing a positive tension of industriousness within city hall.

The public support was vast. Most candidates for local public office during this period included support for waterfront improvements. Most private property owners, although always pushing for more parking, saw the investment value and participated heavily. Public support resulted from meaningful inclusive involvement that translated to a strong sense of public ownership. ■

Jerry Kimball retired in 1995 after 26 years as head of Duluth's Physical Planning Division. He coordinated the forging of the 1985 Downtown Waterfront plan as well as its implementation mainly from 1986 to 1992 and remains an active supporter of city planning.

CHAPTER

42

University of Minnesota Duluth Library

THE "HEART" OF THE CAMPUS GETS A 21ST CENTURY TRANSPLANT

by Kathryn A. Martin

Libraries are the heart and soul of any college or
university. When I arrived at the University of Minnesota
Duluth in August of 1995, I found an eager educational
community desperate for a new library. UMD had a heart that
needed a transplant. Every aspect of the university was, to a
certain extent, compromised by not having a quality library
that the students and the faculty deserved.

That changed when the spacious, four-story, $25.8 million
UMD Library opened in September of 2000. Filled with sunny
reading rooms and 13 miles of bookshelves, the library is on
the cutting edge of information technology, and it is the home
for more than 250 computer terminals. Students with laptops
can access the Internet through wireless hub connections or

UMD

The long-awaited UMD Library opened in 2000. It serves as an "information gateway" for students, faculty and community members where they can access a vast electronic network of information, as well as traditional library resources.

plug into many desktop data ports located in study carrels and classrooms throughout the library. This emphasis on technology more than tripled the library's capabilities to meet student technology needs.

Students find the library's atmosphere inviting, from the high ceilings and the large windows to the comfortably furnished study rooms. The number of students and community members using the library continues to grow, with new services regularly added. For example, library users can receive answers to brief questions through "Ask a Librarian," an e-mail reference service. The library catalog is also online, along with many other electronic resources.

While the new library was built five years after I arrived at UMD, the actual planning for the new facility began in the 1980s. For years, students had complained about studying in the dark, cramped library stacks. The

UMD

The UMD Library is filled with many areas to read and study, such as this spacious, sunny reading room located in the circular tower.

library opened in the mid-1950s after the campus became part of the University of Minnesota system, and it quickly became too small to meet the needs of the rapidly growing enrollment. Two library additions were completed in the late 1960s; ironically, while the UMD community celebrated the completion of the library additions, the facility was already inadequate.

In the mid-1970s, the Health Sciences Library was added on to the library to meet the needs of the students in the new UMD School of Medicine. Since the 1970s, the UMD Library grew in terms of its services and programs, requiring significant office, processing, storage, and public service space. In December 1984, a subcommittee of the Library Policies Committee produced a report requesting additional collection and student study space. In the summer of 1988, UMD established a Long-

Range Physical Facilities Planning Committee to review the capital needs of the campus, which led to a $500,000 planning request for a new library in the University of Minnesota Capital Bonding Request. Included in that request was a report from the UMD Library Policies Committee, which identified major deficiencies that could only be remedied through major remodeling or construction of a new facility. In 1990, the University of Minnesota Capital Improvement Advisory Committee reviewed the UMD Library project and gave it priority status in the system-wide Six-Year Capital Improvement Program.

Meanwhile, the problems in the overcrowded and poorly ventilated library came to a head in 1992 when the Library of Congress Barcoding Project began. About a week into the project, library employees started experiencing eye irritations and infections, skin rashes and breathing problems. The barcoding project stopped, and it was determined that dust and mold spores were literally making many employees sick. In May of 1993, the UMD Library was closed for three weeks so that a private contractor could clean the 450,000 books of dust and mold spores.

In 1993, Chancellor Lawrence Ianni allocated $100,000 from campus resources to create a UMD Library program document, which led to the University of Minnesota Board of Regents adopting a capital budget that included authorization and funding for the development of a facilities plan for the UMD Library. In 1994, a campus-wide task force was created to present an updated needs assessment. Soon after the task force completed its work in January 1995, the State Designer Selection Board awarded a contract for planning and design of the UMD Library project to Stanius Johnson Architects in partnership with Stageberg Partners.

Working intensively with an advisory committee of faculty, administration and facilities management representatives, the consultants completed the pre-design work in the spring of 1995. As part of this pre-design process, the consultants and the advisory committee made library and information site visits to the University of Illinois Grainger Library, St. Mary's College Library, and the DeBartolo Center at the University of Notre Dame. In May 1995, the UMD Campus Assembly Physical Facilities Committee reviewed and approved the project. In October

1995, a few months after I officially assumed my new position as UMD chancellor, the University of Minnesota Board of Regents incorporated the request for planning and construction monies for the UMD Library into the University of Minnesota 1996 Capital Bonding Request.

One of my first challenges as the new UMD chancellor was to help convince state legislators during the 1996 legislative session of the overwhelming need for a new library at UMD. As we often face in northeastern Minnesota, the Twin Cities area legislators tend to look upon our part of the state homogeneously. It was often frustrating to feel like we had to fight against the City of Duluth to have our voices heard in St. Paul.

As part of our legislative strategy, we sent a letter in January 1996 to all 22,000 UMD alumni currently living in Minnesota asking for their support of the UMD Library project. Galvanized by the support of our faculty, staff and students, and with a renewed sense of purpose, UMD received $1.4 million in planning funds during the 1996 legislative session.

The schematic design for the library was approved by the Board of Regents in December of 1996. A year later, the working drawings and bid documents were completed. In 1998, UMD received legislative support for the library, and we broke ground that June.

During the two-year construction phase, we were excited to finally be meeting our goal of facilitating learning for the UMD community into the 21st century. The design has allowed UMD to open its arms to a vast electronic network as well as allowing us to add to our distinguished print collections. We already were one of the nation's premier undergraduate research universities. We already had award-winning programs and dynamic students. This new library helped strengthen what we had, and it has pushed us to the forefront in information access.

The fragmentation of knowledge continues to present a tremendous challenge. We need to make it fast and convenient for students, for faculty and for community members to retrieve data. We need to continue to make our library relevant. Usage of the UMD Library has more than quadrupled since the new building opened its doors. We are proud to give students the chairs, the laptop computer access, the sunlight and the space to go as far as they can dream, and as far as they dare. We built a facility, an information gateway, through which all members of the campus community will pass for many years. ∎

Dr. Kathryn A. Martin became chancellor of the University of Minnesota Duluth in August 1995. Under her leadership, UMD has completed the new UMD Library, Weber Music Hall, and Kirby Plaza, with the Swenson Science Building under construction. Planning is also underway for a new building for the Labovitz School of Business and Economics and an addition to the Recreational Sports complex. UMD is a comprehensive regional university with an enrollment of 10,000 students.

CHAPTER

43

Richard I. Bong World War II Heritage Center

HOW A GRASSROOTS EFFORT
BUILT A CENTER TO HONOR POPLAR'S HERO
& "THE GREATEST GENERATION"

by Christabel Grant

Major Dick Bong of Poplar, Wisconsin, was America's Ace of Aces. During World War II, he piloted a P-38 Lightning through more than 200 missions over the Southwest Pacific and destroyed 40 enemy planes—a record that will never be equaled. He was awarded all the medals possible (except for the Purple Heart), including the Congressional Medal of Honor.

After leaving combat, he enthusiastically took on a new assignment as a test pilot at Lockheed Aircraft Corporation in Burbank, California. Dick was killed when the experimental P-80 jet fighter he was testing crashed on take-off in Burbank,

A hero's wings. Visitors to the Richard I. Bong Heritage Center can see a vintage P-38, the same model of airplane that Bong flew in World War II.

California, on August 6, 1945—the same day an atomic bomb was dropped on Hiroshima. He was 24 years old.

Thousands of people attended Dick's funeral services in Superior, Wisconsin, and many more lined the funeral route to the cemetery in Poplar where he was buried. Wanting to create a fitting memorial for this national hero, a group of businessmen and residents of Poplar formed the Richard Ira Bong Memorial Foundation and began to raise funds. Help came from the Richard Ira Bong American Legion Post #435 of Superior, which in 1948 acquired a P-38 from the Air Force and donated it for the memorial.

Sufficient funds were raised to construct a small Bong Memorial room, attached to the new school gymnasium in Poplar. Dedication ceremonies took place in 1955 with dignitaries attending from around the country.

For the occasion, a team of Air Force personnel from Tinker Air Force Base in Oklahoma City refurbished the acquired P-38, which had been gutted by souvenir hunters over the years. To further protect the plane from vandals, they mounted it on pylons in the schoolyard and put a cover over the cockpit. Since then, people from all over the world have come to visit Poplar to pay their respects to the legendary Wisconsin farm boy.

Over the years, personnel from the Duluth Air Force Base and, later, the 148th Fighter Group of the Minnesota Air National Guard (ANG) coordinated repairs and maintenance to ensure the safety of the aircraft. Their concern grew as they watched damage to the plane increase with corrosion and cracking from Wisconsin's harsh winters and sunny summers.

In 1988, Raymond Erickson, a board member of the Bong Memorial Foundation, led efforts to restore and preserve the vintage plane, now valued at close to $1 million. The organization became incorporated as the Bong P-38 Fund, Inc., and the board launched a fund raising campaign to support the extensive restoration project. At this time a design to enclose the plane in a glass pyramid was proposed but received little financial support. During this period Dick Rose, owner of Discover Wisconsin Productions of St. Germain, Wisconsin, lent his energies and resources to the project until his death in 1994. His major contribution was a Bong documentary film, completed and released by his sons in 1998.

After six years of fundraising efforts, a call for proposals in 1994 resulted in the selection of LHB engineers and architects of Duluth, Minnesota, as the building designers. Their creative approach included hosting a Poplar town meeting to gather the community's perceptions and help crystallize the final building design. Board members approved a design resembling an aircraft hangar, the village of Poplar donated a site on U.S. Highway 2, and the concept of the Richard I. Bong World War II Heritage Center was born. The mission was to honor all those who participated in World War II and provide educational exhibits and programs to help visitors understand the sacrifices made by Americans during that period. Members of the board included Bong family members and the community, with Joyce Bong Erickson, Terry Lundberg, and Raymond Erickson assuming leadership roles.

By this time, the P-38 had sustained considerable damage, so the 148th Fighter Group of the Minnesota Air National Guard (ANG) stepped in to help. They moved it to their headquarters in Duluth where volunteers of the Air National Guard and civilians set to work on the restoration, which would ultimately take three years and 16,000 volunteer hours.

This same year, the board established a steering committee, which included Tom Peterson of Poplar, Bill Ion and Bill Bordson from the ANG, Lew Martin of Superior, and several board members. Consultants advised establishing a full-time paid staff position to undertake the fundraising, so in November 1995, Christabel Grant of Lake Nebagamon was hired as executive director.

Community contributions grew at a slow pace until board chair Terry Lundberg, of Poplar, and Christabel made contact with Wisconsin Governor Tommy Thompson. On February 6, 1998, Christabel met with Gov. Thompson to request $1 million. A week later, Gov. Thompson's office issued a press release announcing $1million in the proposed state budget for the heritage center using Federal Transportation Enhancement funds. Wisconsin Senator Bob Jauch of Poplar provided help and support along the way, particularly in ensuring procurement of the State funds.

On February 28, 1998, the board met to discuss the good news of the governor's commitment and the disappointing news of insufficient financial support from other sources. After much discussion and soul searching, a motion was made to look for a site in Superior, Wisconsin, hoping that a more accessible location would draw more support now and through the years. The motion passed unanimously. Board members at this time included: Chairman Terry Lundberg; President Joyce Bong Erickson, sister of Dick Bong; Vice-President Marge Bong Drucker, Dick's widow; Colonel Curt Jones, ANG ret.; Veda Ponikvar of Chisholm, Minnesota; Bob Jacobson of Poplar; Tom Palkie of Cloquet, Minnesota; Brig. General Raymond Klosowski, ANG; and Christabel Grant.

The decision was received with some dismay by many of the residents of Poplar, who had come to regard the plane as an icon in the village.

The board established a site review committee charged with identifying a location where the heritage center could fulfill its mission. This committee held its first meeting on June 4, 1998. After considering 13 sites within the City of Superior, the committee selected the city-owned site at the junction of U.S. Highways 2 and 53 on the shores of Lake Superior. This site was occupied at the time by the Superior and Douglas County Chamber of Commerce and its visitor center. The chamber director had offered the site for consideration, suggesting the visitor center could be located in the lobby of the heritage center—an arrangement that could prove mutually beneficial.

After board ratification, Christabel presented the site selection to the Superior City Council meeting on August 18, 1998, and requested financial support. The city council approved leasing the site to the board and unanimously approved Christabel's request for a grant of $300,000. Several weeks later, the Douglas County Board also agreed to Christabel's request for a grant and donated $300,000 to the project. When the state funds were approved in 1999, the City of Superior agreed to act as the project sponsor.

> After considering 13 sites within the City of Superior, the committee selected the city-owned site at the junction of U.S. Highways 2 and 53 on the shores of Lake Superior.

Following these major developments, fundraising proceeded more quickly. Richard Bong admirers from around the country responded to the fundraising appeal, and visits from Marge Bong Drucker to veterans associations and aviation groups brought in donations ranging from just a dollar to more than a thousand dollars. Donations came from corporations, foundations, small businesses, and private individuals. As fundraising continued, the board selected the firm of Reuben Johnson and Son to manage the construction, and work began on securing the various required permits. The project almost immediately hit a snag that delayed work for almost a year—the DNR had to review soil surveys of the lakeshore site.

In December 1999, the heritage center received funds to hire its second staff member: A three-year grant from the Duluth-Superior Community Foundation enabled Christabel to hire a curator of collections/education director. This allowed the center to start building a collection of artifacts, collect WWII oral histories, and present the first public programs.

By 2000, circumstances surrounding the center were changing, leading the board to re-evaluate the building's timetable. Inflation caused construction estimates to grow from $2.7 million in 1994 to nearly $4 million in 2000. An additional $1 million was budgeted for design and construction of exhibits. In addition, the World War II generation was fast disappearing, and the declining health of several of the center's staunchest supporters heightened the urgency of moving ahead with the project. The board requested and received a bank loan from the National Bank of Commerce in Superior, guaranteed by brothers Terry and Scott Lundberg—an enormous vote of confidence indicating the long-time commitment to the project of these brothers and their father, Robert. The loan enabled the board to accelerate the construction schedule, and ground was broken on October 19, 2001.

Following recommendations from Dr. Richard Zeitlan, director of the Wisconsin Veterans Museum in Madison, Christabel and Terry Lundberg met with several exhibit design companies. A team led by Craig Sommerville of Split Rock Design Studios in Arden Hills, Minnesota, was awarded the contract. The original plans included several exhibits, including the attack on Pearl Harbor, the Bong family, and the P-38 displayed in a Pacific island setting. Additional exhibits were conceptualized by Christabel to cover all theaters of the war and the home-front story, thus ensuring that the board's vision of honoring all branches of the service was carried through. Ultimately, the Split Rock team constructed fourteen exhibits, as well as creating a space for temporary special exhibits.

Inspiration throughout the project came from Dick Bong's sister Joyce Bong Erickson, her husband and WWII navy veteran Reynold, and Dick's widow, Marge Bong Drucker. In summer 2002, Marge moved from her home of 50 years in Los Angeles to a new home she built on a corner of the Bong family farm in Poplar. Although terminally ill with cancer, she devoted her final years to publicizing the heritage center, meeting with admirers to autograph books and photographs, presenting programs discussing her life with Dick and giving radio and television interviews. Marge died in September 2003, just days after celebrating the center's first anniversary. Six weeks later Reynold Erickson died. The center had lost two of its staunchest supporters.

The Bong Heritage Center's story would not be complete without recognizing the enormous contributions of the personnel of the 148th Fighter wing of the Minnesota Air National Guard and civilian volunteers. They dedicated more than 16,000 hours to restoring the P-38—now widely recognized as the finest example of the approximately 25 P-38s in existence. At the roll-out ceremonies in September 1997 after completion of the project, the base commander, Brigadier General Ray Klosowski, noted the extraordinary contribution of the volunteers: "They performed miracles with tired and corroded metal. When they couldn't fix or find a part, they made a new one... Each volunteer gave the maximum they could to produce an aircraft that would be a fitting tribute

> "...Each volunteer gave the maximum they could to produce an aircraft that would be a fitting tribute to those Americans, represented by Dick Bong, who gave so much when their nation called."

to those Americans, represented by Dick Bong, who gave so much when their nation called."

While the center was under construction, the plane was sheltered at the Anoka County Airport in Minnesota, first at the Polar Aviation museum and later at the American Wings Museum. The P-38 was trucked north to its new home in June 2002 and was unveiled to a standing ovation by thousands of people at heritage center's ribbon-cutting ceremonies on September 24, 2002—it would have been Dick Bong's 82nd birthday.

Today the heritage center receives its financial support from the private sector–donations, memberships, grants, admission charges, gift shop sales and rental of the facility. More than 100 volunteers assist in operations and make an invaluable contribution to the character and the financial health of the facility. The board is working hard to continue in this manner, and staff aspire to earn accreditation for the museum from the American Association of Museums. In keeping with the center's mission statement, all programs and regularly scheduled new exhibits focus on World War II, and WWII veterans themselves assist by giving programs and telling the story in their own words. ∎

Christabel Grant was born in Dublin, Ireland, and earned her M.A. there from Trinity College. She moved to Duluth, Minnesota with her family in 1969; she and her husband now reside in Lake Nebagamon Wisconsin. Christabel's professional life has been in higher education, and she has served on the board of numerous Twin Ports community organizations over the past 35 years.

EPILOGUE

OWN YOUR OWN EFFECTS

by Donn Larson

This book was Monnie's idea. If you like it, he should get credit; if you don't, we'll share the blame. Mainly, I hope the result justifies our prodding and detective work. The learning and reflection on what has happened were certainly worth it to us.

In his introduction Harold Frederick mentioned some omissions. When choosing subjects we had to draw the line somewhere, and we drew a rather wavy one. If our content is just a sampling, at least it is varied. We tried to be regional and many of these projects have an area-wide impact, yet this is mostly a Duluth-centered book. By concentrating on our backyard, we miss some special accomplishments—Wolf Ridge Environmental Learning Center at Finland, Minn., the North House Folk School in Grand Marais, Minn., the U.S. Hockey Hall of Fame, Eveleth, Minn. and the Lake Superior Big Top Chautauqua at Bayfield, Wis. are examples.

Most subjects are civic achievements, yet there are several businesses, some induced by civic action (like the paper mill), others exceptional examples of entrepreneurship, like Maurices and Grandma's. There could have been many more, among them the Chromaline Corporation (now Ikonics), or the Goldfine family's resuscitation of their business interests to become a management company operating 36 motels in 14 states. We left out some specialized enterprises like the Building for Women, the Fitger's complex, the Washington Artists' Co-op, and Northeast Ventures, the Duluth-based community development venture capital pool, and its sibling, Northeast Entrepreneur Fund, both quietly creating jobs. Also missing: how we built flourishing subscriber-supported regional broadcast services, three radio and one TV, as well as our College of St. Scholastica's becoming co-ed, growing steadily, offering progressive new programs and building many campus improvements. Munger Trail and the Hartley Nature Center would also have made interesting chapters. The fact there are enough omissions to fill a second volume helps to prove our point about community initiative.

Our book dwells on successes. To be honest, not everything worked. Just ask about our investment in Duluth Growth Company.

So, what have we learned? We hope there are some experiences in this book that will help others to improve the Northland's economy and quality of life in their new generation. For context, let's recognize a cultural change that happened in the '50s. Certainly there were energetic leaders in the first half of the century, but before and throughout World War II what most folks call a "market economy" prevailed. Growth and change were more reactive, and based less on citizen initiative and involvement. Local and county government adapted to the times and delivered basic services like public safety, streets, utilities and education. Some leaders, like Mayors Magney and Snively, had special vision for parkways and set-asides, but planning, economic stimulants, environmental concern, esthetics, were usually disregarded as part of the commonweal.

Duluthians changed from a commission form of government to the strong mayor-council system in 1956. This fostered a shift in municipal management protocol, expanding government's role beyond meeting essential public needs. Citizens began doing more driving and less riding along. We entered a time when government intervened more in citizens' lives, while citizens began to intervene more in the conduct of public business. In fact, we re-defined public business.

The new form of government gave policymaking responsibility to nine part-time representatives, and consolidated administration of that policy in the mayor's office. The mayor is called *strong* now because he or she oversees all departments formerly divided among bureaucratic full-time commissioners.

This book highlights many examples of the effectiveness of our new form of government. Although to somewhat varying degrees, each of our mayors since 1956 has exerted the kind of leadership intended by our new charter. We've chosen well. These chapters are peppered with mayoral initiative and courage—taking charge.

Another thing this book teaches is the value of entrusting responsibility to appointed lay leaders. Ben Boo talks about this in his chapter on the airport authority. There is little risk and considerable reward in detaching responsibility, but not accountability, from city hall. Duluth's entertainment and convention complex was built and is managed entirely by lay leaders who have our complete confidence and the power to do everything they require except levy taxes. The autonomy of our authorities is a model for other jurisdictions. These boards know when to turn to city hall for guidance and support (the early arena years and early aquarium years are examples).

This book also teaches us to recognize and be thankful for the unselfish energy, resourcefulness and imagination of individual citizens. Some volunteer to serve on the council, boards and commissions. Others, like the Marshall sisters, Jeno Paulucci, Cindy Hayden, Mary C. Van Evera and Kay Slack, are free agents who embrace a good idea and work tenaciously to see it fulfilled. Not all influential people are part of the business and political establishment; we appreciate Eric Ringsred not only for getting back our fog horn, but for his challenges that changed the design of the new tech center and freeway extension.

The integrity and grit of professionals in local government come through in these chapters, too. The caricature of a civil servant with sleeve garters and green eyeshade no longer applies, not with the resolve and talent of starters like Jack LaVoy, Helen Lind, Ernie Petersen or Jerry Kimball on the A team.

Frank Lloyd Wright once advised us to study and admire the good works of others, but "own your own effects." To us this means: respect the experiences in this book but use them as a stimulant for fresh and independent ideas.

It also helps if we choose good mayors, pick councilors who are confident team players having some acquaintance with business and economics, spread the load by delegating to leaders and emerging leaders, and, as you may have noted again and again in the preceding pages, make friends in high places!

Donn Larson, retiring Duluth businessman, was a Duluth city councilor at-large 1959-'67. He also has served on the City Charter Commission, the Arena/Auditorium Administrative Board, the Great Lakes Aquarium Board, the Duluth Superior Area Community Foundation Board, the Lake Superior Marine Museum Association Board and the Duluth City Planning Commission.

INDEX

Photo captions are indicated in bold face type.
Publications are indicated in italic type.

E

Eaton, Robert, F., 44, 106, **108**, 110, 171
Economic Development Administration (EDA), 32, 74, 77, 106, 107, 113, 141, 165, 170
Edgell, Robert (Bob), 46
Edwards & Kelcey, 240
Edward's Shoes, 72
Eisenhower, Dwight D., 237
Ekberg, Donna, 239
Endion Station, 240, 293
Enger Memorial Tower, 219
Enger Park, 219
Enger, Bert, J., 219
Entrepreneur's Ten Commandments, 3
Erickson, Joyce Bong, 306, 309
Erickson, Lewis, 141
Erickson, Raymond (Ray), E., 37, 305, 306
Erickson, Reynold, 309
Erickson, Rondi, 212, 239
Erie Mining Company, 51
Espenscheid interests, 76
Evans, Mary, 141
Evens, Karen, 44

F

Fairhurst, Charles, 212
Family Practice Preceptorship Program, 217
Farr, George, 56
Fastenal Co., 255
Federal Highway Administration, 250
Federal Housing Act, 95
Fedo, John, A., 35, 109, 183, **184**, 186, **192**, 194, 220, 222, **224**, 227, 231, 239, 240, 241, 257, **258**, 290, 296
Fifth Avenue Hotel, 65, **104**
Fifth Avenue West Mall, 59, **60**, 89

Fillenworth, Karen, **92**, 93
Finkelstein, Florence, 93
First and American National Bank, 72, 73, 77
Fisher, Jill, 289
Fitger's Brewery Complex, 241, 313
Flackne, Bob, 75, 77
Fladmark, Orlando (Lars), K., 45
Flaherty, Mark, 62, 249, 256
Flame Restaurant, The, 21, **23**
Fletcher Challenge, 227
Fond du Lac Band, 183
Fond-du-Luth Casino, 183, **184**
Forbes, Phyllis, 193
Forsythe, Robert (Bob), 56
Fosnacht, Donald, 209
Fox, Greg, 44, 274
France, Alfred, E., 51, **78**, 212, 216
Fraser Shipyard, 40
Frederick, Harold, II, VII, 107, 108, 239, 240, 283, 313
Frederick, Ruth, 93
Fredin, Conrad (Mac), M., 6, 113, 140
Fredin, Harriet, 93
Freeman, Orville, 16
Freeman, Michael, 206
Freeway referendum, 239
Freilich, Robert, 290
Friends of the Library, 110
Fryberger, LaVerne, M., 122
Fugelso, Porter, Simich & Whiteman, 129
Fuller, Jr. C. E., 122
Future City—Duluth Tomorrow, 296

G

Gallagher, Annabelle, 20, **22**, 23
Gallery Five, 72
Gates, Joel, 201, 202
Gateway Tower, 64, 69
Gateway Urban Renewal Project, 59, **62-63**, 67
Gee, Robert, 201, 202
Gerlach, Luther, 290

N

T

Y

Z